Corporate Soul

Not everything that counts can be counted, and not everything that can be counted counts!

—Albert Einstein

Corporate Soul

The Monk within the Manager

Moid Siddiqui

⑤SAGE | Response Business Books

www.sagepublications.com

Los Angeles • London • New Delhi • Singapore • Washington DC

First published in 2005 by

SAGE Response
B1/I-1 Mohan Cooperative Industrial Area
Mathura Road, New Delhi 110 044, India

SAGE Publications Inc
2455 Teller Road
Thousand Oaks, California 91320, USA

SAGE Publications Ltd
1 Oliver's Yard, 55 City Road
London EC1Y 1SP, United Kingdom

SAGE Publications Asia-Pacific Pte Ltd
33 Pekin Street
#02-01 Far East Square
Singapore 048763

Published by Tejeshwar Singh for Response Books, typeset in 10/12.5 pts Garamond by Innovative Processors, New Delhi, and printed at Chaman Enterprises, New Delhi.

Fifth Printing 2012

Library of Congress Cataloging-in-Publication Data

Siddiqui, Moid, 1944–
   Corporate soul: the monk within the manager/Moid Siddiqui
      p. cm.
   1. Management. 2. Management—Philosophy. I. Title.

HD31.S5185   2005   658.4'09—dc22   2005014940

ISBN: 10: 0-7619-3297-6 (US-PB)   10: 81-7829-539-3 (India-PB)
          13: 978-0-7619-3297-0 (US-PB)   13: 978-81-7829-539-8 (India-PB)

Production Team: Gargi Dasgupta, R.A.M. Brown and Santosh Rawat

I dedicate this book to Indian sages, Chinese monks, sufis, saints and prophets.

I also dedicate this book to three corporate legends: Jamsetji Nusserwanji Tata—the creator of the private sector; Dr V Krishnamurthy—the shaper of the public sector; and Azim Premji—the promoter of the Indian IT sector.

Contents

PART V
The Wrap Up

Acknowledgements

I started this book in 1998, when I was director HR, in BEML, Bangalore. At that time, I did not make much progress as it needed depth and clarity which I was unable to give. Later, I joined the Nagarjuna Group as executive vice president (Human Potential Development) and got to know K.S. Raju and his son, Rahul very well. In his thoughts I found business sagacity; and gained clarity about spiritual management.

Dr V. Krishnamurthy is a living corporate legend in India. He has always been my source of inspiration throughout my career. I grew under his care and guidance from a first-line executive in BHEL to the director of BEML. I extend my profound gratitude to him.

I thank Chapal Mehra, Managing Editor, Response Books of Sage Publications for his contribution. I also thank my wife, Ruquiya, for all her support.

Every work includes some reflections of others' thoughts and ideas. My work is no exception. I thank all those whose thoughts and ideas I have quoted in this book and also those whose ideas inspired me that might have formed a different pattern of thought in this book.

Moid Siddiqui
reachus@intellects.biz
www.intellects.biz

Part I

Eternal Teachings

Some things are not favoured in heaven. Who knows why?
Even the Sage is unsure of this.

—Lao Tzu

1

Introduction

Mammon versus Buddha: it is tempting to look for two cult figures who best symbolise the critical difference between management theories in the West and the East. Why do I say that? The West believes in results; the focus is always on the ends, and not the means to the end. Western management teaching is driven by 'result orientation', fostering an army of corporate savages insensitive to the larger, intangible goals of life itself.

The people in the East, however, have a different orientation: they are taught the meaning of life and raised on the teachings of the Bhagvad Gita, Vedas, the Qur'an and the teachings of Confucius and Lao Tzu. They are taught to become *karmyogis*, concentrating all their energies on actions and harbouring no expectations about the fruits of their labour. The results, they are taught as children, will flow from the Divine Hand. Over the years, critics of eastern thought have called that fatalism. However, tales of corporate shenanigans and fraud have increased in the world, as modern-day managers have lost their ethical moorings. It is time to revisit such notions and see how eastern philosophy can influence corporate life in general. A beginning has already been made: Japan's management gurus have propounded the theory of kaizen—a focus on process rather than result orientation—which is firmly grounded in eastern philosophy.

Japan should take the credit for sparking interest in process-oriented management theory that became a rage in the 1980s, when a series of economic shocks in the West revealed the poverty of western management thought. Kaizen—the management theory that concentrates on improving the processes rather than achieving certain results— became the new management buzzword. The West scrambled to learn Zen but soon lost interest when they found it couldn't be unscrambled into an easily digestible 'westernised' concept. Zen was not measurable; it could not be reduced to a mathematical formula. The disenchantment with the philosophy in the west stemmed from the fact that it didn't fulfill a single criterion of today's corporate prescriptions.

What followed was a litany of newer buzz concepts that spawned a new corporate vocabulary that was rooted in the achievement of results rather than the improvement of processes. Corporates crunched numbers; they peered at toplines and bottomlines and developed a passion for figures. But a soul-numbing numbers game can never establish an authentic pattern of excellence. It is never quite enough to know that the results were achieved, but rather to find out how they were attained. It is summed up beautifully by the classic black humour in that gag about operation theatres: 'The operation was successful but the patient died'. Why was the operation successful? Because it met the defined criteria. Why did the patient die? Because the defined criteria were wrong for that particular operation.

To stay alive, we need to stay ahead. There is no great victory in winning a race. Anyone can win—at least someone will. The trick is to win without breathing hard. How do

14

you do that? Says the great Wu Wei Master Lao Tzu: 'It is not wise to rush about. Controlling breath causes strain. If too much energy is used, exhaustion follows. This is not the way of Tao. Whatever runs contrary to Tao will not last.'

With their excessive ardour for figures, corporates today have become soul-less organisations. The people in the organisation are seen as just a factor of production. They are pitchforked into a pressure-cooker environment in world-class companies, where they are expected to meet impossible targets and made to feel they are underachievers if they fail to deliver. Companies sweat their human assets to maintain the temperature of the corporate furnace.

It is a throwback to the very dawn of the industrial revolution in Europe in the 18th century. Anyone who reads the history of the manufacturing society realises that its foundation was built on the bedrock of human exploitation. The exploitation was so deep-seated and shameless that it gave rise to Marxism and later resulted in the formation of the Fabian Society in England. Stanley and Beatrice Webb fought for the introduction of 'collective bargaining' as a compromise solution.

But it hasn't changed matters a whit. Today, the information society is built on the same bedrock of exploitation with cyber coolies forced to work for long hours in dehumanising call centres, forced to fake names, accents and attitudes to make themselves 'acceptable' to customers in foreign lands.

That brings me to a simple question: Should the corporate world serve the interests of society and mankind, *or* should society and mankind subsume themselves to the corporate world? We all need to ponder over this question carefully and delve into all that happened with the advent of the industrial revolution in the 18th century. When you search

15

for and find the right answers, you will become a corporate Buddha—the enlightened one.

The corporate world has always been somewhat self-serving and self-centred. It tries to conceal this by spouting off concepts like corporate citizenship and corporate governance—which have more frills than purpose. We talk of value-based organisations and then define commercial gains as corporate or core values. Our thoughts and practices are so corrupted and fundamentally skewed towards bottomline-gazing that they have robbed us of our sensitivity. What we need today is not a corporate guru who can fashion a new-fangled fad but a corporate thinker who can provide lasting wisdom.

But is such a body of wisdom available? Yes it is! Philosophers like Lao Tzu, Confucius, Buddha, Heraclitus, Socrates, Plato and Aristotle have always focused on the innate goodness of mankind and society. These thinkers can direct us to the high road of ethics that will imbue not only our lives but also our corporate governance practices. The road may be less travelled today; but once you get on to the highway of corporate ethics there will be no need to look into the rear-view mirror.

Today, we are caught in a mad rush like a crowd jostling through a narrow tunnel. Arms and legs pummel each other, faces aren't seen and no one quite knows where everyone is headed. In this pell mell, everyone's got to run at the same pace or run the risk of being trampled in the maelstrom. We have no choice but to rush along and hope fervently that we will reach somewhere. 'When you don't know where to go, any road will take you there,' said Buddha wisely so long ago. The irony is that we identify success with the achievement of a goal that we didn't know about in the first place.

Many of us pursue success at great cost to our personal integrity and core values. We are usually unaware of the costs associated with the choices we make to seek a 'successful life'. We prefer to ignore the losses and sacrifices we have made in our relentless pursuit of success: the failed marriages, the broken relationships with our children and friends, and the frost in our hearts for the people whom we profess to love.

It is easier to be a 'careerist' and to keep on chasing the mirage mistaking it for an oasis, than to give some meaning to life and become aware of our potential that is deeper and vaster than all the oceans on this planet. But it cannot be achieved merely through physical pursuits.

The spiritually-challenged corporate pharaohs whose hearts are spiritually empty and minds filled with knowledge that lacks wisdom, who are in an unbelievably dominating majority, have brought the corporate world to a cliff. It is difficult to return, and disastrous to fall. So they teeter on the precipice of half-baked choices. If wisdom finally dawned on them, they might salvage the unsalvageable.

Organisational growth, high production and productivity, market research, market penetration and market creation are some of the important business credos. We learn and teach, 'Enlarge the market for your products... Create a new market for your products...' Now, someone must tell me how do marketing whizzes in the 'war weapons' industry create or enlarge the market for their products? The answer that the management gurus would give is obvious. Each time these corporations enlarge their market pie, mankind will have to experience more bloodshed. As 'roadshows' and 'industrial exhibitions' are organised for the demonstration of industrial products, wars are waged for a similar strategic purpose, demonstrating the capabilities of destructive weapons in real-life situations.

Today, 'war' is a very lucrative and profitable industry; tomorrow human organs harvested from prisoners of war or fresh dead bodies 'produced' during the war might turn into an innovative market. And then, the corporate mavens will be evolving corporate plans and strategies for growth, expansion, modernisation, vertical and horizontal integration and all that sort of thing—always focusing on the need to enhance profitability. The management institutions and consultants will conduct the research studies to add value. Who has the time or wisdom to apply the mind to 'what is right?'

There is a little story that demonstrates very beautifully the futility of such a relentless pursuit of personal profit. A young innocent girl would stand at the graveyard waiting for a dead body to come so that her father, who was a gravedigger, would earn enough money to pay for the day's meals. If no dead body came to the graveyard, the family would go hungry that day. So, each time the girl looked through the window and saw a dead body coming into the graveyard, she would experience immense pleasure. A strange smile would hover on her face. One day when her own father died, people saw the same strange smile on her face.

I put this proposition to you: Are we not trying to put a similar strange smile on the corporate face? The purpose of this book is to create a pure smile that is devoid of need or want—a smile that will heal the corporate soul.

I have divided this book into five parts: In Part I, we see how the teachings of the saints, prophets, sages and sufis are eternal and are relevant to corporates that can envision a world which is not driven by narrow-focused, profit-minded motives. In Part II, we read about the tantalising truths of Confucius and Lao Tzu and how they can build our core corporate values. In Part III, we turn to the entire swathe of

Indian mysticism: from the fuzzy logic of Buddha's argument to the teachings of the Bhagvad Gita and the simple wisdom in the parables of the *Panchatantra.* Part IV treks to the divine oasis in the deserts: it traverses the wisdom pastures of The Torah, the Psalms and the Gospel, turns to the simple and pure way of life propounded in the Qu'ran, which lays down a codified set of principles for business transactions, and comes to grips with the credo of divine love sung by the sufis who are always humble in their knowledge and ever conscious of their limitations. Part V turns to the forgotten philosopher of Greece—Heraclitus. He was the alter ego of Lao Tzu in the West—and they spurned him for Socrates, Aristotle and Plato because they could not comprehend his subtle truth. I conclude with a new concept—intuilogy—that seeks to blend the intuitive wisdom of the old masters like Lao Tzu and Heraclitus with the logic and reasoning of the great masters like Confucius, Plato and Aristotle. It is this balanced knowledge that will take us down the road to excellence and success in the new age.

2

Eternal Wisdom

Him the Sages call wise
Whose understanding is void of desires for results of plans,
Whose actions are burned by the fire of wisdom!

—Bhagvad Gita (IV-19)

Ancient wisdom is distilled from the immutable laws of nature
that are as eternal as the bright sun—the fireball that has been
shining and radiating heat and energy for billions of years.
However, just as every day brings a new dawn, sages, sufis
and prophets come up with new-fangled theories, ideas and
concepts that challenge accepted beliefs and force us to see
things in a new light.

Some of these new-age theorists whip up a warble of
words that fire the imagination for a while and then sputter
out like a guttered flame. Many people have spawned such
false dawns before—and others will do the same in future.

But every now and then, there comes along someone
who is pilloried at the stake as a false prophet by his own

generation but whose ideas and theories have stood the rigorous test of time. History is replete with examples of those who have suffered because they dared to challenge the status quo. It is the intrinsic nature of human society to shun anything that questions established principles. Take Albert Einstein, who discovered a new Cosmos and tried to create a static model of the universe that he called the Cosmological Constant. He was reviled by his peers and his theories came under constant attack throughout his life. Worse, an anti-Einstein organisation was established during his lifetime. But he was never cowed by criticism. When a book titled *Hundred Authors against Einstein* was published, he dryly retorted: 'If I was wrong, then one would have been enough.'

Earlier, in 1916, when Galileo came out with his cosmological discoveries and publicly supported the Copernican theory that planets orbit around the sun, he was charged with blasphemy and condemned by the Catholic Church. Later, he was placed under house arrest for his 'repetitive mistakes'. The manuscript that carried his ideas—which has formed the bedrock of modern Physics—was smuggled out to a publisher in Holland in 1642, just four years before his death.

Other seers have suffered the same fate: Socrates was forced to drink hemlock (a poison), Christ had to bear the Cross, and Prophet Mohammed had to migrate from Mecca because each of them had dared to show the 'false dawn'. Profound wisdom that challenged accepted beliefs and were repudiated as false back then are seen as eternal truths later.

✎ Fundamental Laws ✑

For centuries, wise men have hunted for the fundamental laws of nature that are invisible yet perfect. I have chosen a few that are, to my mind, appropriate to humankind and just as meaningful in the realm of business management: they envelop qualities like purpose, vision, wisdom, values and intuitive wisdom. As I see it, they are intrinsically important to human life and lead to the integral universal path, irrespective of religion, region or resource. Ancient wisdom is akin to eternal principles that are immutable and perfect. The corporate world isn't an alien in the cosmos. It is just one small segment in the same universe. However, it respects no borders. The tentacles of the corporate world spread throughout the globe. Although finite within the globe, it doesn't have any boundaries.

Ancient wisdom takes us to the fountainhead of eternal knowledge. In the Old World, those who attained knowledge from the pure springs were the spiritual scientists. They learnt the truth through spirituality but they didn't know the language of science—logic and mathematics.

The corporate world, on the other hand, is materialistic: it fills its maw with all the resources it can find—minerals, man, machines and money. In its singular pursuit of wealth, it has drifted away from eternal, cosmic principles. It operates under the principles of cold logic and esoteric mathematical formulae.

But over time, these two disparate worlds—the spiritual world and the corporate world—have slowly started converging. As companies begin to look beyond pelf and profits, they have started to talk about corporate governance, ethics and principles, forcing them to look for a brand new set of virtues that are easily found in the spiritual world.

It is important to remember that cosmic principles are perfect but imperceptible. Not everything that we see or hear is entirely true. Our understanding of the world around us is extremely nebulous. Let me illustrate this: with our powerful telescopes we can see galaxies as they existed several million years ago. How do we know that? Stars are millions of light years away—so what we are really seeing is a ray of light that was emitted eons ago. The rays of light from the closest star are about four years old. At sunset, we cannot see the sun but we know it exists. In one sense therefore, what we see doesn't really exist; and if it does, it is almost invisible. That just goes to show how imperfect our vision really is. Call it the cosmic paradox, if you will.

Similarly, in many ways, our understanding of organisations is badly skewed. The increasing complexity and the blinding pace at workplaces puts people constantly on edge. It creates the feeling that things are careening out of control; this also signals our failure to understand a deeper reality of organisational life and of life in general. Human beings ultimately need to be happy wherever they may be. Working in the pressure-cooker environment in the corporate world, especially in world-class companies, people feel badly stressed, suffocated and unhappy. That is when they need to turn to Nature to find a balm for their stressed-out lives.

Our changing knowledge about the cosmos has impacted our thoughts and approaches to life. From this we distil a new wisdom—a corporate wisdom. Just as our knowledge about the cosmos mutates, corporate wisdom and practices change as well. It is interesting to see the parallels: the ideas of Galileo (1564–1642) about the cosmos were a lot different from Isaac Newton's (1642–1727). Again, Newtonian theories about the cosmos—which were essentially based on the principle of gravitational theory—were a lot different from the perceptions of Albert Einstein (1879–1955) and Stephen Hawking (1924) who posited concepts like gravitational fields and the String Theory which talks about heavenly bodies being held together in great harmony with unseen 'connectedness'.

So how did all this impact business management theories? The gravitational approach—controls—gave way to gravitational attraction—or collaborations. And the String Theory taught us that the business pattern warrants an understanding of the big picture—connectedness.

Supervision and control—the buzzwords of an older generation of businessmen—drew their inspiration from the gravitational force theory that was propounded by Isaac Newton. Participation and involvement were the shibboleths of a later generation that had grown on Einstein's theory of the cosmos. Today, the world of business has hitched its coattails to Stephen Hawking's ideas about the cosmos, where everything is inter-connected under the laws of the 'String Theory'. Suddenly, people in the corporate boardrooms have started talking about the 'Big Picture'—a frame that has since been enlarged to cover the broader discourse over 'Eco-Systems'. As knowledge grows, perceptions change.

But here is where we come to the paradox: there is a wealth of ancient wisdom that seems to be frozen in some sort of a time warp. It remains as relevant today as ever: the challenge is to yoke corporate wisdom of the New Age to ancient precepts about life as a whole. It is time for us to turn to the past, while seeking solutions to the complex problems of tomorrow.

ᴈ Eternal Truth ᴂ

Status quo is akin to conventional wisdom—it stands for stagnation. Eternal wisdom, on the other hand, is dynamic—it flows from eternal truth which is timeless, ageless and bottomless. The urge to discover a new horizon takes you down the road to eternal truth. The quest for the eternal truth depends crucially on how much you long for it.

The Sufi thought reflects dynamism and it flows from eternal wisdom.

Sufism emerged among the Shiite Muslims in the late 10th and 11th centuries, borrowing ideas from Buddhism, Christianity and Neoplatonism. How many of us really understand and believe that in the will of man is a unique power of longing which is so strong that it can turn the mist in ourselves into the sun? How then, can we accept the status quo that is the product of conventional wisdom as a substitute to the power of longing?

> *The significance of man is not in what he attains, but rather in what he longs to attain.*
>
> **—Kahlil Gibran**

One can learn about the eternal truth but may not be able to explain it constructively through the use of language. 'Tao that can be told is not Tao,' says Lao Tzu. It is much the same with eternal truth.

There is a rhythm in the universe with the planets moving regularly in a defined path. Everywhere, there is a law of rhythm and everything conforms to the cosmic principles. Corporate leaders and entrepreneurs ought not to use oars to propel the boat; they must learn to navigate.

Managing a business is like painting a big picture and not just clicking snapshots. Often a 'tag' or a 'buzzword' emerges like a fad and just as quickly fades away. These 'tagged'

> *It is only when you hunt for It that you lose It.*
> *You cannot hold It, but equally you cannot get rid of It.*
> *And while you can do neither, It goes on its way.*
>
> **—Yung-Chia Ta Shih**
> **(A Chinese philosopher)**

business practices and business processes stay in isolation like snapshots—and become evanescent moments in time.

They do not paint a big picture on the canvas. When you start counting trees, you lose sight of the beautiful forest. Managing a strategic business is like seeing the big picture.

Each doctrine, each bit of philosophy, each principle of business management is basically truthful. But each principle is like a glass pane—you can see the truth through it but it remains between you and the truth as an unseen barrier. Each principle in isolation stands for some truth but it also divides the eternal truth.

One should learn to discriminate the real from the fake; winnow the true from the false. The world rests on truth. The corporate world cannot hope to bypass the universal truth. We should try to live in truth because truth is the highest refuge. Sometimes what we think is real turns out to be a mere chimera. In our anxiety to fatten corporate bottomlines, we window-dress to mask the truth. Don't chase profits—like a mirage it will outfox you. Profit cannot be the sole motive of an organisation.

✆ Profit is the Residue ✆

People often assume—quite wrongly—that a company exists only to make profits. It is true that profit is important for a company's survival and growth, but it cannot be the sole reason and the *raison d'etre* for its existence. Managers need to concentrate on the game and keep an eye on the ball. And, of course, once in a way, look up at the scoreboard.

Often, like an ostrich sticking its head into the sand we refuse to see the reality. It is a form of self-deception and deflects us from our basic purpose in life. Such digression takes place when we diverge from the cosmic principles and ignore ancient wisdom. The cosmic principles are simple and truthful.

We live them; we breathe them. Yet, ironically, when we want to find solutions either in life or business, we tend to look elsewhere.

Most entrepreneurs and chief executives today behave much like the musk deer. Without a sense of direction, they scatter about in a mad rush to find that cutting-edge that will keep them ahead of the others. In the process, they burn themselves out in a futile search. Like the stupid musk deer, they end up chasing shadows; they plot, spend and acquire assets to knit together a huge empire that will satisfy their insatiable egos; and in the process they run themselves into the ground. They are exhausted in the end and find little joy or satisfaction after years of being part of the chase.

> *As the stupid musk deer, so also man is running through the endless maze of sense-objects, earning, spending, acquiring, hoarding, wasting all and striving for more, only to get himself exhausted. He ultimately dies because of his own exhaustion, without finding the joy and satisfaction he is seeking.*
>
> **—Swami Chinmayananda**

Take time off to reflect and introspect. Think in peace. Try to understand the rhythmic cosmic principles with intellectual neatness and you will find yourself on a different plane—far higher than anything that money or material gains can give you.

I should not be misunderstood: of course money-making and profitability are necessary in business. But profit is not an end in itself and should not oblige people to sacrifice their values or compromise their conscience. Today, the corporate world is abandoning talk about business management and choosing instead to focus on corporate governance. Corporate leaders have started to realise the importance of values. There has been a major shift in perception also. Earlier, there was a Darwinian concept in business: only the fittest survive; now it is tinged with a Confucian thought: only the virtuous thrive.

Those who believe in material gains must know that wealth comes from different sources. The source is just as important as the stream of revenue. In purely economic terms, it has the same value. But it is just as important to know where the dollar comes from. Values are very important in business; it is important to earn your dollar from the right sources—and this theory meshes well with the spiritual commandments of Buddha enunciated in his eight-fold path.

Buddha's Eight-fold Path
• *Right Belief*
• *Right Thought*
• *Right Speech*
• *Right Action*
• *Right Means of Livelihood*
• *Right Meditation*
• *Right Efforts*
• *Right Remembrance or Memory*

There is so much to discover beyond material gains that one need not put his feet precisely where everyone else has gone before. Robert Frost makes this clear in his poem *The Road Not Taken*:

> Two roads diverged in a wood, and I—
> I took the one less travelled by,
> And that has made all the difference.

One need not go astray like the musk deer. Have the confidence that you can do the job unaided—and that is the only way you can ensure that you will not go down the beaten track. Gain new heights and discover new horizons.

One has to discover his self. But first one has to ask oneself whether there is more to ourselves than mere physical beings. If we feel that we are indeed superior to physical beings,

28

then it would call for some introspection. This test applies to all human beings including corporate entities. Once we become aware of our superior Self, we will better appreciate our purpose of being human beings and working for corporate entities.

> *We are not human beings having a spiritual experience. We are spiritual beings having a human experience.*
>
> **—Ken Blanchard**

Unfortunately, most of us take life as a physical journey and get so absorbed in it that we forget our mental, emotional and spiritual needs. We wrongly assume that it is during this physical journey that some of us may be touched by spirituality. But the truth is that spirituality brings with it a completeness, a sense of peace. Imagine the blissful pleasure that we would find if we discover that life itself is a spiritual journey and it is during this journey that we experience physicality. Once this eternal wisdom sinks in and touches the soul, the whole purpose of life will change in the temporal and corporate worlds. Remember, money-making is the residue, not the sole purpose of a corporate entity.

≪ Eternal Wisdom ≫

Ancient wisdom is fathomable, yet beyond the grasp of a logical mind. Today's corporate covens believe too much in logic. Mathematical equations are used to describe the indiscernible. Human behaviour, which is extremely complex, is explained through equations. Intelligent Quotient has given way to Emotional Quotient and now there's talk of the Spiritual Quotient—IQ, EQ, and SQ. What next? Will it be Cosmic Quotient—CQ? The other day, my son Feroz called me from Singapore to ask whether I could lead a session on

Adversity Quotient—AQ, they call it. It seems once something becomes a buzzword, corporate thinkers try to devise new-fangled extensions!

We coin new words and develop inventories and numerical measures to assess what we have hardly grasped ourselves. We little realise that mathematics is the language of science which cannot, *ipso facto*, be applied to human potential and human behaviour. Business management theories evolved in the Age of Science; so the corporate leaders adopted the same numerical patterns to explain management processes. Gradually, corporate wisdom distanced itself from ancient wisdom. But we forget that life is not a numbers game.

Ancient wisdom gives us the insight to make a divine distinction between cause and effect. It allows one to delve into the roots to resolve problems. Most problems emerge at the roots that cannot be seen. They crop up without flashing a warning signal on the CEO's table. Ancient wisdom succeeds where corporate wisdom does not, by helping us see the unseen and hearing the unheard.

In the new age, we grapple most of the time with the effects, without understanding the causes. We only see the 'effects' and try to find solutions to the problems we encounter. Such solutions provide only partial relief and problems will crop up again in some other form. And then we might say, 'Today's problems are yesterday's solutions.'

Once we fail to address the cause of the problem when we first encounter it, we fail to reconise a new problem as a solution of the past. An inexperienced manager attacks the problem of high inventory costs and 'solves' the problem—except that the sales force now has to spend 20 per cent more time responding to angry complaints from customers who are still waiting for delayed shipments. What apeared to be a solution wasn't one at all. While clamping down on costs, we fail to see the invisible hidden cost of exercising such rigorous controls. Business management is not just a game of tidy figures.

The truth is always simple, yet it cannot be seen. Certain experiences in life are unbelievable. But that does not discount the quality of the experience. We cannot understand the subtle truth with the aid of hardened logic or lifeless science. I don't pretend that what I am saying is easy to comprehend: it certainly won't be if you are conditioned to think in a particular way. Ancient wisdom is in perfect balance with the cosmic principles and can be aligned to the corporate world. All it needs is an intuitive ability to understand the subtlety of truth.

Ancient wisdom has no past and no future. It is frozen in time. It has an Old World purity. When I talk about the virtues of ancient wisdom it is not a fantasy.

We need to develop a new perspective. The corporate argot already has a term that connotes this: it is called 'eco-approach'. Plunder the ancient gold mines of wisdom, virtue and values, and you will find the solutions to both life and the corporate world in the new age...

Part II

Chinese Vista

'Chinese philosophy' is a unique blend of intuitive wisdom and practical knowledge, based on logic and reasoning that the Chinese have associated with the images of the sage and the king. Such a fine balance is peerless.

Two sages were born in China almost around the same period: Lao Tzu and Confucius. Lao Tzu pleaded for intuitive wisdom, while Confucius emphasised logic and reasoning. Chinese sagacity is a blend of spiritualism and worldly affairs.

3

Wu Wei—The Dance of Change

Managing a country is like cooking small fish. The more you stir them the less their shape can be maintained.

—Lao Tzu

❦ Change Dynamics ❧

'Change or perish'— then
'Change and perish'—now

Before we speak of change, we must first understand its dynamics, or else failure is inevitable. The art of Wu Wei is all about change dynamics.

Wordsworth said: 'Child is the father of man'. It is one of the most perspicacious statements I have heard. A lot of our understanding about the universe ultimately connects with what we heard, saw or learnt in our childhood.

Similarly, my limited understanding of Wu Wei was revealed to me by a few sparrows one summer day during my childhood.

One day my sister and I discovered a baby sparrow that had fallen out of the nest that had been built in a cavity in the ceiling of our house. The baby sparrow's parents perched on the ground and made encouraging chirps to try and inspire the young one to get up and fly. The baby sparrow made several feeble attempts but was unable to do so.

We watched the scene for a while. Soon, we wanted to become active players and decided to help the sparrow. My sister took the lead and I obediently followed her. To comfort and warm the baby sparrow, we first wrapped it up in cotton gauze and then made several abortive attempts to feed it. My sister twisted a piece of cotton gauze and soaked it in milk. I forced open the beak of the baby sparrow and she attempted to pour in the drops. The tiny bird resisted but we went on forcing our goodness upon it. The sparrow's parents hovered around us and chirped in protest but not loud enough to force us to abandon our 'compassionate' experiment.

After a while, the sparrows decided to abandon their child. They flew away. As one can guess, the baby sparrow died, leaving us dumb struck!

Wisdom dawned: there are certain things in life that we must allow to occur without intervention. When we turn impatient and try to make things happen, we sometimes hamper the process and destroy the product. Manifestation needs no intervention. It follows the law of rhythm. Flower buds bloom with a smile at dawn when the dewdrops plant their subtle kiss. One must learn passion and fantasy from Nature—and that is the art of Wu Wei!

There are many lessons in Nature that are relevant for the corporate world. You cannot rush change. In the new age, several companies have perished because their Chief Executive officers (CEOs) have tried to manage change without understanding the underlying paradoxical 'change dynamics'—the dynamic stability. The ancient art of Wu Wei is akin to dynamic stability.

The corporate world is on the cusp of a new epoch. Our memory of the past is weak and we cannot 'remember' our future. Are we smart enough to change our outlook? Or, should we depend on a crystal ball to tell us what awaits us in the future?

ⓦ The Death of Scientific Management ⓦ

The death of so-called 'scientific management' is certain. This raises an inevitable question: was management ever a science? The answers vary depending on what you understand management to mean. If it is about people, management can never be a science. Dealing with people and getting the best out of them is an art, and not a science. Business management is most unpredictable—the only certainty is uncertainty.

> We are at the end of one period of "building modern organizations, and at the beginning of a new period".
>
> —**Peter Drucker**

Work-study, job evaluation, ergonomics and value engineering are just a few small slices of a big pie.

Unfortunately, what has happened is that the small slices have hogged all the attention. Here is my proposition: it is the tail that wags the dog and the banana that eats the monkey. If that sounds ludicrous, tell me why technology has become such a huge article of faith with corporates? Companies have reached a point where they are ready to mangle their business strategies to mesh with the available technologies. Should it not have been the other way round? Today, most of us are standing upside down and, therefore, think that the upright person is actually standing on his head. When our concepts and approaches are skewed, the right appears to be grossly wrong.

We have developed a fetish of trying to project 'business management' as a science. Blame it all on Fredrick Winslow Taylor (1856–1917) who coined a catchphrase—'scientific management'. There is, of course, another deeper cause why we consider management as a science. Business management came into existence when science was at its ascendant. 'To be scientific' was a matter of great pride: it signified a 'modern' outlook. Science grew and prospered and gave primacy to logic and reasoning over wisdom, virtue, intuition and ethical values. So, when business management took birth during the age of science, it acquired her DNA! It adopted logic and mathematics as its mother tongue as science knew only these languages.

Mathematics is the language of science. We have complicated business management by trying to explain everything in terms of equations. We even attempted to define human behaviour through numbers and intelligence through quotients—Intelligent Quotient, Emotional Quotient, and now Spiritual Quotient. Like blacksmiths, we hammered out the subtlety and became insensitive to the softer and finer aspects of management.

> *Business Management is not "Rocket Science"; we have chosen world's more simple profession.*
>
> **—Jack Welch**

We forgot that 'intangibles' represent the flip side of management. Intangibles are not the kith and kin of science. We have also forgotten that 'intangibles' make the 'tangibles'. Science dislikes dealing with anything that is abstract. 'Keep it simple' is the new-age message for business leaders: simple vision articulation; simple communication; simple systems; simple processes; simple measures...

What is the life span of science vis-à-vis the cosmic age? The 'scientific era' that we boast about is not even a nanosecond in terms of 'cosmic time', which dates back to 10 to 20 billion years. In contrast, the lifespan of modern science is just a few hundred years.

The beginning of humankind is assumed in the Pliocene epoch (5 million to 1.8 million years ago); manlike apes appeared around 5 million years ago! Even human civilization is more than 10,000 years old. Such an understanding should sober us up before we express our infatuation with science. Virtue and wisdom are age old; science is a mere suckling! We are at the end of one period of scientific management—'building modern organisations'—and at the beginning of a 'new period'.

What is this new period? What will it look like? Whom shall we worship? There are a host of such questions...

Let me make a wild guess. The emerging post-scientific/ post-modern era of business management will be the era of ethics and spirituality where purpose, vision, values, virtue, wisdom will be the new gods of worship. Creativity and innovation will become essential attributes for managers who wish to thrive in

> *We are going to see companies increasingly assume that "What they stand for" in an enduring sense is more important than what they "sell".*
>
> **—James Collins and Jerry Porras**
> *(Build to Last)*

the chaos amidst uncertainties. We will move from 'denominator management' to 'numerator management': so 'cost effectiveness' and 'downsizing' —the buzzwords of today—will fall by the wayside. The focus will be on healthy growth and happiness and prosperity of the stakeholders—customers, employees, shareholders, vendors and society.

Both business ideology and business character will undergo a major change. In the new age, a magical alchemy will emerge from a unique blend of the 'culture of discipline' and 'entrepreneurial ethics'.

◖ The Age of Uncertainty ◗

There is no sure-fire, cure-all, snake-oil remedy in business management, and certainly no crystal ball to predict the future.

Those who claim to be 'corporate prophets' are simply snake charmers or charlatans. It is part of an elaborate charade: like snake charming which is a massive deception. All snakes are deaf. So, how do they dance to the tunes of the charmer? They sway to sinuous movements of the charmer. It is much the same with the so-called corporate prophets. Entrepreneurs shape their strategies for the future firmly believing in their predictions. It is not as if the management gurus predict the future; they posit a course of action for companies. Sometimes, their theories catch on and everyone moves in that direction. In a way, they simply create a new 'corporate consciousness' that brings about the real change.

Tom Peters coined a slogan: 'Leap then look'!' Suddenly, everyone started leaping without looking. It turned into a mad scramble to find the new buzzword, catch the next trend, ride the next wave. Speed has become the dominant factor: we have divided time into milliseconds, microseconds, nanoseconds, picoseconds, femtoseconds, and attoseconds. Today, even one-millionth part of an attosecond can be measured. The high rate of productivity and fast growth rate resulted in a cancer in the sense that it has created imbalances. Cancer is a kind of rapid and unwanted growth. When products were produced in surplus disproportionate to market demands, consumption needs and affordability, producers did not know what to do with the surplus stocks! So, they tried to enlarge the pie: consumers were persuaded to eat more than their stomachs could digest, develop new habits, and splurge on new products ranging from technology to soft drinks! Thus, we have started consuming our future by not only eating what would have been consumed by the next generation but also by exploiting natural resources in an indiscriminate manner, thereby depriving future generations of a healthy ecology. The corporate prophets did not forecast a future of this kind: they had only predicted speed! They did not even have a clue about the consequences of their advice.

Nothing illustrates this better than a story for nursery children. A chicken was running about crazily. A rat asked, 'Why are you running?' The chicken replied hysterically, 'Hurry up, hurry up, the sky is going to fall...' and the rat followed the chicken. A cat saw them running and asked, 'Why are you running about madly?' The rat replied, 'Hurry up, hurry up, the sky is going to fall' and the cat followed the rat and the chicken. They were then joined by a dog, a donkey, a horse, and a camel. It had soon swelled into a huge cavalcade that was rushing about as the 'sky was about to fall'. No one stopped to think: 'Can this mad rush save us if the sky really caves in? Can we go beyond the territory canopied by the sky?' When we act thoughtlessly, the brain stops functioning. The corporate world is caught up in a similar mad rush—no one has the time to pause and think why everyone is running helter-skelter. If you stop, you will be trampled upon. But is this speed dynamic? Certainly not. The

irony is that even at this fast pace, each runner is 'static' in relative terms. You remain where you are in relative terms because the competitors are all running at the same speed.

In life, as in business management, 'moderation' has its own significance. One must have time for reflection. People of wisdom understand this and follow what is known as the 'universal law of energy response'—the manifestation of a set pattern of cause and effect!

The road that leads to the future is paved with uncertainties. Uncertainty is the only certainty. The future is a perfect mystery. The future is very fuzzy. Let me try and put it in simpler words.

The future appears before us in 'patterns'. 'Once' is an instance; 'twice' is a coincidence. But three or more times make a 'pattern'. The only way to understand the future is by switching to a 'pattern-seeking/pattern-finding' mode. One such pattern that management gurus have discovered through experience can be distilled into a basic premise: what was applicable yesterday is not appropriate today and will surely not be fully relevant tomorrow. This hasn't happened once or twice but many times. So, it has formed a pattern. We understand our present and evolve systems and business

> *A cloud does not know why it moves in just such a direction and at such a speed ... But the sky knows the reasons and the patterns behind all clouds and you will know too, when you lift yourself high enough to see beyond horizons.*
>
> —**Richard Bach**
> *(Illusions)*

processes based on reasons that make a lot of sense to us. We religiously follow these systems and processes. Time passes and things change. The original reasoning for generation of systems and processes may no longer exist but because the systems are still in place, we continue to follow them until new awakening strikes and we realise 'it will not work anymore'.

The other reliable way to look into the future is by fully understanding the present. Unfortunately, we tend to look into the future while still living in the past, without even *wanting* to understand the present. When we fail to recognise the patterns of today, we cannot make even a wild guess about what might happen tomorrow. So, understand your present to reach the future.

There is another approach: I call it the 'bellwether approach'. Today, the US is undisputedly the front-runner and its actions are aped by the western world, Japan and ASEAN countries. In one sense, the US' yesterday is the today of the advanced European and ASEAN countries, and shall be the tomorrow of other developing countries.

But a subtle change is beginning to take place: a section of corporate America is creating a new pattern by leaning towards spirituality and ethical values. It is the US again (not its politicians but its corporate covens) that wants to lead the corporate world into a new age that is filled with sagacity. It is ironic that countries in Asia—which have always had a rich spiritual tradition—will again ape the US to find its ethical moorings in its Eastern and Oriental wisdom.

❦ Change and Wisdom in a New Age ❧

Time cannot be sliced into past, present and future. Every new age is a continuous, seamless, timeless eternal present. Both past and future dwell in the new age. When I say new age, I mean a continuum. We have created the words—past, present and future—to sharpen our common understanding.

No one can say when the old economy ceases and the new economy emerges.

The new age is an integrated game. IBM makes computer hardware; but you can't operate those computers without software. That is where Bill Gates and Microsoft come in. So, in one sense, IBM needs Bill Gates, and Bill Gates will always need Andy Grove (founder of Intel, which makes computer chips). Grove will always need Akio Morita of Sony and so on. Like the temporal world, the corporate world is also inter-connected and inter-dependent.

So what is new in this New Age? To understand the new age, we must first understand the present as a continuum, and not in terms of time slices. However, we need to name these segments as past, present and future, to enhance our understanding. There is absolute tranquillity in the present moment. The 'eternal present' is the *sine qua non* of the new age.

> *In this spiritual world there are no time divisions such as the Past, Present and Future for they have contracted themselves into a single moment, the Present where life quivers in true sense ... the Past and the Future are both rolled up in this Present moment of illumination, and with all its contents, for it ceaselessly moves on.*
>
> —DT Suzuki

The future is an absolute enigma—an unknown miracle that man must wait for. The other way to look at the future is to see it simply as 'the past modified by the present!' One may accuse me of saying two paradoxical things in the same breath. But what we call truth is nothing but a paradox. For, instance, the subatomic particles are matter and energy simultaneously. Readers will witness such paradoxical statements quite often in the subsequent chapters. I can assure them that

44

what may appear to be paradoxical on the surface will not be conflicting or contradictory statements. Understanding 'Koans' (paradoxical truth) lets one understand the truth. In the new age, the test of superior intelligence will be the ability to hold two paradoxical ideas and keep them in absolute harmony.

Eastern mysticism has developed several ways of dealing with the paradoxical aspects of reality. Lao Tzu's *Tao Te Ching* was written in an extremely puzzling, seemingly illogical style. But the purpose of the book was meant to arrest the reader's mind and throw it off its familiar track of logical reasoning.

> *The violent reaction on the recent development of modern physics can only be understood when one realizes that here the foundations of physics have started moving; and that this motion has caused the feeling that the ground would be cut from science.*
>
> —**Heisenberg**

Tao Te Ching is full of intriguing contradictions and its compact, powerful, and extremely poetic language takes the readers entirely into a different plane. It explains through words what words cannot explain!

All that I have mentioned, and am likely to mention here, may seem irrelevant and out of context with the theme of this chapter. But such a prelude is essential to understand this profound art. To understand Wu Wei one must possess

> *I remember discussions with (Niels) Bohr which went through many hours till very late at night and ended almost in despair; and when at the end of the discussions I went alone for a walk in the neighbouring park I repeated to myself again and again the question: Can Nature possibly be so absurd as it seemed to us in the atomic experiments?*
>
> —**Heisenberg**

intuitive wisdom and a deeper insight to understand a paradox. What was taught in ancient times as a 'koan' has today become a scientific reality. Most new-age managers will be amazed to learn that Niels Bohr and Werner Heisenberg—the founders of quantum theory in physics—experienced exactly the same paradoxical situation of a 'koan': the subatomic particles turned out to be matter and energy simultaneously! This new awakening provided space for spirituality in science. Today, physics has become metaphysics and technology is searching for its soul to stay alive.

In the new age, terms like 'inner self', 'unspoken' and 'unseen' and 'ineffable' will have their appropriate places in business management. The new age will witness more 'spirituality' and ethical values. A spiritual revolution in the corporate world is ready to erupt.

> *Over time, America has transformed from a technically comfortble place into a technically intoxicated zone ... Technology feeds our pleasure centres physically and mentally, but its intoxication is squeezing out human spirit, intensifying our search for meaning.*
>
> —**John Naisbitt**
> *(High-tech; High-touch)*

The new age revolution does not remain confined to oriental philosophy and spirituality. There is a huge search for spirituality in the world today, especially in the US. There is a growing realisation that it is time to have more spiritual power than development of technology and science. Love and truth will be the most dominating ethical values in business. Performance without virtue will be taken as an act of the devil. Performance through virtue will be a common business practice tomorrow.

Where has the mad race brought us? Today, the US is facing a unique business paradox—the cost of medical treatment is too high; medical centres and hospitals are going bankrupt! It is time to shift from illness to wellness. This new awakening will act as some sort of a 'singularity' to create a new big bang in the corporate world.

❦ The Dance of Change ❧

The corporate world is morphing. Let me try and explain this metamorphosis by using the metaphor of trapeze artists in a circus. Metamorphosis is not just about 'managing change'; it is rather a more natural process. 'Managing change' in a corporate sense is typically with human intervention. The art of Wu Wei explains how change can be managed without human intervention. One must first understand the dynamics of change—the dance of change.

I watched my first circus show one summer evening along with my parents. The show began with jugglers performing a variety of feats. Watching them was great fun— jugglers, acrobats, gymnasts, and clowns. Then, came the trapeze artists. Charming girls swung from one crossbar to another. The clown mocked them and raised a joyous fizz. The girls caught the clown and tossed him from one crossbar to another like a ball. Amid all the fun and slapstick humour, the clown missed the crossbar and fell. The crowd whooped in joy enthralled by the 'falling feat', little realising that it was a deadly fall. When it dawned on them, there was a hue and cry. Many years have passed but I have never been able to forget the deadly fall of the clown.

Today, I understand the dynamics of change—the dance of change—through the acrobatics of the trapeze artists. Swinging from one bar to another is not easy. What we hold tightly is the crossbar of the accomplished past. What swings towards us is the crossbar of the unseen and uncertain future.

47

The space between the two swinging bars provides an 'anchorless' moment. Managing change is all about managing this anchorless moment. Managing change is a trapeze act. During my three decades of experience in corporate India, both in public and private sector companies, I have been an unfortunate witness to three such deadly falls. These three organisations (mis)managed change and perished. Why do I say 'mismanaged'? This is because they did not realise that managing change is all about managing the 'anchorless' moment in a trapeze act.

When a trapeze artist lets go off one crossbar, she holds her breath until she gains a firm grip over the other swinging bar. Managing change is managing this 'uncertainty'. What will happen to me? What will happen to my company? These anxieties need clear and satisfactory answers. If they are convinced by the answers, the 'anchorless' moment creates excitement. If they are not convinced, the same moment creates breath-ceasing anxiety. Those who can convert 'anxiety' into 'excitement' succeed. The process of change is that simple, but most practising managers and entrepreneurs have little or no understanding of it.

The process of natural change is seamless; there is no anxiety in being 'anchorless' as there is no managed transition. But managing change with human intervention is difficult because in doing so, one tries to swim against the current. When we try to manage change, we don't even try to locate the 'cornerstone'. If you remove one wrong stone, the whole structure will collapse. We are not extra cautious while effecting change. We assume that this is just another business activity, which is a fallacy. Lao Tzu, the Old Master says: 'Be alert, like men crossing a winter stream; be alert, like men aware of danger!'

Each dawn passes through perfect darkness. Each dusk appears out of the fading brightness. Between the black and the white lie many gradients and nuances. At dusk, dawn or puberty—at every stage of transition or rite of pasage—there is always twilight. Twilight is hazy. Managing twilight is managing the future. But to see through the twilight needs great wisdom—intuitive

> *Oh God! Give me the courage to change what I can; the serenity to accept what I can't; and the wisdom to know and accept the difference.*
>
> —**Swami Vivekananda**

wisdom. The art of Wu Wei is all about gaining intuitive wisdom to understand the dynamics of change—the dance of change on nature's rhythms.

Awakening is the seed of transformation. When one transforms, a self-transformation of a grander kind takes place. When we talk about the metamorphosis of the new age, it is more a transformation than managing change or shaping the future. It is more a process of manifestation—unfolding of nature. Change may hurt; manifestation never hurts. It is a natural process. It is a divine process. Can such divinity be made a part of the transition when it comes to business? My answer is, 'Yes'.

⍦ Dynamic Stability ⍦

Dynamic stability is a corporate paradox. What the Bhagvad Gita calls 'action in inaction' and the Sufi Kahlil Gibran terms as 'going in staying', help explain 'dynamic stability' with a spiritual touch and philosophical flavour.

Sometimes change is more effective when it hurts less. That's where a new approach to change—dynamic stability—

49

> *My house says to me, "Don't leave me, for here dwells your past."*
> *And the road says to me, "Come and follow me, for I am your future." And I say to both my house and the road, "I have no past, nor have I a future.*
> *If I stay here, there is a 'going in my staying'. And if go, there is a 'staying in my going'.*
> *Only love and death change all things."*
>
> **—Kahlil Gibran**

comes in. The art of Wu Wei can be understood better if one can understand what we mean by 'dynamic stability'. Change, if not managed smoothly, is so disruptive that it can tear an organisation apart.

GE started with what one may call, 'creative destruction' in the 1980s.

Later, when wisdom dawned, the same Jack Welch brought transformation with a human touch that was far less disruptive. GE's success story owes much to dynamic stability. Jack Welch was a voracious reader. I suspect some of his later practices in GE were the result of his inspiration from Lao Tzu's *Tao Te Ching*. Lao Tzu has been the source of spiritual stimulation for many corporate leaders and modern spiritual gurus.

> *Achieving* dynamic stability *is more difficult than ramming big, hairy, auditions changes through an organization, in much the same way that it is more difficult to end a war with negotiations than with an atomic bomb. But dynamic stability has the great advantage of leaving survivors. It allows change without fatal pain.*
>
> **—Eric Abrahamson**
> *(Change without Pain)*

50

Shakespeare said, 'They stumble that run fast.' People of wisdom realised that while managing rapid changes, one must know when to slow down. They also realised that continual but relatively small changes that involve the reconfiguration of existing practices and business character— tinkering—rather than the creation of new ones, prove to be less painful and more effective. Change is constant—it has remained all the time with us. But the idea of change itself is changing. Corporate people are increasingly becoming aware of Wu Wei.

You can't change the universe. It is sacred and perfect in its own way. There are certain truths that even the sages do not understand. Therefore, the sages avoid extremes—both excesses and complacencies. Both Buddha and Lao Tzu speak in the same tone when it comes to 'moderation'. Buddha's middle path is no more an ancient wisdom; it has become a corporate wisdom—a corporate metaphor. 'Moderation' is a modest beginning of the art of Wu Wei.

The seed of change is paradox. It needs both movement and stillness at the same time. It requires patience and urgency simultaneously. 'Pacing' is necessary for smooth transition. One needs to bring constant personal and corporate change as an 'on-going process' rather than as 'one-time' surgery. The art of Wu Wei subscribes to the former and opposes the latter.

I believe the new age can be managed better through the Art of Wu Wei. Big and small changes must be allowed to happen at the right intervals. The art of Wu Wei is not 'inaction'. It is an art to discover action in 'inaction' and 'inaction' in 'action'.

◖ The Soul of Wu Wei ◗

What is Wu Wei?

'Manifestation' is the soul of Wu Wei. To explain this complex concept in simple words, I borrow the text from Gordon L. Zineithwicz's article, *The Tao and Art:* 'As a plant emerges from hiding within the seed beneath the earth and erupts upward toward the light of the sun, reaches maturity, flowers, dies, and returns to the earth, so all things natural are continually in a process of coming to be and passing away, prospering and declining, appearing and disappearing, rising and falling, emerging and returning.'

Things come to be in nature the way an infant is born of its mother, through non-action (Wu Wei). The bud blossoms, dewdrops fall early in the morning, the fragrance of flowers wafts with the breeze, winds blow, clouds move: Nature works through non-action. Wu Wei does not mean 'doing nothing'; Wu Wei means 'doing without forcing'. Nature does not make, does not form things, as a craftsman forms material into a pre-determined shape. Nature just manifests.

Wu Wei is an ancient Taoist art of living, practised by most of the Chinese monks in the good old days. As mentioned earlier, Lao Tzu's work mostly reflects Wu Wei— the law of manifestation without or rather beyond human intervention. 'Wu Wei is essentially the process of accepting and harmonising with the "flow". Just as you can't catch water in a net, there is no set of rules, no matter how flexible, extensive or subtle, that can capture flow,' explains Peter Merel.

The art of Wu Wei is based on the universal law of energy response—let cosmic forces play their role polarising

opposite poles. Let things happen without human intervention. Let life unfold and unfurl.

The other day I received an e-mail from my cyber-friend,
Charles. He enclosed an attachment—Butterfly. The creator
of this marvellous text of wisdom requested Internet surfers
to send the message to their friends to show them how much
they cared. I 'pay forward' the good turn that I received from
Charles.

The Butterfly

*One day, a small opening appeared in a cocoon; a little boy sat
and watched the butterfly for several hours as it struggled to force
its body through that little hole.*

*Then, it seemed to stop making progress. It appeared as if it
had gotten as far as it could and it would not go any further. So
the little boy decided to help the butterfly; he took a pair of scissors
and opened the cocoon. The butterfly then emerged easily.*

*But the little boy continued to watch because he expected that, at
any moment, the wings would open, enlarge and expand, to be
able to support the butterfly's body, and become firm. Neither
happened! In fact, the butterfly spent the rest of its life with a
withered body and shrivelled wings. It never was able to fly.*

*What the little boy, in his kindness and his goodwill did not
understand, was that the struggle required for that butterfly to get
through the tiny opening, was God's way of forcing, fluid from the
body of the butterfly into its wings, so that it would be ready for
flight once it achieved its freedom from the cocoon.*

Manifestation allows things to happen. You cannot
always make things happen. There's a divine distinction
between the two. The wisdom that lets you understand the

difference between the two is the secret of success. A winner knows when to act and when not to act. In life, there's a time to be aggressive and a time to be passive, a time to work and a time to rest, a time to hurry and a time to wait and watch. The universal law of energy response is not static. Manifestation is 'dynamic stability'.

A business leader needs to develop an intuitive eye that can see 'action' in 'inaction' and 'inaction' in 'action'. What I call 'manifestation' is much the same as active 'inaction'. People of wisdom understand this implicitly. They allow things to manifest for they see action in 'inac-

> *He who sees "inaction" in "action" and "action" in "inaction" is a man of established wisdom and a true performer of all actions.*
> —Bhagvad Gita

tion'. What is 'action'? What is 'inaction'? Even the wise are sometimes confused. It is hard to understand the course of action.

Let me try to explain this by borrowing from Albert Einstein the concept of 'frame of reference'. 'Action' or 'motion' has relevance with the 'Coordinate System'. It makes a marked difference when the seer and the seen are in two different 'Coordinate Systems' (CS), and when they are in the same 'Coordinate System'—what appears to be 'motion' could appear 'motionless'. In a moving train my co-passenger is 'motionless' with respect to me, but a person sitting in another halted train will find my co-passenger and me in 'motion'. And if his train also moves and picks up the speed of my train and both the trains run parallel to each other, we all three will be 'motionless' again.

The art of Wu Wei is 'wisdom in practice' that gives you the required patience to wait, watch and allow things to happen keeping a sharp focus on your objectives. This art enables you to chip in effortlessly without exerting. It lets you make your place and contribution in the 'occurring event' naturally.

In simple words, the art of Wu Wei is a Taoist practice of not working 'against the grain of things', of waiting for the right moment without forcing anything unduly. All that you have to do is to remain alert and focused on your purpose, and sooner or later the right opportunity will knock on your door, things will start falling into place. In simple words the art of Wu Wei is all about 'total harmony with nature'. This art is a reflection of six tenets of Taoism:

- Don't force things on people
- Be unmovable—let events flow over you
- Maintain the universal balance—Yin and Yang
- All things are one, interrelated
- Ideally, one should desire nothing—desires upset equilibrium
- The art of Wu Wei—action through inaction

❧ Tai Chi Tu' ❧

Tai Chi Tu'—Yin and Yang—is the seat of Chinese vista and the soul of Taoism. Tu' means symbol; Tai Chi refers to two dynamic natural forces—Yin and Yang.

As a metaphor they mean two sides of a hill range; shady and sunny. Yin is the shady part that is cool and tranquil. Yin represents all feminine traits: calmness, tranquillity, serenity and stillness. Yang is the sunny portion of the hill range. It is dazzling and hot. Yang represents all masculine traits: robust, mighty, active and vibrant. Yin has the seed of Yang and Yang has the seed of Yin. In a fishlike figure, these seeds are shown as the eye of the fish. These seeds of 'opposite traits' grow and Yin transforms into Yang and Yang transforms into Yin over time. Yin and Yang also represent the life philosophy. Neither the clouds nor the sunny days will ever stay; they give way to each other. The bright day comes out of the dark night and the bright day gives birth to a dark night. The Chinese believe that Yang, having reached its climax, retreats in favour of the Yin and vice versa. The ancient Chinese saw all changes in nature as manifestation of the dynamic interplay between the polar opposite—Yin and Yang.

> *The universe is sacred. You cannot improve it. If you try to change it, you will ruin it. If you try to hold it, you will lose it. Therefore, the sage avoids extremes: excess, and complacency.*
>
> —Lao Tzu

The Chinese feel that whenever a situation develops to its extreme, it is bound to retreat and become its opposite. At dusk the cock announces dawn; at midnight, the bright sun. This basic belief has given them courage and confidence in times of distress. Chiefly due to these two reversible opposite poles of Tai Chi, they have become cautious and modest in times of success. It has led to Buddha's doctrine of the golden mean, in which both Taoists and Confucians believe. 'The sage,' says Lao Tzu, 'avoids excess, extravagance and indulgence.'

Our own language echoes the wisdom found within the concept of Yin-Yang. Bad luck becomes good luck and crisis contains the opportunity for growth. We can choose to cooperate with this complementary set of opposites by not denying, suppressing, or struggling against unwanted discomfort or pain but rather by accepting all facets of our existence, 'good' and 'bad', as the natural flow of Nature.

The up and down path of the Tao can also be called the 'principle of reversion'. Eventually, any state of being reverts or returns to its opposite. Any extreme is a turning point, a threshold, a limit. When a thing has reached its limit, it changes into its opposite. This happens because it contains within itself the seed of the opposite. Tai Chi explains the 'change dynamics' of Nature. The Wu Wei masters lean towards the Nature and gain wisdom from Nature. All of us see how Nature manifests, but we don't learn from it. We know that as summer progresses, the days grow longer while the nights grow shorter. Finally, there comes the longest day. The reversal begins after it reaches the apogee. This way Nature sustains and remains in existence. It does not allow itself to go too far; it does not allow one extreme to stay at the expense of the other.

A wise person is guided by Nature. He knows the secret of Nature's mode of acting (Wu Wei, non-action). The wise person imitates this naturalness. He is not pushy, aggressive, or violent. He does not seek excessive pleasure for it reverts to pain. He does not seek great wealth for it reverts to poverty. He does not seek political power of fame for it also reverts. He does not even strive to be a Confucian Chun-tzu. Let me explain how the Confucian approach differs from Taoist belief in terms of Tai Chi—the soul of Wu Wei.

I have talked about Yang and Yin—the two polar opposites. On the active side are heavens, light, activities, form, etc. For Confucians there is a time to act and a time to remain inactive. But Taoist belief is exactly the opposite. A Taoist Wu Wei master waits and allows manifestation to take its course and lets his deeds emerge spontaneously and naturally, as day flows from night. In the West, Heraclitus was impressed with Wu Wei and adopted this model for his philosophy, but Plato chose Confucian Chun-tzu. The West has forgotten the

57

genius Heraclitus and remembered only Plato. So, it becomes difficult for them and for those who drink management wisdom from the western cup to understand and follow Wu Wei as it runs counter to all their learning and beliefs. As for corporate India, it is more western in its thoughts and practices than the western corporate world. Having reached its material limits, the US may turn in the opposite direction sooner than India. Corporate America will make peace with Nature early as it has been quarrelling with it all along.

Like Tai Chi, which represents the true equilibrium of Yin and Yang, Wu Wei is all about the right equilibrium. It is like the right tension in a bow that is drawn neither too tight nor too loose. If you sharpen a blade too little, it will not cut. If you sharpen a blade too much, it becomes dull.

Equilibrium is the soul of Wu Wei. One can create melody only when the strings of the musical instruments are neither too loose nor too tight. When the strings of the heart are very loose, the heart will not sing the song of life.

✍ 'Non-action' is not 'No-action' ✍

Confucius philosophy, known as Chun-Tzu, provides a bit of action to the Art of Wu Wei. He believes that there is a time to act and a time to refrain from acting, a time to speak and a time to remain silent, a time to move forward and a time to hold back. But one needs to act. 'Nature needs to be cultivated and polished. Unformed human nature is good, but consciously formed and disciplined or refined human nature is still better.'

Some people misunderstand the art of Wu Wei as 'doing nothing'. They don't understand the deeper meaning of non-action. Wu Wei means doing without forcing, and without con picuously acting as per plans, which does not mean that one should not act. In fact, Lao Tzu opposes only 'too much' interference. He was not against action *per se*. He believed that too much activity interferes with the creative process, and too much planning kills spontaneity. Both Nature and human nature are ruined by too much interference. He firmly held the view that too much cultivation destroys the land, too much government corrupts the people, and excessive 'moral training' turns people into robbers.

'A common translation of Wu Wei is "not doing"', writes Kiel Hodges. He later emphasises how 'not doing' can be a better option. 'When a problem arises, many people feel they have to "do something" about it and they do something that is counter-productive because there are no productive alternatives—except "doing nothing" which people don't see as an alternative.' And when people intervene, they do not allow a chrysalis to evolve into a butterfly.

'More subtly, Wu Wei is "not doing" in the sense of not "contending, competing, arguing, ranting, boasting, invading, and winning". So you might choose to do something subtle that others would discount as nothing at all,' suggests Hodges.

To put Wu Wei into a business context, Peter Drucker said that the important thing is not to 'do things right' but to 'do right things' i.e. the choice of 'what to do' is more important than 'how to do'. I think the application of Wu Wei would say that there may be nothing which is right to do at a particular time.

Buddha said, 'Don't just do something; stand there!' It means sometimes it is better not to intervene. One must have the wisdom to decide when to intervene and when not to. We must understand that when someone chooses not to decide or not to act, he still has made a choice. It is important to distinguish Wu Wei from passivism. Wu Wei is not pushing, nor just standing there, but harmonising with your partner in order to dance.

The origin of Wu Wei has led to an interesting debate. The term itself is Taoist, from Lao Tzu, coming as a reaction against Confucius' (Kung Fu Tzu) concept of 'Li', meaning order. 'But the notion (Wu Wei) is older still,' argues Peter Mere. 'You can see plenty of it (Wu Wei) in Bhagvad Gita, which antedates Buddha by three Millennia.'

I take issue with assertion that 'the Bhagvad Gita was within three millennia before the time of Buddha'. Buddha (563–483 BC), Kung Fu Tzu who is popularly known as Confucius (551–479 BC) and Lao Tzu (born in 604 BC) belong to the 6th century BC, whereas Mahabharata, the classical Sanskrit epic, was probably composed between 200 BC and AD 200, as per the concise *Columbia Encyclopedia*. Needless to say that the Bhagvad Gita is part of the Mahabharata. Yes, the Vedas and some of the Upanishads antedate the Buddha, but the Bhagvad Gita was composed a few centuries after the death of Buddha. My advice is that we should not take away the sweetness of Chinese Vista largely created by Lao Tzu and Confucius (Kung Fu Tzu).

> *The sage tells us: Accept disgrace willingly. Accept being unimportant. Do not be concerned with loss or gain. Love the world as you love your own self. Then you can truly care for all things.*
>
> **—A Tao thought**

Wu Wei is an unforced, spontaneous natural action (not in conformity with artificial standards) that allows the true nature to emerge. In fact the Wu Wei masters are great change makers. Wu Wei masters, in a sense, are the mid-wives of Nature; out of pregnant emptiness they seek manifestation.

They can see many things in nothing. They can see action in inaction. They can see movement in stillness.

In life, sometimes, one must follow the art of Wu Wei, waiting for the right moment and getting into the process effortlessly. Look for the right moment without forcing anything unduly. Otherwise, you will either be killing a 'baby sparrow' or making the 'butterfly' a withered creature.

> *The stillness in stillness is not the real stillness. Only when there is stillness in movement can the spiritual rhythm appear which pervades heaven and earth.*
>
> —Lao Tzu

Fritjof Capra, a renowned physicist and the author of many books, believes in and practices the art of Wu Wei. He writes in his *Uncommon Wisdom*, 'I sought to heighten my intuitive awareness and to recognise "the patterns of the Tao"; I was practising the Art of Wu Wei, that is, of not working "against the grain of things," of waiting for the right moment without forcing anything unduly... I knew that all I had to do was remain alert and focused on my purpose, and sooner or later the right people would cross my path.' In his famous book, *The Tao of Physics*, Capra writes, 'Those who follow the natural order flow in the current of the Tao. Such a way of acting is called Wu Wei in Taoist philosophy, a term which means literally 'non-action', and which Joseph Needham translates as "refraining from activity contrary to nature", justifying this interpretation with a quotation from Chuang Tzu: "Non-action does not mean doing nothing and keeping silent. Let everything be allowed to do what it naturally does, so that its nature will be satisfied."

If one refrains from acting contrary to nature or, as Needham says, from 'going against the grain of things', one is in harmony with the Tao and thus one's actions will be successful. This is the meaning of Lao Tzu's seemingly puzzling words, 'By non-action everything can be done.'

'Managing less is managing simple.' There are simpler ways to lead organisations, the ones that require less efforts and cause less stress than the current practices.

The law of manifestation does not allow any intervention. Don't think you can take over the universe and improve it? 'I do not think it can be done,' says the Old Master. The universe is managed by 'non-action'. The Supreme Truth manages through 'non-action'. 'Tao does not act yet nothing is left undone.' What is this miracle? If this miracle works at the macro level, why shouldn't it work at the micro level? Peter Senge's *Systems Thinking* is one such great work about 'non-action', which has been little understood even by corporate masters and practitioners. 'Systems Thinking' is an ideal situation where no systems would be needed. When events take place in the universe, one believes in the unseen hands of the supreme power that is behind all cosmic processes—the processes that have some well-designed underlying pattern. When there is a cloud mass, the sky darkens and an earthy smell hangs in the air and we know that it will either rain or it is raining somewhere nearby. We also know that after the heavy downpour, the runoff will feed into the groundwater miles away, and the dark sky will turn blue and clear again! All these events are distant in time and space, yet they are all connected within the same pattern, what we call 'eco-system' in the new age terminology.

The actions of the 'Wu Wei master' thus arise out of his intuitive wisdom, spontaneously and in harmony with

> *Tao is non-action. Yet nothing is left undone.*
> *Practice "non-action", work without doing.*
>
> —**Lao Tzu**

his environment. He does not need to force himself, or anything around him, but merely adapts his actions to the movements of the nature. Wu Wei also implies action that is spontaneous, natural and effortless. It refers to behaviour that arises from a sense of oneself as connected to the others and to one's environment with invisible bonds. It implies an experience of going with the grain or swimming with the current—going with the flow of Nature. Tao exhorts us to 'experience ourselves as part of the unity of life'.

'For the past 2000 years, traditional western thinking has been dominated by a dualistic, either-or approach: either something is good, or it is bad; desirable or undesirable; someone is an ally or an enemy,' writes Ted Kardash in his article 'Taoism—Ageless Wisdom for Modern World'. 'We perceive experiences to be either positive or negative and we expend much energy in trying to eradicate what we consider to be negative. From a Taoist point of view, this is like trying to erase the negative current from electricity because it is not positive.'

The western outlook is based on the assumption that humans are all separate entities, existing apart from each other and from the surrounding environment. For this reason, one does not feel bad while abusing people or exploiting nature. 'Te' meaning 'virtue', on the other hand, implies a trust and belief in one's own inner nature and in the interconnectedness of life. Today, scientists, not spiritualists, have been endeavouring to formulate the 'bootstrap theory' or 'string theory' to prove the underlying 'interconnectedness' of the animate and inanimate things. With this, Taoism, and especially the Art of 'Wu Wei', has become increasingly popular with Americans. The other reason for leaning towards Wu Wei is the growing stress within the corporate world. As corporate life is becoming more stressful and complex, leading to mounting crises on personal, local, corporate and global levels, the search for the means to obtain peace and tranquillity has grown. They naturally seek solutions that will restore them to a more balanced, harmonious and satisfying way of living, both in real and corporate life.

Managing simple is managing best. We are all searching for simplicity and striving for a stress-free business management. As per a study, Bangladesh and India top the list when it comes to stressful management practices—Singapore rests in tranquility at the bottom among Asian countries following the least stressful practices. Singapore—the only 'intelligent country' of the world—has discovered the worth of simplicity and made the process very simple. To my mind, the matchless success of Singapore lies in discovering and excavating the golden wisdom from the ancient era—the art of Wu Wei!

Wu Wei also implies action that is spontaneous, natural, and effortless. To allow Wu Wei to

> *What is "action"?*
> *What is "inaction"?*
> *As to this, even the wise are confused.*
> *Therefore, I shall teach thee such action,*
> *By knowing which thou shalt be liberated from evil.*
> *Verily, the true nature of action should be known,*
> *As also of forbidden action and of inaction;*
> *It is hard to understand the course of action.*
> —**Bhagvad Gita (IV-16 & 17)**

manifest in our lives may seem like a Herculean task. However, if we pause to reflect on our past experiences, we will recall many instances when our actions were spontaneous and natural, when they arose out of the needs of the moment without thought of profit or tangible result. In life, we follow Wu Wei unknowingly. We follow it but forget. 'The work is done and then forgotten. And so it lasts forever,' says Lao Tzu.

Wu Wei is not 'non-action'; it ensures that our actions are truly spontaneous, natural, and effortless. We thus flow with all experiences and feelings as they ebb and flow. We know intuitively that actions, which are not ego motivated but are in response to the needs of the environment, lead towards a harmonious balance and give ultimate meaning and 'purpose' to our lives. Such actions are attuned to the deepest flow of life itself.

To stay alive we have to stay ahead. There is nothing great in winning the race. Anyone can win—someone will win anyway. The trick is to win without breathing hard. Ancient wisdom shows you how to win without breathing hard. Managing a big corporate house is like cooking a small fish. The more you manage and exercise

> *It is not wise to rush about. Controlling the breath causes strain. If too much energy is used, exhaustion follows. This is not the way of Tao. Whatever is contrary to Tao will not last.*
> **—Lao Tzu**

controls, the less their operations get aligned to the market-driven corporate world. So, stir less to manage with delicacy for superior performance in the new age.

❦ Do Little ❧

'Managing less is managing better': this will be the mantra for the new age. The new age will be managed through the art of Wu Wei. Ancient wisdom is eternal. Wisdom will dawn and people will find action in 'inaction'. A new horizon will be discovered at that eternal moment. It will mark the start of putting the Art of Wu Wei into practice.

4

The Power of Purpose

Life is not worth living,
Without a purpose or meaning.

—Buddha

Life is all about purpose. If you can articulate your goal in
life, you can chart a course for it. You first need to establish
the purpose and the means will automatically follow. If the
purpose is noble, the means will have to be honest. Some
people say, 'There is no right way to do the wrong things.'
Let me flip that round: 'Right things cannot be done through
wrong means.'

I have spoken earlier about the need to mine the lode
of ancient wisdom. But before you can do that, you need to
establish the purpose of your mission. This is the hard stuff:
it involves a high degree of introspection and reflection. There
are two ways you can do this. I call them the Inside Out and
Outside In approaches.

The Inside Out approach begins with a simple existentialist question: 'Why do I exist' or 'Why does my organisation exist?' We first try to identify the meaning or purpose of our life or the corporate life, and then find the means to accomplish the purpose. Once you have articulated the purpose, you can start looking for the means to manage the external environment—tapping into resources, building networks and honing skills. This journey begins from 'within'. If the purpose is profound and powerful, one needs to exert very little. The power of purpose makes things happen.

The other approach is Outside In. Here we start by taking all the external factors into account—the available skills and competencies of the people within the organisation and our peers, the salary structure, job descriptions: in short the whole caboodle that makes an organisation tick. Then we hunker down to the task of determining what can be feasibly achieved given our available resources.

The Outside In approach thus helps us to create a vision by understanding the resources that are available. In this approach, the focus is on 'resources', and aspects like meaning or purpose are shoved into the background.

Both approaches have their benefits—and it really isn't a toss up between the two. You could just as well blend the two approaches. The underlying truth is that there isn't a sure-fire remedy or a one-size-fits-all strategy to deal with tough situations, either in life or in organisations.

Having said that, in this chapter we will focus on the Inside Out approach.

Buddha, who was born in the 6th century BC, passionately believed that life had a meaning and a purpose. People could lead meaningful lives if they understood its underlying purpose. It is much the same with organisations. Purpose is the driving force—both in personal and corporate

67

lives. The organisations that will flourish tomorrow are the ones that have discovered the purpose of their existence.

It is an ancient belief that each soul when incorporated into the body makes a promise to the Supreme Truth—a covenant—to pursue an agreed purpose in life. However, once it enters the temporal world, it is blinded and deflected from its purpose by material comforts, glamour, fame, greed, lust and the other enchantments of a worldly life. The soul, which is imprisoned within the human core we call the 'body', turns it back on its agreed commitment. But once in a while, the soul whispers to the mind and the body and reminds them of the committed promise. This creates perturbation that prompts one to begin the search for meaning in life—and the quest harks back to the promise that the soul had made to God at the time of incarnation. It is this quest that had transformed Siddhartha to Buddha. Each organisation is also committed to such a promise—which is sometimes clearly articulated in its articles of association—that forms the purpose of its existence. If there is no purpose, the organisation is not worthy of existence.

> *If you don't seek meaning, no vision can drive you to excellence.*
>
> —**Ken Blanchard**

✎ The Power of Vision ✐

Let me pop a simple question at this juncture: 'Is a nation's positive image of the future a consequence of its success?' Or is it the other way round? Can a nation's success be attributed to its positive image of the future? You could just as well ask the same question about an organisation.

You could well accuse me of indulging in some sort of linguistic acrobatics. But that isn't really true: these are two different and opposite perspectives. Any organisation's success is the consequence of the positive image of the future—the very purpose of its being. A positive, profound and strong vision lends excellence or world-class status to an organisation.

You first need to create a positive and profound vision. A visionary is a dreamer who espouses values and still remains steadfast to the objectives. Softly create your vision, lucidly articulate your vision, passionately own your vision, and untiringly drive your vision to fulfilment. The significance of a person is not in what he attains, but rather in what he longs to attain.

> *The angels know what too many practical men eat their bread with sweat of the dreamer's brow!*
> —**Kahlil Gibran**

Purpose creates the vision. Purpose can also flow from the vision. It works both ways. Nations with a vision have grown strong. Nations without a vision have gone astray. What applies to nations applies equally to people, both in their personal and corporate lives. A powerful vision is like a rope that helps you cross the river. Just as a rope connects both banks of a river, vision helps you stay connected with the future—the other bank of the river.

Vision without action is like a dream. Action without vision will lead you astray. When you don't know where to go, any road will take you there. It is only vision with action that changes the world. Each of us is gifted with the ability to make the difference. This ability is your intuitive wisdom.

Vision shapes the future. It defines the purpose that fills your heart with positive emotions and eventually governs your actions. A sense of mission helps you achieve your goals.

Values pave the righteous path. Wisdom provides the required sense to take the right decisions. Sagacity makes your soul rich and instils humility and sobriety in your life. The challenge is to yoke body, mind and soul and achieve pure and wholesome synergy. The sages of yore joined these faculties to discover the truth. They knew the art of discovering the truth from within.

> *If you don't know where you are going, any road will take you there.*
> —**Buddha**

Management mavens today talk about the need to create a 'strategic vision' for an organisation: it is a mental map for the whole organisation that goes far beyond the blueprint for a particular product or operation. This vision statement is usually articulated in very simple words but has a powerful impact on the organisation and its people. John F. Kennedy inspired NASA with just one simple but profound sentence: 'Put a man on the moon by the end of the decade.' It was not just a sentence; it was a complete vision captured in a simple sentence.

Akio Morita of Sony inspired his people with just one simple sentence that led to the creation of the Walkman which revolutionised entertainment. He said: 'Produce a palm-size tape recorder at the price to suit a young person's pocket.' No other product has had as profound an impact on our lives as the Walkman: it provided music on the run!

Honda wanted to develop an eco-friendly car and he shared his vision with his managers in these words: 'You eat and drink, you leave your waste behind, and someone has to clean it up...Well! What we need to do with these vehicles is not to produce any waste in the first place!'

IBM had deeply miscalculated the power of computers: in the early 1970s it had never imagined a situation where

computers would be on everyone's desks within the fore-
seeable future. It didn't think people or companies would be
able to afford it; so it stuck to mainframes. By the time it
realised its mistake and lumbered into the desktop market, it
already had a number of competitors. One of them was
Toshiba whose CEO articulated his dream succinctly: 'Build
me a product that does not exist, using technology you do
not have. If you do manage to produce the hardware, there
will not be any software available for it. You must compete
in a market dominated by IBM and you must beat other
Japanese companies... Oh, yes! And you must bring the
product to the market in two years.'

There's a footnote to this story: in December 2004, IBM
announced a deal to sell its PC and desktop business to Chinese
giant Lenovo—dropping out of the race because of the intense
heat of competition.

Does a company become visionary just because it has a
vision statement? The vision statement is a good first step,
but it remains just a step. Although a journey of a thousand
miles begins with a single step, one ought not to forget that
the same single step is also required for its completion. Many
leaders make a good beginning but dry up as failures.

Over the years, fewer and fewer corporate leaders are
able to articulate a vision; they settle for slick and colourful
PowerPoint presentations. Moreover, purpose stems from the
heart, and the heart cannot be hired. Many organisations try
to create purpose for their organisations by hiring consultants.
All they add is needless confusion.

John Rock, general manager at a leading multinational,
makes a very wry comment about the practice of hiring
consultants: 'A bunch of guys take off their ties and coats, go
into a motel room for three days, and put a bunch of words
on a piece of paper—and then go back to business as usual.'

Once the vision statement is created with the help of a consultant, it remains frozen on the notepads. 'A mushy mission statement,' says Jack Trout, the author of *The Power of Simplicity*, 'is an indication that a company doesn't know where it's going.'

One can also learn from fairytales that are usually packed with wisdom. Lewis Carrol's *Alice in Wonderland* is a remarkable tale that is full of wit and wisdom. When Alice can't find her way out of the maze, she asks the Cheshire Cat, 'Could you tell me, please, which way I ought to go from here?' The Cheshire Cat replies, 'That depends on where you want to go?' Alice says, 'Really, I don't know!' 'Then it doesn't matter which way you go,' says Cheshire Cat. 'Anywhere you go will be somewhere other than this place.'

> *People usually fail when they are on the verge of success. So give as much care to the end as to the beginning;*
> *Then there will be no failures.*
> **—Lao Tzu**

Often, people fall agonisingly short of their goals. They start well but do not know how to finish strong like a long-distance runner. They tend to concentrate on the start and tend to remember the initial stanza of the Old Master: A journey of a thousand miles starts under one's feet. Ancient wisdom teaches you that you need to give as much care to the end as to the beginning—and that is what the new-age terminology 'finitiative' is all about—encompassing everything from the initiation of a project to its completion.

✎ Dare to Dream ✐

Encourage dreaming. A dream is the first step towards the ordained path. Even daydreaming is good. There is nothing wrong in building castles in the air. Unless you create a mental map you cannot go on—daydreams are the blueprint for the future. A daydream is a beautiful vision packed with emotions and filled with energy.

An ancient parable holds true even today. A man had a strange dream and he went to a soothsayer and asked him to interpret it for him.

The soothsayer told the man, 'Come to me with dreams that you see when you are awake and I will tell you their meaning. But the dreams of your sleep belong neither to my wisdom nor to your imagination.'

A dream is a daring adventure—a journey that takes you far. It is only when you hold a dream in your heart that you can reach the stars. A dream is a beautiful vision that looks beyond what you can see. It lifts you and guides you and makes you grow strong within. Dreams help you to be all you can be!

Recognise your dream; it is a secret reflection of your true self. Be aware of your dream; it is a threshold that leads to a wonderful future!

✇ Give Meaning to Life ✇

One should look for meaning in life. This holds true for the world of business as well. Great corporate visions are created only when they are invested with meaning. Ancient wisdom says that the only obligation we have in life is to discover the 'self'.

Life is not worthy of living without a purpose or meaning. The significance of a corporate leader is not in what he has achieved, but rather in what he longs to achieve.

Let us understand clearly that there is always a gulf between man's imagination and attainment. Only his longing can help him bridge this chasm. No longing remains unfulfilled when pursued with single-minded determination.

The monks, saints, sufis and prophets of ancient times—whom I call spiritual scientists—had purity of thought and unmatched wisdom that

> *When you long for blessings that you may not name, and when you grieve knowing not the cause, then indeed you are growing with all things that grow, and rising toward your greater Self.*
>
> **—Kahlil Gibran**

remain as relevant today as they did then. The corporate world has only now started to rediscover the wealth of knowledge that has lain buried for years. These spiritual scientists include Socrates, Lao Tzu, Confucius, Buddha, Solomon, Aristotle, Plato, Heraclitus and a host of other mystical masters whose words of wisdom are frozen in time.

'Great talents ripen late', says the Old Master. Like good wine, wisdom matures with age. It is not easy to understand the simple words of the ancient philosophers. As explained in the previous chapter, one needs to be fully tuned to their thoughts before they can understand 'koans'—the paradoxical truth—and thereby gain insight. It requires a deep understanding to appreciate the oxymoronic truth hidden

> *The perfect square has no corner;*
> *Great talents ripen late;*
> *The highest notes are hard to hear;*
> *The greatest form has no shape.*
>
> **—Lao Tzu**

in statements like 'Going up is coming down', 'Going far is coming back', 'yield and overcome', 'bend and be straight', 'stay empty and remain filled', and 'wear out and still be as good as new'.

Ancient wisdom is pregnant with such paradoxes. Science has now discovered that life itself is a paradoxical truth. The sub-atomic particles of atom are both matter and energy at the same time. It now depends on how you see yourself—as a product of matter or energy. Those who see themselves as product of matter focus on the physical self and life has no great meaning for them. But those who consider themselves to be the product of energy focus on their spiritual side and find infinite meaning in their lives.

In *Man's Search for Meaning*, Victor E. Frankl shares his unique experience of people who find the power of meaning in their lives. Just before they were due to be executed, condemned men in Nazi concentration camps would harbour the illusion that they would somehow be reprieved at the very last minute. Hundreds of them never survived; but Frankl says the ones who did invariably had a dream—a deep desire to do something with their lives. 'All those who survived through were those who had something significant to do in future,' he says. It was this power of meaning that kept them going and turned to be the cause of their ultimate survival. Frankl writes that two persons—both scientists—decided to commit suicide. 'We have nothing to expect from life,' they said. But Frankl made them realise that the world still expected a lot from them: both survived when they learned to believe in this.

Frankl describes three powerful ways to give meaning to one's life. The first is by carrying out a mission or creating a charitable institute to help poor and sick persons. Mother Teresa's mission is the best example of this. The second way is by experiencing an emotion that transcends self. 'Love is the only way to grasp another human being in the innermost core of his personality,' says Frankl. The third, and most important way, that is less practised, is by choosing an attitude

75

towards 'unavoidable sufferings'. It is not the situation that creates pain or pleasure, it is our attitude towards the situation that determines whether we suffer pain or gain pleasure. 'Avoiding pain or seeking pleasure is not the basic tenet of life. The basic tenet is to see meaning in life,' says Frankl.

A Sufi was going through the worst days of his life, but still remained quite happy and content. Someone asked him how he remained happy while suffering. 'I am suffering because God has willed it so. His will is my will. How can I look for pleasure that is not His will?'

Frankl also describes a situation where a person can find meaning in suffering. His friend lost his beloved wife and was inconsolable. One day Frankl asked his friend, 'What would have happened had you died and she survived?' His friend said, 'It would be unbearable for her!' Frankl said, 'Then thank God who saved your wife from the unbearable suffering.' In an instant, his friend had found meaning in his suffering and it changed his life.

❦ Develop Your Personal Signature ❧

It is not enough to know what you expect from life. It is more important to realise what life expects from you. The purpose of life is not to gain pleasure or to avoid pain but rather to find meaning in your life and shape its course.

Barbara Glanz, author of *Dozens of Little Things you Can Do to Regenerate Spirit at Workplace,* suggests that one way to maintain your identity and give meaning to your life is by 'developing your personal signature'.

'One of the ideas I stressed was the importance of "adding a personal signature to your work"—something that differentiates you from all the other people who do the same thing you do,' says Glanz.

Each individual and each organisation can develop their personal signature. 'A Northwest Airlines baggage attendant decided that his personal signature would be to collect all the luggage tags that fall off customer's suitcases which, in the past, have been tossed into the garbage. And in his free time he sends them back with a note thanking them for flying Northwest.' This is one of the many examples in Glanz's book.

'There is nothing better for a man than to rejoice in his work,' says the Bible (Ecclesiastes 3:22). One can rejoice in one's work if he or she inscribes a personal signature, creating a distinct identity for himself or herself. It is good to do what you like, but it is great to like what you do with a passion. Here's what a sufi saint says: 'If you cannot work with

> *Sing and dance together and be joyous, but let each of you be alone ...*
>
> *Stand together not too near together for the pillars of the temples stand apart .*
>
> —**Kahlil Gibran**

love but only with distaste, it is better that you should leave your work and sit at the gate of the temple and take alms of those who work with joy.'

Once you find meaning in your work and decide to do it with your personal signature, you would not know when you have already done the impossible. 'Start doing with

> *If you are called to be a street sweeper, sweep streets even as Michelangelo painted, or Beethoven composed music, or Shakespeare wrote poetry. Sweep streets so well that all the host of heaven and earth will pause to say, "Here lived a great street sweeper who did his job so well".*
>
> —**Martin Luther King, Jr.**

passion what is necessary, then what is possible,' says St Francis of Assisi, 'and suddenly you are doing the impossible.'

A personal signature puts a stamp of your identity on whatever you do no matter how quirky it might be. One corporate manager staples a tissue of Kleenex every time he has to send out a distasteful memo to his subordinates!

I would like to relate my own strange experience here. I had gone to Mumbai on a holiday where I was staying with the Khans. One Sunday, my hosts decided to have breakfast on the beach at Juhu. There were seven of us and we squeezed into the family car and headed there.

When everyone else was busy arranging for breakfast, I decided to stroll barefoot down the beach. Looking out at the vast and placid Arabian Sea, I was lost in thought. The silence was broken by a shriek. A woman was yelling at her children and warning not to go near an old woman wandering about the beach in a suspicious manner.

Another family had come to the beach to enjoy the holiday. Children were building sandcastles as they so often do. The pretty picture had been broken by the old lady who had a long, wicked nose like the witches in fairytales, grey hair that blew in the wind, and torn clothes. She looked like a tramp: she yelled and screamed while picking up things from the beach and putting them in a bag. The anxious mother warned her children to run back as the old lady was moving towards them. 'Come back,' she shouted. 'Stay away from that old lady.'

I was curious. I moved towards the old lady to see what she was doing. To my amazement, I found she was picking up glass shards and other detritus that littered the beach.

'Why are you doing this?' I asked. The mysterious old lady said, 'It is my life-mission to pick up the bits of glasses

78

and other sharp pieces from the beach lest children should cut their feet and bleed. Children are dear to my soul. I lost the only child when I was a young widow...' She was yelling and cursing those who didn't have the civic sense not to litter the beach and display concern for humanity.

She had developed a very divine personal signature that gave meaning to her life that had been wracked by personal grief. It is not a 'small or big task' but your 'concern and passion' that makes the mission nobler.

Here's another interesting story that illustrates the power of the passion to do something that will change the world around you.

One day a scientist strolled along the beach and noticed a young man who appeared to be dancing. He was picking up something from the ocean and hurling it into the ocean: it was so rhythmic that it looked like a well-choreographed dance.

The scientist approached the young man and asked, 'What are you doing?' The young person replied, 'Throwing starfish into the ocean. The surf is up and the tide is going out. If I don't throw them back, they will die.'

'Son,' said the scientist, 'Don't you realise there are miles and miles of beach and thousands of starfish? You can't possibly make a difference!' After listening politely, the boy bent down, picked up another starfish, and threw it back into the surf. Then, smiling at the scientist, he said, 'It made a difference for that one.'

The words of the young man haunted the scientist throughout that night. Wisdom dawned: Don't choose to be a mere observer in the universe; choose to be an actor in the universe.

Unless you discover or give some meaning to your life, it is not worth living. Each of us is gifted with the power to make a difference. On the corporate strand, one will find a lot of starfish that wait for the people of wisdom who can spot their inner wounds and so heal them. If you can heal one wounded soul in your organisation, you have thrown a starfish wisely and well.

5

Build on Values

In a state, pecuniary gain is not considered to be prosperity; its prosperity will be found in righteousness.

—Confucius

What does prosperity mean to you? How do you measure it? What yardstick do you use to measure your achievements against your peers?

If you are honest with yourself, you will admit you generally equate prosperity with material well being, if not wealth. In all probability, you would not consider a man to be prosperous if he has lived a life that is rich in values—a life laced with high moral principles. Nor are you likely to believe that someone has done well in life unless he has attained tangible material gains—a posh bungalow, a Mercedes Benz, loads of jewellery, a good stock portfolio, and a large bank balance.

Likewise, an entrepreneur measures his success by focusing on the bottomline. We do not lay great store by values, ethics, morality or dignity. Nor do we assign any value to intellectual neatness. Intellectual integrity makes no sense to most of us.

We have been conditioned to do our sums carefully—tap the most advantageous situation, value everything in terms of money, calculate the price of everything and give away nothing. We focus only on that which we can take to the bank or tot up as material gains.

Alas! The simple truth evades us most of the time. We immerse ourselves in a rat race and lose sight of the dictum: 'In a rat race, the winner is after all a rat.'

❦ Five Packs of Rice ❧

I am reminded of a true story of the Chinese poet Tao Yuanming who lived in the 4th century (AD 365–427) who was a man of substance.

Tao was a minor official in a far-flung district who did not attach great value to rank and refused to kowtow to his superiors. One day, a senior inspector arrived on a tour of the district. Tao's subordinates advised the poet to call on the inspector and pay his respects. The poet said with a sigh, 'For five packs of rice, I cannot bow before a country bumpkin and petty man!' The legend goes that he quit office the same day.

One may think Tao was silly to have stood on his dignity and refused to behave like a sycophant. But that's not the point. The point is, 'Did he think his material well being was more important than his sense of right and wrong?' The obvious answer is: 'No!'

I am not suggesting that everyone should follow Tao's example. I merely want to emphasise that whenever you feel low and believe you are losing out in the rat race, think about

Tao and then try to listen to what your heart says: 'Is it worth breaking your back for five packs of rice?'

Success is often measured by material wealth. However, it should be the other way round: material well being is just a by-product of success which is attained by espousing strong moral values such as selflessness, consideration for others, truthfulness, honesty and other values.

> *When you accumulate virtue with continued practices, you do not see the good of it, but in time it will function;*
>
> *If you abandon right and go against truth, you do not see the evil of it, but in time you will perish.*
>
> —A Zen saying

Take the case of Japan. Its economy was devastated after World War II but it rose from the ashes because the proud Japanese people had a set of common core values that became a part of their lives. Consideration for others, honesty, caring, responsibility and humility are just a few values that deserve mention.

Societies decay when people adopt unethical attitudes. Likewise companies that compromise on values and try to make money through unjust means are more likely to collapse. Enron and Tyco are just a few examples of companies that have collapsed in recent times because of accounting shenanigans and their executives' failure to ensure probity in all their actions.

An age-old adage asserts, 'Stiff and unbending is the disciple of death; gentle and yielding is the disciple of life.' Values stand for life and vices for death. Unethical practices hamper agility and liveliness which are the main attributes that one needs to survive in a world that is punctuated by intense competition.

83

Self-respect and self-esteem are not ego-related attributes. There is a true story of a famous Urdu poet Mirza Ghalib whose talent was applauded not only by his friends but also by his countrymen. At one point in his life, Ghalib was going through a very bad patch and he did not have the means to make both ends meet. His family was on the brink of starvation. At such a critical juncture, one of his friends, who was the principal of a school, offered him a position as an Urdu teacher in his school. Ghalib was a renowned poet and most schools invited him to share his profound knowledge with their students. His friend suggested that if Ghalib accepted the offer, he would earn money as a teacher which was quite a respectable way to earn a livelihood. Ghalib agreed. On the very first day, Ghalib reached the school but did not get down from the palanquin. The school peon, who had come to carry his portfolio, asked him what the matter was? Ghalib said that when he had been invited to the school on previous occasions, the principal used to come to receive him and he was waiting to be received. The school peon told Ghalib that earlier he used to come as a poet—the guest of honour—so the teachers and the principal used to welcome him at the gate; but today he had come as a teacher—a servant of the school. As a result, the principal would not come to receive him. Ghalib didn't think for a moment and decided to return saying, 'I thought as a teacher I would earn more honour. I would not do anything that robs me of my honour.' For Ghalib, dignity and self-esteem were more important than money. He preferred to starve rather than compromise with the dignity that he deserved as a poet.

Like Tao Yuanming, Ghalib preferred not to break his back for five packs of rice.

Never think small. Think big. If you stretch your arm to pluck a few stars from the sky, you may not get one, but at least you will not end up muddying your hands. Self-respect and dignity are time-tested values that pay off in the long run. Never break your back for five packs of rice.

◖ The Sea is not Calm ◗

'When the sea was calm, all ships alike showed mastership in floating,' Shakespeare wrote in his play *Coriolanus*. We live in turbulent times that severely test the survival instincts of most companies.

The pace of change in the new age and the growing complexities of doing business persuade us to believe that the corporate world a decade ago was calm and peaceful. We work today at a dizzying pace; we mistakenly believe that speed is the only way to navigate our way through the turbulent ocean.

> *When you combine a "Culture of Discipline" with an "Ethic of Entrepreneurship", you get the magical alchemy of great performance.*
>
> —**Jim Collins:** *Good to Great*

Jim Collins, author of *Built To Last* and *Good to Great*, says one needs to blend the 'culture of discipline' and the 'ethics of entrepreneurship'. Every company in the world has some 'culture' that it can call its own and follows some norms of 'discipline'. But only a few companies have a rich blend of both: a 'culture of discipline'.

They say, 'It takes time to grow in wisdom'. The adage could just as well be applied to discipline: It takes time to grow in discipline. Only sustained efforts can create what Collins calls the 'culture of discipline'. 'When you have disciplined people, you don't need hierarchy. When you have

85

disciplined thought, you don't need bureaucracy. When you have disciplined action, you don't need excessive controls' (Jim Collins: *Good to Great*).

An organisation can achieve great performance only when it creates a 'culture of discipline' and espouses values. No alchemist can turn copper into gold, but a corporate can achieve magical alchemy when it adopts a culture of discipline that is deeply imbued with values. Remember, 'profit' is the residue and not the *raison d'etre* for an organisation. When you pop the question: 'What does an organisation stand for', the immediate reply should be 'Values'.

The real challenge today is to deal with the value dilemma—the dilemma between goals and strategies, and values. Remember, you can debate over goals and strategies, but values are not negotiable.

Goals get people going; but 'values' sustain and give meaning to business. Take a stand in life. When you pause at the crossroads, always follow the path that is paved with values. When the 'value system' is clear in your mind, decision making becomes a lot easier.

Many companies espouse certain values at the start, but they go astray when the harsh realities of doing business spread the canker of

> *The path of the just is like the shining sun,*
> *That shines ever brighter unto the perfect day.*
> *The way of the wicked is like darkness: They do not know what makes them stumble.*
>
> **—A Psalm**

invidiousness down to their foundations. When it comes to the crunch, they compromise on these values. When the going gets tough, that is when you need to cling harder to your values. That is what differentiates the champions from the also-rans.

86

When the sea was calm yesterday, you did not feel a great need for values and wisdom that bring you a long-term benefit over time. Today, the sea is raging and the only way to thrive in chaos is to follow the path dictated by values. Values are the ways you measure the correctness of your direction. Look back over time and you will find that the only companies that have survived for a long time are the ones that have cherished values. The only ones that will survive in the rocky days ahead are the ones that are able to see the future through the prism of ancient wisdom and old age values.

⚙ Hold Values to create Values ⚙

Values are both the means and the ends. To build value-based companies, one needs to make values that walk.

> Ask: Why do I exist? *Purpose.*
> Ask: What do I stand for? *Values.*
> Ask: What guides us? *Conscience.*

Without determining the boundaries of purpose, without developing a corporate conscience, and without distilling knowledge into wisdom, no company or commercial organisation can hope to survive in the future.

A commercial organisation is an organism. It has a body with flesh, bones, soul, and a conscience. It resides in the cosmos and, therefore, the cosmic principles remain deeply relevant.

Like an organism, an organisation also has a lifecycle. Few large corporations live even half as long as a person. A survey conducted by Royal Dutch/Shell revealed that one-third of the firms in the 'Fortune 500' in the 1970s vanished within the next decade. A study conducted by James C. Collins and Jerry I. Porras says, 'Companies that enjoy enduring success have core values and core purpose that remain focused while their business strategies or practices endlessly adapt to the changing world. Core values are the essential and enduring central tenet; core purpose is the organisation's reason for being.' One can discover the core values and core purpose by looking inside. They have to be authentic. You can't fake them!

Later, Jim Collins and his team discovered that the companies that grew from being just 'good' to 'great' had lots of values in the 'black box'. Why did he use the term 'black box'? This is because values are immeasurable and remain invisible; what people get to see are the results after the transformation. Most of the time we see transformation but don't quite understand the value-based efforts that caused the transformation.

The 'outside in' approach suggests that you must choose the right people who will build the core values within the organisation. Ignoble people cannot bring you nobility and purity; a wrong person cannot do the right things and lead you down a righteous path unless he or she attains enlightenment. Men of wisdom can cause miracles in any organisation.

Ability, competence and attitudes alone cannot take you there. Ability is the skill to apply what one has learned. Competence is the ability and the desire to apply what is learned. Desire is the attitude that makes a skillful person competent. Sadly, many skilful people are incompetent because they lack wisdom.

What is wisdom? Knowledge, skills, competence, and the will to do something are all excellent traits—but you need that almost ineffable quality called commonsense.

> *First, those who manage well the circumstances, which they encounter day by day; and those who judge situations appropriately as they arise and rarely miss the suitable course of action.*
>
> *Next, those who are honorable in their dealings with all men, bearing easily what is unpleasant or offensive in others, and being as reasonable with their associates as is humanly possible.*
>
> *Furthermore, those who hold their pleasures always under control and are not unduly overcome by their misfortunes, bearing up under them bravely and in a manner worthy of our common nature.*
>
> *Most important of all, those who are not spoiled by their success…*
>
> —Socrates (470–399 BC)

Commonsense is the ability to see things as they are and do things as they ought to be done with perfect timing. We are born with five senses—touch, taste, sight, smell, and hearing. But men of wisdom have a sixth sense that takes them beyond the five sensory perceptions. This sixth sense is intuitive wisdom. In common parlance, one can call it 'commonsense'—the ability to differentiate between right and wrong, virtue and vice. Wisdom is just an abundance of commonsense.

The first duty of the corporate world in the new age is to infuse wisdom through teaching and practice. Trade, technicalities, strategies and even entrepreneurship are all secondary factors. A robust corporate discipline is the *sine qua non* for success in the new age.

Both values and wisdom create soft assets within the organisation that will last for a long time. It is difficult to understand the real worth of the 'soft assets' with a mindset that is just tuned to see only material side in business—the net worth of hard assets. One can understand the softer aspects and finer things in management affairs only through intuitive wisdom and by loosening the grip over logic and conventional wisdom. Business management is not merely a numbers game.

🖙 Values and the New Age 🖎

In the New Age, customers will not just look for the quality of the product; they will also look at the company's image: 'What does it stand for?' Ethics and values will have more importance than products and service. The focus will be on the 'credibility' of the company. Once the value system is clear, business decisions will be honest. Once you choose the right path you can never go astray.

> We are going to see companies increasingly assume that "what they stand for" in an enduring sense is more important than what they "sell".
>
> —**James Collins and Jerry Porras**
> *(Built to Last)*

To understand all this, take a look at some companies that have been able to rise to the top of the corporate totem pole by dint of the strong value system they were able to create—and which their customers strongly identified with.

Sony, which is now a household name in the global market, started of by making pressure cookers. It morphed into a company that wanted to 'experience the sheer joy of innovation and the application of technology for the benefit and pleasure of the general public' (James C. Collins and Jerry I. Porras: *Built to Last*).

In the early 1950s, Japanese companies were known to produce cheap products of doubtful quality. Sony wanted to change that image: not only its own but also the world's perceptions about Japan. 'Fifty years from now, our brand name will be as well known as any in the world; "Made in Japan" will mean something fine, not something shoddy' (Akio Morita: *Made in Japan*).

Sony lived three core values: First, 'Elevation of the Japanese culture and national status'. Second, 'Being a pioneer—not following others; doing the impossible'. And third, 'Encouraging individual ability and creativity'.

The core purpose of Walt Disney is 'To make people happy'. It lived the core values: 'Preservation and control of the Disney magic' and 'Creativity, dreams, and imagination'. Numerous examples of excellent companies can be quoted in support of a direct link between ethical values and their prosperity.

Unfortunately, today we tend to underplay the importance of values. While the bottomline is important for a company's survival, one needs to go deeper to discover the real reasons for existence! John Young, former CEO of Hewlett-Packard, said in 1992, 'We distinguish between core values and practices; the core values do not change, but the practices might. We have also remained clear that profit—as important as it is—is not why the Hewlett-Packard Company exists; it exists for a more fundamental reason!'

The alignment of a company is based on values. Alignment means being guided first and foremost by one's own internal compass, not the standards, practices, conventions, forces, trends, and buzzwords from the outer world.

In the early 1980s, Ford Motor Company found itself 'reeling, bleeding red ink from wounds' (James C. Collins and Jerry I. Porras: *Built to Last*) that had been inflicted because of the battering it received from Japanese competitors. Naturally, the Ford team went into a frenzy to come up with

91

emergency measures to staunch the bleeding and keep the company alive. The company came back on track only when the supreme team discovered its MVGP—Mission, Values, and Guiding Principles. 'There was a great deal of talk about the wrong sequencing the three P's—Profits, Product and People. It was decided that people should absolutely come first [product second and profits third].'

Success in any organisation is all about the utilisation of untapped human energies. The only way to tap this energy is to make people your partner. The only way to do this is to create some meaning in their activities and show concern for them. Preserve the core; stimulate progress!

Today companies need a new vision, a new faith and a new confidence in business ethics. One need not reinvent the wheel. Just rediscover the purpose of your being in the corporate world. Ask 'Why you exist?' Once you understand the purpose of existence, it will make all the difference. Remember, both time and direction are built into the purpose. Purpose and values are twin sisters.

✉ Values and the Intellect ✈

Values relate to the heart while strategies are the result of intellectual impulses. Today, everyone tends to focus on resource utilisation and business strategies—both of which are key attributes of the mind. Sadly, we remain imperfect even in the application of mind. I hear management gurus say, 'Business management in simple terms is all about managing resources'.

I do not find that a credible explanation. And I will argue thus: If I were to play chess with Vishwanathan Anand— the world champion—who do you think would win?

Obviously, I can't beat the world champion. But, wait a minute. He has the same resources on the chessboard as I do. Both have 16 chessmen; one uses black pieces, the other white. Anand doesn't have a single chessman extra: he is got one King, one Queen, two Rooks, two Knights, two Bishops, and eight Pawns. The game begins. He makes a few moves in his match with me and cries 'Checkmate!' The game is over! I hear management gurus say, ' Business Management in simple term is all about *managing* resources. But *managing* in the sense of mere acquisition of resources is not enough to get success. What is more important is how you utilise these resources to an optimum extent. To buttress this I argue, that resources are not sufficient to attain success; what matters is how you manage the resources! To manage resources, one must acquire competence. To win the game one should play it honestly—cheating will disqualify the player or an athlete.

There are four kinds of human energies—physical, intellectual, emotional, and spiritual. For 200 years or so, we exploited only the physical energy and skills of people while we created the industrial society. In the past two decades or so, we have entered into what we call the information or knowledge society that considers an idea as an intellectual capital and time as a resource. We have harnessed only the physical and intellectual energies; our emotional and spiritual energies have remained largely unutilised.

In the new age, it will no longer be enough if we just tap our physical and intellectual energies. We will have to learn to live with uncertainties; we shall be required to acquire skills and competencies that the business sector has not even conceived of till now. We shall be required to discover horizons beyond our vision; we shall be required to scale unknown heights. But to conquer the unknown—the future—one will have to follow the path paved with values. There will be no other route to success.

93

✎ Join Mind and Heart ✎

The 'spiritually challenged' business leaders will be distinctly uncomfortable in the new age. The corporate world will witness a 'spiritual revolution' that will be far more powerful and earth-shaking than the industrial revolution. To understand the fusion of spirituality and business, one must understand the human potential.

'Human energy is like the energy of light,' said Ken Blanchard in his book *Mission Possible*. One may harness the energy to light a bulb; it glows and drives away darkness. However, the same light energy, when used as a laser beam, cuts through even a thick steel plate. The same law applies equally to human energy. It is time to synergise the emotional and spiritual strengths and inspire people to make an emotional investment in the company.

People will have to have a heart. The mind alone will not take you very far. Business leaders need to hone their emotional skills as well if they are required to survive and work with dignity. It is the heart that helps identify values: it defines how people want the world to be and how they want to live in that world.

Professor Michael E. Porter of Harvard Business School has redefined the very concept of competition in the 21st century. He believes that we will need a 'Big Bang'. To ignite the process of development, several things need to happen all at once. 'We need to articulate a more integrated future through oriental values,' he asserts. The Big Bang will usher in path-breaking ideas with groundbreaking strategies, and will keep business ethics in sharp focus.

People assume wrongly that a company exists simply to make money and that the only way to make money—and quickly—is by compromising on values. It is foolhardy to believe that companies need to sacrifice their values at the altar of Mammon. To win, the player must concentrate on the game and keep his eye on the ball rather than on the scoreboard. If you run after money and ignore values, success, like a mirage, will outfox you!

The clarion call is already being heard: Companies must be groomed to take risks without stultifying their principles and sacrificing core values. The managers must be freed from the shackles of bureaucratic practices and in unequivocal terms that they are paid to adopt risks and ask questions, and not turn into a bunch of yes men. 'An ostrich that buries his head in the sand has a bigger problem than a limited vision; its rear end is an enormous target!,' says Ricardo (Semler, author of *Maverick*).

Be bold, without losing your humility. Providence loves both humility and boldness and will assist you in ways you cannot imagine. They say God loves humility and favours the prepared mind! The business leader in the new age will need to have a blend of humility and boldness, and competence and commitment. Above all, he must be honest, compassionate and loving.

It is time to preserve the core values; we need to improve the things that exist and innovate for the future. While establishing long-term strategies, we need to be sensitive to the demands in the short term. One must allow the past and the future to co-exist with the present. The spiritual volcano in the corporate world will erupt only when the bureaucrats reinforce their faith in values.

An entrepreneur can no longer concentrate on money or material well being to the exclusion of every thing else and hope to succeed in the future. If we mess with our values, we will be big-time losers.

For the past 20 decades or so we have been managing things with our minds. Now, we need to learn to manage things with our hearts. This is the moment when we need to redefine our compact with our souls and unearth a side that we have ignored for a very long time. We need to work with our minds and our hearts: I call this, 'managing through sense and soul'.

ᘓ Build on Values ᘒ

How should we deal with our ethical problems? Let's face it: We will increasingly need to address ethical issues in the future—the issues that we have either ignored or pushed under the carpet.

This is best illustrated by the story related by Sir Adrian Cadbury, former chairman of Cadbury Schweppes PLC and best known for the formulation of the Cadbury Code, a code of best practices which has served as a basis and inspiration for corporate governance reform around the world. It also reveals that there is no simple, universal formula to deal with ethical problems.

We will have to choose from our own codes of conduct what rules to apply to a case in hand; the outcome of those choices defines who we are.

'In 1900, Queen Victoria sent a decorative tin with a bar of chocolate inside to all her soldiers who were serving South Africa. These tins still turn up today, often complete with their contents, a tribute to the collecting instinct. At the time, the order faced my grandfather with an ethical dilemma. He owned and ran the second-largest chocolate company in Britain, so he was trying harder and the order meant additional work for the factory. Yet he was deeply and publicly opposed to the Anglo-Boer War. He resolved the dilemma by accepting the order, but carrying it out at cost. He therefore made no profit out of what he saw as an unjust war, his employees benefited from the additional work, the soldiers received their royal present, and I am still sent the tins,' said Sir Adrian. 'My grandfather was able to resolve the conflict between the decision best for his business and his personal code of ethics because he and his family owned the firm which bore their name.'

Only men of wisdom know how to resolve such a value dilemma. Values live in the dewdrops of wisdom. Knowledge shrinks as wisdom grows!

As mentioned earlier, the significance of a person is not in what he attains, but rather in what he longs to attain. Softly create your vision, lucidly articulate your vision, passionately own your vision, and untiringly drive your vision to fulfilment. Never laugh at someone's dreams. Encourage daydreaming. A dream is a daring adventure, a journey that will carry you far—for if you can hold a dream in your heart, surely you can reach a star!

Conscience belongs to the heart and not the mind. Without a corporate conscience no organisation can have an enduring future. However, you also need to realise that there is a cost to keep the corporate conscience alive. Ethical behaviour involves a high cost; but in the end, it always pays off.

A word of caution: you cannot yoke ethics to the desire to improve profits. A participant at a symposium sponsored by Business and Society Review put it very succinctly: 'To be ethical as a business because it may increase your profits is to do so for entirely the wrong reason. The ethical business must be ethical because it wants to be ethical.'

We should understand this clearly: you cannot quibble over business ethics. It is only when you desist from cutting corners with the whole business of ethics that you can expect to achieve long-term benefits. The real creative part of business ethics is to discover the ways and means to do what is morally right and socially responsible, without wrecking one's career or company.

C.K. Prahalad, popularly known as 'Mr Core Competence', foresees a new form of team-oriented organisations— teams that behave not as a 'herd of sheep' but as a 'pack of wolves'. I would add these new team-oriented organisations will not only acquire the shared vision but they will also promote shared values.

> *Wolf packs contain highly different set of skills; they are extremely flexible in the way they haunt, have a clear hierarchy and are very clear about the goal.*
>
> **—C.K. Prahalad**

Cockburn, former managing director of Royal Mail— the largest employer in Britain with the largest distribution fleet—sent out an admirable message to his employees that could apply just as well apply to other companies: 'Why don't we try to be world-class? Why should we not become a beacon of best practices?'

Without deep-seated values and inspired people, no one can develop a world-class organisation in the new age. The prosperity of tomorrow's commercial organisations will depend on the human and ethical values they are wedded to and their ability to create commercial value through their people and not merely by husbanding resources, technology and hard assets. The real assets of the

> *You owe more than gold to him who serves you. Give him of your heart or serve him.*
>
> **—Kahlil Gibran**

company will not be the fixed assets; the soft assets will assume primacy.

Ford's 3P's will serve as the guiding star: People first!

It takes time to grow into wisdom. Likewise, it takes time to build trust in any organisation by constantly living values. Trust begets trust. Mistrust creates mistrust. Ricardo Semler, the CEO of Semco in Brazil, makes this point clear in no uncertain words: 'I would rather have a few thefts once in a while than condemn everyone to a system based on mistrust. Have thefts and timecard cheating increased or decreased? I don't know, and I don't care! It's not worth it to me to have a company at which you don't trust the people with whom you work!'

With corporate governance being on top of the agenda, Total Ethics Management (TEM) is rightly emerging as industry's newest buzzword. Anil Sachdev, the former managing director of Eicher Consultancy Services and the soul of the TEM movement in India, makes the invisible principles of business ethic vividly clear. Here is how he explains it: 'How does TEM help the bottomline? The logic is simple—business ethics is pro-profit because it reduces transaction costs in the economy and is good for the firm as well as for the stakeholders. For instance, in the export market, the man who delivers on time and keeps his commitments is the one who gets the repeat order... The negation of ethical values in business in real terms works out to 10 to 20 per cent drop in performance.'

No business organisation can hope to become an exception to the universal truth and the cosmic laws. The new millennium belongs to those who embed ethical values in their business practices.

The leader must develop an eagle's eye and look beyond the horizon. A business leader needs to develop two aspects—

intuition and faith—if he wants to succeed. These are two traits that the current lot of corporate bureaucrats have learnt to view with a great deal of suspicion. Organisations must clearly and constantly demonstrate 'fairness'; 'Fairness' for employees is like 'quality' for customer—it takes years to build but collapses with a single incident.

Don't mock at values for they lead you to the path of Supreme Truth. 'Strange that we all defend our wrongs with more vigour than we do our rights,' says Kahlil Gibran.

Recharge yourself by living values. Learn business management from the books of ethics and scriptures. Learn from everyone and from every incident. Trust what Swami Vivekananda once said: 'Every soul is potentially divine'.

6

The Practice of Virtue

By their stillness become sages;
by their movements kings.

—Chuang Tzu

Chuang Tzu was born 200 years after Lao Tzu's death and was a disciple of the great Chinese philosopher. He is best known for his aphorism that beautifully encapsulates what we call the Chinese Vista, that stillness makes a person a sage, and movement a king.

The two great Chinese sages—Lao Tzu and Confucius—were proponents of this essential duality in life. Lao Tzu spoke about stillness while Confucius always tried to add movement to stillness.

During the 6th century BC, Chinese Vista was developed by blending the thoughts that flowed from the two pure fountainheads—Taoism and Confucianism. Lao Tzu and Kung Fu Tzu (popularly known as Confucius) brought this unmatched balance to humankind. One drew the people's attention to intuition, the other laid emphasis on reasoning. One sought sagacity in tranquillity, the other spoke about virtue in action. It was like the two great impulses in life itself: the Yin and the Yang. You could conceive of Lao Tzu as Yin and Confucius as Yang. One developed sages, the other created kings.

Confucius believed that the perfect path was paved with virtue. This is a universal truth that applies as much to the past as the present.

As in life, so in the world of business: we need the kingmaker as much as the sage developer. Yang, the masculine impulse for action, has for long overshadowed the Yin—the female impulse for intuition. It is time to re-establish the perfect balance between these dual impulses. We have had the kingmakers in the corporate world; we need a new order of management monks in the new age. This chapter will discuss the forces of Yang and provide a counterpoint in the next chapter which deals with the aspects of Yin.

In this chapter, I will also try to bring to the fore the Chinese concept of virtue and wisdom. But before I do so, let me explain the Chinese Vista.

ᨆ Chinese Vista ᨆ

Chinese Vista is a unique blend of intuitive wisdom and practical knowledge based on logic and reason.

The Chinese have two powerful images—the sage and the king—that they associate with everything in their lives. It imbues every aspect of their thought process, their lives as well as the way they run their businesses. Such a balanced mix is unparalleled anywhere in any epoch. Chinese sagacity is steeped in both spiritualism and worldly affairs.

Taoism was basically concerned with the observation of nature and the discovery of the way. For lack of a better word, Lao Tzu calls it Tao. The originator of Taoism was Lao Tzu, which literally means the Old Master. He was a contemporary of Confucius.

Lao Tzu and Confucius counterbalanced intuitive wisdom and illustrious virtue.

About 200 years after the death of Lao Tzu, his thoughts were further developed by Chuang Tzu. Lao Tzu had said, 'The Tao that can be told is not the eternal Tao'; Chuang elaborated on this thesis and claimed that the person who seeks to know and the one who tries to explain are both ignorant and do not know Tao. What he meant was that intuition is simply seized upon; one cannot explain nor can one understand it.

> *If one asks about the Tao and another answers him, neither of them knows It.*
> —**Chuang Tzu**

Zen is the kernel of Chinese Vista. The Zen masters taught their disciples to understand the idea without remembering the words. The worst disservice that western business management practitioners have done is to try and explain the undefinable. They have coined words to explain the concepts and created an entirely new argot.

> *Fishing baskets are employed to catch fish;*
> *But when the fish are caught, the men forget the basket.*
> *Snares are employed to catch hares;*
> *But when the hares are caught, men forget the snares.*
> *Words are employed to convey ideas;*
> *But when the ideas are grasped, men forget the words.*
> —**Chuang Tzu**

103

The Zen masters believe that we need the finger to point at the moon but, once that is done, we need not trouble ourselves with the finger. This may sound elliptical and confusing, but it really isn't. Management theories and all the buzzwords that they spawn help us grasp a concept: once we grasp the concept, we must forget about the buzzwords just as an angler needs to forget about the baskets when he has caught the fish.

One must learn to throw away the crutches when one gathers enough strength to stand on one's feet. Unfortunately, we cannot seem to do that and we continue to parrot the definitions and mouth inanities till the next buzzword comes along.

A map is not a territory—we just need it to explain an idea of space. In one sense, it is just a figurative device. Most people will understand this implicitly. However, they cannot learn to extend the same idea to management concepts that are also figurative expressions required merely to explain an idea.

Most of us mistake the organisational design for the organisation itself. If you see an organisation and learn to keep people in sharp focus, you will find each organisation is a living entity. An organisation is also packed with sensitising vibrations and powerful emotional feelings. An organisation has both a body and a corporate soul. However, if you mistake the bricks and mortar for the organisation, then it becomes an inanimate entity.

Zen refuses to acknowledge emptiness in anything. Even an empty glass is seen as being filled with nothingness. Isn't it ironic that the sages of yore understood this concept long before Einstein established this as a scientific fact and changed the Newtonian notions about the cosmos? Unlike Newton, Einstein believed that the cosmos was filled with an electromagnetic field. When the cosmos itself is a living entity that is full of energy, how can an organisation be viewed as an inanimate being?

Like human beings, each organisation is an evolved being that has consciousness. The level of consciousness varies depending on the awareness of business leaders and people within the organisation. If an organisation's level of consciousness is low, it doesn't mean that the organisation is lifeless. When values die, the organisation still breathes like a human being and survives even after losing its value system. To be 'non-virtuous' and a 'non-living being' are two separate things; one must understand this clearly. The organisational consciousness has a bandwidth—I call this the 'physical' to 'universal' perspective. This bandwidth can also be seen in terms of a 'physical' to 'spiritual' perspective. There is a four-tiered hierarchy of organisational consciousness: physical perspective, intellectual perspective, emotional perspective and spiritual perspective. Only an evolved organisation attains corporate wisdom.

Knowledge shrinks as wisdom grows. Much depends on the business leader and his level of maturity. To attain such maturity, one should programme his rational mind to an intuitive mode of tranquillity. The intuitive mind creates an inconceivable awareness. The environment is experienced in a direct way without the help of conceptual thinking.

Chinese Vista is monotheistic—it is based on a singular ultimate reality that underlies and unifies the multiplicity that we observe. The Chinese believe that though 'complete', 'all-embracing', and 'the whole' are three terms, the reality they seek to express is the same—which they call Tao. Tao is the cosmic whole—the cosmic process—that involves everything. In its original cosmic sense, Tao is the ultimate, indefinable reality. Do not take the conditioned image on the surface as

105

a fact; it is a chimera! Try to gain an insight into the truth that lies within.

🍂 Universal Equilibrium 🍂

A key concept in Chinese thought—universal equilibrium—is all about learning to strike a perfect balance between reasoning and intuitive wisdom. It means looking at the future and accepting implicitly that uncertainties are wild cards. Chinese cultural heritage conditions the people to accept that there is nothing like a predetermined event: either they have already occurred or will occur. They strongly believe that there are some events that no one could have foreseen, like the tsunami tragedy in December 2004 that killed over 150,000 people across Asia. At the same time, their faith in universal equilibrium gives them immense confidence. Neither the good nor the bad times will continue. It is this abiding faith that keeps them going.

An insight into Confucius' *Analects* and Lao Tzu's *Tao Te Ching* will bestow wisdom on corporate leaders in the new age. The two books virtually counterbalance two modes of human philosophy—reasoning and intuition.

Legend surrounds the life of Kung Fu Tzu (Confucius), but modern scholars base their accounts mainly on the *Analects*, a collection of sayings and dialogues apparently recorded by the disciples of Confucius. As you read this great work, you will notice the phrase 'The master said...' all too frequently. Obviously, Kung Fu Tzu would not have used this phrase, had he authored *Analects*. Multiple authorship characterises all the great spiritual works and is not unique to *Analects*; *Tao Te Ching*, Bhagvad Gita, Upanishads and even the Bible have been written by multiple authors over a considerable period of time. It is all a question of roots. For that matter the entire philosophy of Socrates was put on paper by his disciple, Plato. Socrates was unlettered.

According to the *Concise Electronic Columbia Encyclopedia*, Kung Fu Tzu (Confucius) was born in the feudal state of Lu, in modern Shandong province. It was probably because of his reformist teachings that he held only minor government posts. In the midst of warfare and tyranny, he used a system of morality and statecraft to bring about peace and stability, and create a just government. His supposed doctrines are embodied in Confucianism. His teachings that contributed towards the making of an honest and morality-filled empire remain just as relevant to company managements that seek long-term goals.

These ancient works—*Analects* and *Tao Te Ching*—are typical of the Chinese way of thinking. They are written in a dialect of the Chinese language which itself is typical and matchless. 'Many of Chinese words could be used as nouns, adjectives or verbs, and their sequence was determined not so much by grammatical rules as by the emotional content of the sentences,' observes Fritjof Capra, a modern physicist. Such a dialect takes the finite words to an infinite plane of thought and understanding that other languages can never hope to reach. We are groomed and brought up within the narrow grammatical confines of writing correct English which takes precedence over emotional expression. Capra discovered that the Chinese sound symbols hold a strong, suggestive power. The real intent is not so much to express an intellectual idea, but rather to influence the listener. Similarly, the written characters are not just an abstract sign, but are organic patterns—a gestalt!

The oldest written records in Chinese could be tracked down to the 14th century BC. But the Five Classics of

Confucianism stand out; the only book that matches it is the classic literary work of Lao Tzu—*Tao Te Ching*. These Five Classics consist of the Spring and Autumn; the Book of Changes—a system of divination; the Book of Rites, which describes a ceremonial and ideal state; the Book of History; and the Book of Songs—a collection of poems on war, love, and peasant life written in a simple style. Like any other classical Chinese poem, the verses of the Book of Songs are also short and suggestive. *Analects*—the collection of his thoughts and philosophy—has been written in the form of a dialogue.

We are underprivileged because we are able to read only the English versions of these great works. In translation, we lose the images that the Chinese philosophers used to express themselves. 'It needs a combination of all the translations already made and many others not yet made, to reveal the riches of Lao Tzu and Confucian Analects in their original forms,' says Fung Yu-lan.

✉ Virtue is the Root ✈

Confucius teaches us to illustrate virtue, to renovate the people and to rest in the highest excellence.

'Virtue is the root; wealth is the result,' says the great master. To obtain results, you need to trace your way back to the roots.

It is not just botanical entities that have roots: even things and affairs have their roots and branches, let alone human beings whose moorings are more visible. To know 'what is first and what is last' will lead us to what the Great Master calls Great Learning. Commercial organisations have flesh and bones, heart, mind, soul and conscience, emotions and intelligence; business activities have their roots, and their branches bear the fruits.

An organisation must be imbued with virtues if it wants to be a happy entity and a great place to work. How does one go about creating one? You first need to address the roots.

All too often we try to manage the 'effects' without understanding the 'causes'. When the problem crops up again,

---

Wishing to illustrate "illustrious virtue" throughout the kingdom,
  They first put their own states in order.
Wishing to put their own states in order,
  They first regulated their families.
Wishing to regulate their families,
  They first cultivated their persons.
Wishing to cultivate their persons,
  They first rectified their hearts.
Wishing to rectify their hearts,
  They first sought to be sincere in their thoughts.
Wishing to be sincere in their thoughts,
  They first extended to the utmost their knowledge.
Such extension of knowledge lays investigation of things.
  Things being investigated, knowledge became complete.

—**Confucius**

---

we say: 'Yesterday's solutions, today's problems!' We refuse to acknowledge that our approach was wrong in the first instance since we dealt with the problem only at the surface and did not go down to the roots. Confucius says: Go to the root cause; don't deal with it at the superficial level. The Japanese 'Ishikawa diagram' that shows 'cause and effect' is a reflection of Confucius' philosophy.

When you want to manage an organisation, first acquire all the information by tracing things back to their roots. Only then can you proceed with the objective of achieving excellence. Let me elaborate on this in the Confucius style: once their knowledge is complete, their thoughts become sincere. Once their thoughts are sincere, their hearts are pure. Once their hearts are pure, their true personalities emerge. Once their true personalities emerge, their families are regulated. Once their families are regulated, their states are properly governed. Once their states are properly governed, the whole kingdom becomes tranquil and happy.

Just go back to the roots: if you tackle the problems at the elementary level, you can achieve all the objectives that you set out to achieve. If a manager ignores the root of the problem and focuses more on a short-term objective like maximising profits, he will only end up wrangling with the people working under him. Managements often focus on results and profits without tackling the root cause of the problems that beset the organisation.

In business management, human resources are the roots of the organisation, profit-making is the result. Profit can never be the rationale for a company's existence; it is the residue. Henry Ford understood this well and formulated the doctrine of the three P's—People first, then Production and Profit last. Like a ruler, the business leader should first take pains to reinforce his own virtues. A virtuous person wins over people. Once you have won the hearts of the people, you acquire genuine power that will help you create wealth. That wealth will provide the resources to meet expenditure and the residue will be the profit.

Let us now turn to the metrics for measuring performance. Managers must understand that their organisation's measurement system strongly affects the behaviour of the employees. They must also understand that the traditional financial accounting measures like Return on Investment

110

(ROI) and earning per share can give misleading signals for continuous improvement and innovative activities that today's competitive environment demands.

✉ P for People ✉

P stands for people, not profit. Those who treat their people as a profit-generating resource will soon wither. If you take care of people, they will give you their sweat and blood. According to a Chinese saying: 'Regard your soldiers as your children, and they will follow you into the deepest valleys; look on them as your beloved sons, and they will stand by you even unto death.'

If you involve your people, you will gain both in terms of earning their commitment and reducing time cycles for accomplishing tasks. Decision making proceeds to action. You may spend

> *The royal domain of a thousand Li is where the "People" rest. The twittering yellow bird rests on a corner of the mound. When it rests, it knows where to rest. Is it possible that a man should not be equal to this bird?*
>
> —Confucius

a lot of time in getting your people involved, but you will save a lot of time when you enter the second phase of 'action'. When you involve your people, you are sending out a signal: 'I care for you; I care for your views'. Such a gesture will earn you a lot of love and respect.

Pecuniary gain is not prosperity; prosperity must be found through righteousness. A complete business leader is a fount of virtue. People look upon him with veneration. There is no room for quibbling or self-deception. A leader needs to

111

be aware about how the people regard him. He must always keep a watch on himself and his actions.

> *Never has there been a case of the sovereign loving benevolence, and the people not loving righteousness.*
>
> *Never has there been a case where the people loved righteousness, and the affairs of the sovereign have not been carried to completion.*
>
> *And never has there been a case where the wealth in such a state, collected and in treasuries and arsenals, did not continue in the sovereign's!*
>
> —Confucius

❦ The Power of Awareness ❧

Self-deception is self-seduction! The opposite of self-deception is self-awareness. They say the honeybee, at certain times of the year, can shift its hormones and completely reverse its age through its unique power of awareness. One must be aware of the good and the bad. Awareness is a double-edged sword. It provides both pleasure and pain. Virtue lies in understanding and becoming aware of what is happening around you. You need to be sensitive to the virtues of the men of wisdom as well as the meanness of the evildoers.

> *There's no evil to which the mean man will not proceed, but when he sees a superior person, he immediately tries to disguise himself, concealing his evil, and displaying what is good.*
>
> —Confucius

An old sage once said: 'People grow old and die because they see others grow old and die'. The power of awareness has never been explained so vividly.

Belief creates biology. 'Despite the thousands of hours of old tapes that programme our responses, we continue to live because awareness finds new ways to flow. The positive side of awareness--the ability to heal—is always available,' says Deepak Chopra, the author of *Ageless Body, Timeless Mind*.

A business leader should be aware of his allies, opponents, adversaries, bedfellows, and fence-sitters. Be aware of your opponents and adversaries. But beware of the fence-sitters. Let me elaborate what I learnt from Peter Block.

There is a distinct difference between an opponent and an adversary. In the matrix, the opponent does not always agree with the leader's views but his loyalty towards the leader and the organisation remains unquestioned. An adversary, on the other hand, is not only disloyal to the leader but also picks holes in everything. Opponents are good and trustworthy for they create a purposeful and positive conflict that provides light rather than heat. Adversaries are negative in thinking, approach and action. They only create bad blood and heat within the organisation. But the worst of the lot are the fence-sitters who wear different masks and are the most unpredictable people.

Sincerity and insincerity flow from your thoughts. What is truly within will manifest itself sooner or later. Like the Buddha, Confucius lays stress on the mind as the supreme organ of the body. When the mind expands, the body is at ease and the heart soaks in tranquillity. 'Therefore the superior man (leader) must make his thoughts sincere,' advises Confucius.

If one sees only what light reveals to the eye, and hears only what vibrates the eardrums, then in truth one does not either see or hear. The inner self is invisible to the outer eye. Virtue soothes the inner self. Virtue is your interior and behaviour is your exterior. Rectify the mind so that it can understand the inner self before it guides you on how to deal with external issues. Inner clarity resolves external problems. There are three eyes—the eye of the flesh, the eye of the mind, and the eye of the soul. The mind, in the normal course, believes and takes inputs through our eyes, which I call the eye of the flesh. It can also think and see through the eye of the mind to gain intellectual impulses. But what really brings insight to the mind is what we see through the eyes of the soul—or the third eye.

When you go through a difficult time, you often feel low or insecure. That is when you need to remind yourself that you are a multi-sensory person and can rely on the power of your brain and your soul. It is the awareness of this inner strength that makes all the difference between a great manager and an ordinary one.

A swollen mind is no better than a negative mind. Let me share an episode to illustrate this point. A cocktail party had been organised at a leading hotel in India's garden city, Bangalore by Eicher Management Consultancy, which was opening a new branch in the city. I had gone there to represent my company—which called itself the timekeeper to the nation and was a prospective client. When the so-called intellectuals meet, they tend to boast. So did I. At that time I was involved in developing a Productivity Improvement Program (PIP) for the company with the assistance of global consultants—Japanese International Cooperation Agency (JICA). F.K. Fakkuda a well-known Japanese consultant, was helping me with the implementation of 5S (Seiry, Seiton, Seico, Shitsuke and Suketsu), PPORF (Practical Program of Revolution in Factory), and PIP as the HRD missions within the company. As I spoke, I saw the sparkling eyes in the audience that spoke more than their tongues would. I shared with them my unique venture—*The Roadmap to Excellence*—a video film that I had scripted, directed and produced with the conviction that each employee of the company would see at least three times. 'You see, carrying a mission of this kind in a multi-product, multi-unit company like ours, with 30 manufacturing units and a workforce of 30,000 is a challenge for me and my team,' I said while ending my presentation. A budding young consultant at Eicher, said, 'We too are working on these missions for the production business groups of our company. But we have not reached the stage where we can start covering the employees; we are still going through these missions for the family members of our employees. We start HRD programmes with the family members and then decide how we should proceed with the employees.' That is when I realised that all these years I had been carrying out my HRD programme the wrong way round—HRD must begin with the families of the employees and only then enter the workplace. It is again a question of going back to the roots.

Awareness is the seed of transformation; awareness is powerful. There is no point working on the exterior without going into the interior. If you have to develop a virtuous group of leaders, you have to change their mindset first. You cannot create a virtuous business

> *Only by perfect virtue can the "perfect path", in all its course, be made a fact.*
> —Confucius

character without rectifying the individual minds. Virtue leads to a focused direction and perfects your path. There is no right way to do a wrong thing.

Let me reinforce this idea with the thoughts of the great master: 'That peach tree, so delicate and elegant! How luxuriant is its foliage! This girl is going to her husband's house. She will rightly order her household. Let the household

115

be rightly ordered, and then he may teach the people of the state... In his department there's nothing wrong; he rectifies all the people of the state. But, when the ruler (leader), as a father, a son, and a brother, is the model, then the people imitate him... The government of his kingdom depends on his regulation of the family.'

The power of awareness is strong. Awareness is the seed of awakening. Transformation can take place only when you are truly awakened. Just make people aware of the truth to bring about transformation for a grander cause. But for pure awareness one must develop purity in the mind, heart and soul.

> *What a man dislikes in his superiors,*
> *Let him not display in the treatment of his inferiors;*
> *What he dislikes in inferiors,*
> *Let him not display in the service of his superiors;*
> *What he hates in those who are before him,*
> *Let him not therewith precede those who are behind him;*
> *What he hates in those who are behind him,*
> *Let him not bestow on the left;*
> *What he hates to receive on the left*
> *Let him not bestow on the right.*
>
> **—Confucius**

An organisation can face no greater bankruptcy than the lack of a role model. Many organisations have perished as a result; many more will vanish tomorrow. Monetary losses can be borne, but not a poverty of virtues. Take care of the intangibles; the tangibles will take care of themselves!

One can extend Confucian thoughts to one's personal life. 'Serve your father, as you would want your son to serve you. Serve your elder brother, as you would require your younger brother to serve you. Set the example by behaving towards a friend as you would require him to behave towards you.' Both life and business are so simple. We make them complicated by applying too much thought and little wisdom.

The key to success is simple: Treat your juniors as you wish to be treated by your seniors; treat your seniors as you wish to be treated by your juniors. I have purposefully avoided the words superiors and subordinates, as they no longer enjoy any currency in the corporate vocabulary.

Be compassionate towards your people! If you neglect your people, you will sink in disgrace. Confucius says when a ruler gains the hearts of the people, he gains a kingdom; if he loses their hearts, he loses the king-dom. You can extend this thought to organisations.

> *You owe more than gold to him who serves you. Give him of your heart or serve him.*
>
> —**Kahlil Gibran**

I have seen many rich organisations stumble because they lost their intuitive wisdom and illustrious virtues when they com-promised on human values.

ᦄ Corporate Sages for a New Age ᕳ

It is my belief that sages and monks will thrive in the new age. People will call them management monks or management sages.

The old buzzwords won't work: there will be little faith in transactional leadership or transformational leadership; inspirational leadership will be the model for tomorrow. Charismatic leadership will find no place; heroic managers who are insensitive to the feelings of others and sensitivity, will feel suffocated and look for places to hide.

Interpersonal relationships will assume greater significance in the new age. The 1990s belonged to Jack Welch, just as Lee Iacocca kicked up such a storm in the 1980s with his thoughts. They became icons for managers across the world. Jack Welch later went on to condemn heroism in management affairs.

No matter how talented a manager might be, the one phrase I hate to see on his evaluation is: 'He has trouble getting along with people!' Managements should be worried about such people. 'If an executive cannot get along with his peers, what good is he to the company?' asks Iacocca. We must not forget that as a manager, his function is to inspire other people. If he cannot do that, he is in the wrong position. Heroic managers excel by over-reacting and creating a crisis before dealing with it in order to gain an edge over others. 'Doing nothing is far better than managing a situation into a crisis,' says Alec Mackenzie, the author of *Time Trap*. The great master in the 6th century BC expressed his resentment against those whom we call heroic managers today!

Solicitude, watchfulness, and adjusting with time and people are virtues. Stiff and unbending is the disciple of death; the gentle and yielding is the disciple of life. Stillness

> *I would not have him to act with me, who will unarmed attack a tiger, or cross a river without a boat, dying without any regret. My associate must be the man who proceeds to action full of solicitude, who is fond of adjusting his plans, and then carrying them into execution.*
>
> —Confucius

and tranquillity set things in order in the universe, says a sage. Moderation is the way of sages.

Wisdom lies in moderation. Both Buddha's mid-path and Confucius' 'mean' stand for moderation in life. Moderation has no spikes, thorns or sharp edges that will hurt the other. 'An accordance with the nature is called the path of duty; the regulation of this path is called instruction.'

A good leader does not treat his juniors with contempt; in a crisis, he does not seek favour from his superiors. He rectifies himself and seeks nothing from others so that he has no dissatisfactions. He does not murmur against Heaven, nor grumble against his people.

When Germany collapsed and the earth shook under his feet, Adolf Hitler blamed his subordinates. John Adair writes in his book *Great Leaders* how, 'When the roof fell in, Hitler castigated the German people for letting him down...' The great master says he who does not transfer his anger; he who does not repeat a fault is the superior person. We must learn to take our successes to heart, and our failures to our heads so that we never repeat the mistakes we make.

The new age managers can turn into corporate sages if they just introspect—no meditation is required. Introspection is the basic evaluation technique for a leader. In archery, we have something of what it takes to become a superior man. When the archer misses the bull's eye, he turns round and seeks the cause of his failure within himself. The virtuous thoughts of Confucius bestow a new wisdom upon us to manage a new age. We can learn the art of leadership from an archer. When you attain success, open the window wide and look for someone to whom you can give credit; when you encounter failures, look into the mirror and own up responsibility.

I read someone defining business management as, 'Risk-taking, risk-taking, risk-taking...' I agree; 'No risk, no gain'. But the virtuous leaders follow the cosmic principles. Risk-taking is distinct from committing suicide. Risk-taking is within the defined parameters of the path that takes you to success; it doesn't run counter to the cosmic principles. When you flout the cosmic principles, you meet failure and disaster.

The virtuous leader is quiet and calm, waiting for the right time and opportunity; he does not wish to start a journey unless he sees a clear goal. On the other hand, the leader without virtue walks a dangerous path looking for lucky occurrences.

Confucius was the epitome of humility. He never claimed to be a man of illustrious virtue; though he was. Here is a nugget of his wisdom:

> *The way of the superior man is threefold, but I am not equal to it. "Virtuous", he is free from anxieties; "Wise", he is free from perplexities; "Bold", he is free from fear.*
>
> **—Confucius**

Be free from anxieties;
Be free from perplexities;
Be free from fear.

'Success comes to those who dare and act,' said Pandit Jawaharlal Nehru, the first Prime Minister of India.

A sage-leader is one who knows himself! Knowing the self is grander. 'I will not be concerned that men do not know me; I will be concerned at my own want of ability'; that is a deep thought that only sage-leaders can have.

Gone are the days when one used to see whether a person fit the job. In the new age, one needs to go beyond job fits; you need to look for righteousness in managers and find men of virtue who will not go astray. They are the only ones who can become the leaders of tomorrow. Character will play an important role tomorrow, far more important than competence. Not only the character of the leader but also the character of the organisation will assume significance.

An organisation grows rapidly under a virtuous leader. Righteousness is determined by one's actions. It is important to do right things; it is even more important to honour someone who does something right and reward him for his selfless contribution. Sincerity is the right way.

> *In a high situation, he does not treat with contempt his followers. In a low situation, he does not court the favour of his superiors. He rectifies himself, and seeks nothing from others, so that he has no dissatisfactions. He does not murmur against Heaven, nor grumble against men.*
>
> —Confucius

We tend to concentrate on the effects without going into the causes, responsible for those consequences. We often forget that 20 per cent of the causes are responsible for 80 per cent of the effects, good or bad.

We should remember that:

- Virtue is the root which leads to the right path; material gains are the result
- Virtue, like awareness, is soundless
- The man of virtue is one of wisdom
- Virtue is the interior; behaviour is the exterior

There is no right way to do a wrong thing. Only virtue can lead you to the perfect path.

✎ The Big Picture ✐

The roots of Gestalt Therapy—a school of psychology that interprets phenomenon as an organised whole rather than as aggregates of distinct parts—in management affairs can be traced to 1930. It maintains that the significance of a structured whole does not depend on its specific constituent elements; thus, a drawn figure still has meaning when there are gaps in the drawing. It lays emphasis on the invisible patterns, which has a substantial bearing on the organisational behaviour. It presupposes that a person's inability to successfully integrate the parts of his personality into a healthy whole may lie at the root of psychological disturbances. In Gestalt therapy, the analyst encourages clients to release their emotions and to recognise these emotions for what they are.

The Gestalt phenomenon seems to be the integrated part of Confucius' concept of virtue! To regulate one's conduct, go down to the root.

The commonality between Confucius' philosophy and Gestalt Therapy is revealed from the following text in the Book of Poetry and *Analects:*

'In all things, success depends on previous preparation and, without such previous preparation, there is sure to be failure. If what is to be spoken be previously determined, there will be no difficulty with them. If one's actions have been previously determined, there will be no sorrow in connection with them. If principles of conduct have been previously determined, the practice of them will be inexhaustible.'

The learning horizon expands when one prepares the mind. To be fond of learning is the first step to knowledge, said the Great Master. Isn't this the basic assumption that Peter Senge makes in his *Fifth Discipline* while defining the various learning disabilities and emphasising that the prerequisite to creating a learning organisation is to create the mindset first!

Some are born with knowledge; some acquire it after years of study; and others attain it after experiencing the pain of ignorance. Likewise, some use their knowledge with a natural sense of ease; others with a desire to gain advantage; and still others through strenuous efforts. Confucius believed that the knowledge acquired after a painful feeling of one's ignorance is as good and worthy as the knowledge that comes with birth or through hard study. He further believed that the knowledge that is applied with strenuous efforts is as good and worthy as the knowledge that is applied with a natural ease or with a desire to establish one's advantage.

Those who acquire knowledge with painstaking efforts create wellsprings within themselves. These leaders are honoured and admired.

Transparency is a great virtue. Let me underscore some of Great Master's reflections on transparency and shared vision.

'Do you think, my disciples, that I have any concealment? I conceal nothing from you. There is nothing, which I do that is not shown to you, my disciples—that is my way.'

Transparency and openness are the cardinal traits for a virtuous leader. Today seniors expect that their juniors should take them as their 'guru' and maintain the 'guru-disciple' relationship. However, they should ask themselves whether they really give their best to their juniors and share all their knowledge and corporate wisdom while grooming them. The superior leader examines his or her heart that there may be nothing wrong there, and that he or she may have no cause for dissatisfaction with himself.

Socrates said: 'The small man thinks of favours, which he may receive.' Confucius says: 'The mind of the superior man is conversant with righteousness; the mind of the mean man is conversant with gain. The leader must learn how to lose to win. He is there not to make the gains, but to gain from his giving.'

123

The virtuous will be sure to speak correctly, but those who speak well may not always be virtuous. Men of principle are sure to be bold, but those who are bold may not always be men of principle!

Confucius said, 'When we see men of worth, we should think of equalling them; when we see man of a contrary character, we should turn inwards and examine ourselves.' I haven't found a better description of benchmarking—a buzzword that has crept into management texts.

Bureaucratisation is the biggest threat and the singular cause of failure for most of the business organisations. Systems *per se* are not the obstacles—the problem lies in their blind application. It is at moment that the rule of clerks begins. Amazingly, the great master had analysed the configuration! 'Where the solid qualities are in excess of accomplishments, we have rusticity; where the accomplishments are in excess of the solid qualities, we have the manners of a 'clerk'.'

Knowing ignorance is strength; ignoring knowledge is sickness, said the Old Master Lao Tzu. I am not the one who was born in the possession of knowledge; I am the one who is fond of antiquity and earnest in seeking knowledge there.

⚑ Virtue is Soundless ⚑

We live in times of great uncertainties. The time ahead will throw up surprises unknown to mankind. You cannot expect the uncertainties to display a red flag on your table before disaster strikes...

The Fang bird does not come warily;
The river in flood sends forth no map!

124

Every changemaker has to bear the cross, or drink hemlock. Confucius also faced resistance during his lifetime. A madman of Ch'u, Chieh-yu, came near Confucius' carriage singing as he walked...

> *The phoenix, the phoenix...*
> *His prestige has gone down!*
> *Don't say he hasn't tried:*
> *For he may get there yet:*
> *But he should quit,*
> *Oh, he should quit:*
> *It's much too dangerous:*
> *In politics today!*

Confucius alighted and wished to converse with him, but Chieh-yu hastened away so that the Great Master could not talk to him. This incident finds mention in *Analects* (18:5).

Confucius is known as the Moses of China (Moses: 13th century BC) and his *Analects* as the tablets bearing the commandments. But the Moses of China had no promised land where he could lead his people. He prescribed 3,300 rules of conduct as the way of living virtue. He offered prescriptions for peace and order. These prescriptions are cosmic and, therefore, apply to the world of business world also.

❦ What is Perfect Virtue? ❧

Chung-kung asked about perfect virtue. Confucius said, 'It is, when you go abroad, to behave to everyone as if you were assisting at a great sacrifice; not to do to others as you would not wish done to yourself; to have no murmuring against you in the country, and none in the family.'

Virtue is the mother of ten thousand things; virtue is the root to ten thousand plants of happiness. 'Riches and honours acquired by unrighteousness are to me as a floating cloud,' says Confucius.

Socrates, the Greek philosopher who is generally regarded as one of the wisest men of all time, chose to drink hemlock (a poison) rather than abandon virtue. He neglected his own affairs, and instead spent his time discussing virtue, justice, and piety wherever his fellow citizens congregated. He equated virtue with knowledge of the true self, holding that no one knowingly does wrong. He looked upon the soul as the seat of both a waking conscience and moral character, and held the universe to be purposively mind-ordered.

His criticism of the Sophists and of Athenian political and religious institutions earned him many enemies. In 399 BC, Socrates was tried for corrupting the morals of the Athenian youth and for religious heresies. He was convicted and, resisting all efforts to save his life, willingly drank the cup of hemlock given to him. Plato in Apology, Crito, and Phaedo describes the trial and the death of Socrates.

One wonders whether it was simply a matter of chance that before Confucius died in 479 BC in China, another prophet of virtue, Socrates, had risen in 469 BC in Greece pursuing the same mission?' While we pretend to seek knowledge and wisdom from the prophets from the past, do we introspect enough about the scams and ripoffs in this age? We have become morally bankrupt and, in these circumstances, we have no choice but to go back and learn from the teachings of the old sages.

These sages were spiritual scientists and some were prophets to mankind. Socrates used to say that he spoke to mankind because the Lord had commanded him to do so. Likewise, Confucius used to claim, 'God begot the virtue in me!'

126

Confucius in his *Analects* underscores the virtuous business practices. To rule a country of a thousand chariots, there must be reverent attention to business, and sincerity; economy in expenditure, and love for men; and the employment of the people at the proper season.

Confucius believed in purpose and effectiveness and not empty rituals. When Confucius was very ill, Tzu Lu requested that prayers be offered. 'Is that done?' the Master asked. 'It is,' Tzu Lu replied. 'The litany says, 'Prayers have been offered for you to both earth and sky spirits.' The Master said, 'My prayers have been offered long since... If God was not moved by that, ritual prayers would add nothing.' What Confucius meant was his existence for teaching virtue was the greatest prayer. If Heaven could not be moved by his devoted actions, how could it be moved by the ritual of a simple prayer?

Confucius spoke about strategic vision 2500 years ago— long before it became fashionable to do so. He who runs the government by means of virtue may be compared to the Polar Star which keeps its place and all the stars turn towards it, said the Great Master. Can there be a better expression to emphasise what we in today's world call strategic vision? Like the North Star, strategic vision keeps its place and all business strategies and business activities turn towards it.

If the people are led by laws, and uniformity is sought to be achieved by meting out punishment, they will try to avoid the punishment, but will have no sense of shame. If they are led by virtue, and uniformity is sought by the 'rules of propriety', they will have a sense of shame and will become good.

It was a wise man who said: 'There is no greater inequality than the equal treatment of unequals.'

But do we make systems and formulate management strategies as rules of propriety? There's another question mark on what we mean by equitable treatment. Johnston's Law probably comes closest to the rules of propriety: If you treat everyone the same, what varies is the satisfaction. To achieve equal satisfaction, you must vary the treatment.

Here is a virtuous thought from the Great Master to mull over:

> *The superior man thinks of virtue;*
> *The small man thinks of comfort.*
> *The superior man thinks of the sanctions of law.*

7

Tai Chi—The Perfect Balance

At dusk the cock announces dawn;
At midnight, the bright sun.

—A Zen saying

The Chinese use a symbol—Tai Chi—to represent cosmic balance. Sages belonging to various ages and different faiths have searched for this difficult, almost elusive, aspect. Hinduism, Buddhism and Islam strive to find that fine balance between cause and effect. Lao Tzu gave this perfect balance a name: the universal law of energy response.

Perfect balance is now a *sine qua non* for business management as well. Lopsided growth can be extremely harmful.

⚜ The Polar Opposites ⚜

Chinese mysticism draws sustenance from the impulses of Yin and Yang—the feminine and masculine energies that underpin life itself. Tai Chi T'u is the symbol that reflects the cosmic balance between Yin and Yang. The ancient Chinese saw all changes in nature as a manifestation of the dynamic interplay between these two polar opposites.

The Chinese see the cosmos as a singular, inseparable reality that rests on an inherent duality represented by Yin and Yang. The concept of Tai Chi T'u has deeply influenced eastern management thoughts and practices.

> *In the transformation and growth of things, every bud and feature has its proper form. In this we have their gradual "maturing" and "decay", the constant flow of transformation of change—Tai Chi.*
>
> —Chuang Tzu

Yin and Yang are the counterbalancing halves of the ancient Chinese symbol Tai Chi T'u, which represents the shady and sunny parts of a hillock. Yin, the shady side, exemplifies feminine values like stillness, receptiveness, yielding, tranquillity, repose, calmness, quietude, and other feminine-qualities. Yang, the sunny side, typifies masculine values like assertiveness, vigour, movement, courage, and other masculine-qualities.

'From the very early times, the two archetypal poles of nature were represented not only by bright and dark, but also by male and female, firm and yielding, above and below,' observes Fritjof Capra, a modern physicist. 'Yang, the strong, male, creative power, was associated with Heaven, whereas Yin, the dark, receptive, female and maternal elements, was represented by the Earth. The Heaven is above and full of movement, the Earth—in the old geocentric view—is below and resting, and thus Yang came to symbolise movement and Yin rest. In the realm of thought, Yin is the complex, female, intuitive mind; Yang is clear and rational male intellect. Yin is the quiet, contemplative stillness of the sage; Yang the strong, creative action of the king.'

Yin is something that Lao Tzu calls the intuitive mind; Yang is what Confucius conceives as the rational intellect. These balancing symbols (Yin/Yang) are meaningless unless you can conceptually accept that Yin contains within itself the seeds of Yang and vice versa. When Yin reaches its climax, it retreats in favour of Yang; when Yang reaches its apogee, it wanes in deference to Yin.

This basic belief has given the Chinese courage and confidence in stressful times. Equally, it has moulded their character so that they become cautious and modest in times of success. They draw strength from Buddha's doctrine of the golden mean in which both the Taoists and Confucians believe. 'The sage', says Lao Tzu, 'avoids excess, extravagance and indulgence.' The Chinese consider the unity that lies behind Yin and Yang as Tao and see it as a process that ensures the interplay of their diverse energies. Yin and Yang represent the two poles that set the limits for the cycles of change.

✍ Balancing Intuition and Intellect ✍

Chinese wisdom is both holistic and balanced. Business management, however, lacks a holistic approach and balanced growth.

Global management theories have spawned a culture that tends to respect masculine virtues represented by Yang and have tended to give short shrift to the feminine qualities represented by Yin.

We idolise assertion over submission, vibrations over tranquillity, logic over intuition, digital logic over fuzzy logic, analysis over synthesis, reasoning over perceptivity, evidence over prudence, competition over collaboration... Yang over Yin, in a nutshell.

We discount the value of the intangibles that Yin represents. In the new age, this will need to change; the balance will tilt towards Yin virtues. The intangibles will come into sharp focus to bring about a cosmic balance. One must acknowledge the latent truth: the intangibles create the tangibles.

Our management style today is Yang-dominated: it is rational, aggressive, and masculine! The belief in science is Yang. We never seem to tire of talking about scientific management, rationality, and logic. The softer, feminine characteristics that are represented by Yin—values, wisdom and virtue—are not the sort of things that aggressive ex-

> *The valley of spirit never dies;*
> *It is the woman, primal mother.*
> *Her gateway is the root of heaven and earth;*
> *It is like a veil barely seen.*
> *Use it; it will never fail.*
>
> **—Lao Tzu**

ecutives have any patience or respect for. It is time that 'Yinism'—which Lao Tzu calls the valley of the spirit—is understood and given adequate importance in management affairs and business practices in order to achieve the cosmic balance that is sadly missing today. It is time we learnt the art of counterbalancing Yin and Yang in business practices. We must understand the values of feminine virtue and develop a respect for it first. This should not be misconstrued to mean that we need to employ more women at the workplace; rather it should focus on what we term the intangible, softer aspects of business. Today, managements have developed the massive pectoral muscles of male-dominated virtues that now need to be counter-balanced with a heavy dose of feminine characteristics.

132

The harmony between Yin and Yang is Tao. Tao is the cosmos; it is the cosmic truth. The corporate world cannot pretend that it can remain insulated from this universal truth. The Yang-oriented management style will now have to wane and allow feminine virtues to imbue the culture of companies. That is the only way that they will be successful in the future.

Chinese Vista considers every human being as *Chu-goku*, which literally means the centre of the universe. Most organistions would recoil with horror if they were told to consider their best employees as the 'centre of the universe'. *Chu-goku* enables us to see things in a new perspective. Imagine for a moment that each capable worker was regarded as the centre of your company. Consider that each one of them is in harmony with the organisation and its larger vision and vice-versa. If all of them together can create a vision for the future, they will own it, nurture it and build it. They will, in that sense, become the centre of our universe. It changes the entire outlook; it helps companies find the delicate balance between 'management pride' and 'workers' dignity'.

✎ The Present and the Future ✍

There is a growing need to achieve cosmic equilibrium in every sphere of business management, including a balance between the present and the future. Tai Chi gives us the wisdom to strike the desired balance between today and tomorrow.

Improve the present; create the future. Improve 'What Is'; create 'What isn't'. It isn't easy to improve today, and design tomorrow. We tend to snatch at the future while living in the past and without understanding what surrounds us. To keep pace with the future, one needs to understand the present first.

133

Corporate executives tend to concentrate on the present—riding the highs and lows of quarterly performances. They look at the trees and do not see the wood. The future belongs to those who can develop a corporate perspective—the people who can look beyond the numbers and see the distant patterns. Sadly, very few executives have either the time or the attitude to develop a long-term perspective. But why blame them alone? Most organisations measure the performance of individual employees through the prism of numerical targets and achievements.

'On an average, senior managers devote less than 3 per cent of their time to building a corporate perspective on the future. In some companies, the figure is less than 1 per cent,' says C.K. Prahalad in his book *Competing for the Future*. To manage balanced cosmic growth, business leaders have little option; they must be willing to devote considerably more time and spend more energy on creating a corporate perspective. If they fail, the organisation will crumble even though all the financial metrics seem to be on an upward curve at least for sometime.

Conceptualising the future, or seeing what others cannot see, provides you a distinct status and gives you the competitive edge. Today, if you do not devote time to build the future, you will be forced to do so tomorrow in a pressure-cooker environment. Sometimes, the violent forces disrupt even the most well-planned strategies. The only way to succeed is to develop a perspective for the future or, as the Chinese would say, follow the cosmic path—Tai Chi.

✎ Short term and Long term: The Great Gulf ✐

Ken Blanchard posits a solution in his book *Mission Possible*: 'Many companies are experiencing the downside of that rollercoaster ride today. We need to work smarter. Organisations today must have two strategies operating at once. The secret of constant growth is to start a new Sigmoid curve before the first one peters out.'

He suggests the creation of two teams—the 'P' team to improve the Present, and the 'F' team to innovate the Future. Before the P sigmoid of the Present team peters down and the curve starts moving downwards, the F sigmoid of Future team must activate. In this way, the two sigmoids of the Present and the Future can keep the company always fresh and alive.

Tai Chi counterbalances the imbalances. A balance must be struck between the needs of today and the requirements of tomorrow through continuity and innovation. Kaizen implies incremental development and it maintains continuity. However, we cannot afford to ignore the second law of thermodynamics—if not corrected, things move from order to disorder. To overcome this natural phenomenon, one needs to apply the technique of total productive maintenance (TPM). Through TPM, you can ensure that things do not spin out of control.

Thus, companies need to apply Kaizen to ensure continuity with incremental progress, and use TPM to prevent decline. To create the future, you need to trigger innovation. You cannot have one without the other. Al Dunlap, former chairman and CEO of Scott Paper Company, said: 'There are three types of executives in the world. There are those who can get short-term results and haven't a clue where they're going to take the company in the future. Conversely, there are those who have a great ten-year plan but are going to be out of business in ten months. And then there are those who can get short-term results in conjunction with a vision for the future. These are the good ones. But they are in unbelievably short supply.'

While developing the 'long-term' plans, you need to be perceptive to the highly demanding short-term standards. Take the bull by its horn and face the current challenges posed by the short-term standards. Simultaneously, you need to create long-term plans and strategies with an eye on the future. Discover the core values and core purpose of your company and live by them. Concurrently, make your people sweat, innovate and discover lest they get trapped in the 'we have arrived' syndrome. 'Creative tension', where pressure is the norm and challenges are compounded, is a powerful mechanism to stop people from becoming complacent.

A vision always goes beyond the numbers that are typically found in long-term plans. Business management is not a game of numbers. Nor is it a game of rules and procedures. It is all about managing people by winning their hearts and prevailing over their souls. It is about managing the process by overriding the bureaucratic barriers and demolishing the vertical blocks of disciplines that hinder the horizontal flow of process. It is all about managing the place where your market exists by understanding the strengths of your competitors and internalising the environment. It is about managing the Future by allowing your Past and Future to coexist in your Present.

✎ Intellect and Passion ✍

Likewise, balance the intellect (your Yang) and passion (your Yin). Singapore, the solitary intelligent country in the world, faces a unique problem. A few years back the government had realised that Singaporeans were growing into robots. Technology, which is devoid of any spirituality, has turned Singaporeans into commercial and economic beings. In their relentless pursuit of technology, they have lost touch with human feelings and values. This sparked grave concern. I understand a $ 6 billion project was launched called 'Smile Singapore'. The great builders of the first intelligent country are aware of the cosmic balance—Tai Chi—and they are making an all-out effort to pour emotions into their hearts. John Naisbitt wrote in his famous book *Megatrends* about the need to balance 'Hi-touch' with 'Hi-tech'; everybody has read it and then forgotten about it. The Singapore government is the first to have tried to put it into practice.

In 2002, the Singapore government launched another mission to strike a unique balance called 'Remaking of Singapore'. The cardinal aim is to make their youth realise that the five C's—Career, Condominium, Credit Card, Club and Car—are not the only things in life to aspire to. There is life beyond 5 Cs that is richer in quality. The purpose of the project is to balance material outlook with value-orientation.

Singapore needs to find new ways to make a living. In remaking Singapore, we need to go beyond economics:

- *What kind of Singapore will make Singaporean proud?*
- *What values must we preserve?*
- *How do we strengthen our multi-racial, multi-religious society?*
- *How do we prepare Singapore politically, culturally and socially to survive in the 21st century as a nation?*

—Convener of Remaking Singapore

Singapore is perhaps the sole example where everything is 'process oriented'. They know how to allow things to manifest like the need for balance between material and emotional happiness.

⍋ Balancing Human Energies ⍰

Emotional energy is more powerful than the intellectual energy. If emotional strength is blended with the intellectual prowess, it creates a unique synergy that can help overcome any obstacle. 'Human energy is like the energy of light,' says Ken Blanchard. 'When it is dissipated, as in the average light bulb, it gets work done in an average way. But when same energy is focused and concentrated in a single direction, as with a laser beam, it has the power to cut through any kind of obstacle.'

There are what we call 'moments of truth' when the fine cosmic balance between emotional and intellectual energies are achieved. Every contact with a customer is an opportunity for a positive moment of truth. The marketing person should ask himself: with every interaction with the customer, am I drawing him closer or putting him off? Am I the kind of person who accepts others and builds bonds to establish long-term relationships? The answer should come from the bottom of your heart and not from the top of your mind. Unless your intellect blends with emotions, the 'moments of truth' cannot happen. No mission can succeed unless and until it is carried out at the emotional level.

Tai Chi reflects the natural process of transformation—manifestation. Today the management gurus have understood the meaning of seamless transformation and they have coined a phrase to explain it: dynamic stability. Managing change through dynamic stability is purely an adaptation of the natural laws of manifestation in terms of Tai Chi and Wu Wei.

❦ Business Disciplines ❧

Business can no longer be run by adopting a unifunctional approach. Unfortunately, right from Adam Smith's time we have been groomed to think and manage in compartments—personnel, finance, production, marketing, material management, engineering, and R&D. However, Cartesian logic doesn't apply here: the whole isn't greater than the sum of the parts. Excellence in each discipline does not automatically translate into excellence of the company. Integration and coherence are more important. If each musician performs best when he plays alone, the combination of the players will not result in melody. Melody is nothing but the space between the two notes. How does one create this space? 'Process orientation' will be the focus of tomorrow.

❦ Upside, Downside ❧

Companies tend to focus on a set of metrics to evaluate performance. One of the most commonly used measurement models is ROI, a formula that has two components: a numerator (turnover, growth, expansion) and a denominator (investment, capital employed or manpower). Most companies strive to increase the numerator, and decrease the denominator.

'Top management people know well that raising net income is likely to be harder than cutting assets and head counts,' observes C.K. Prahalad. A business leader needs entrepreneurial skills, intuitive values, insight, acumen and a sense of direction to increase the numerator. He must envision the changing pattern of market and shifting needs of customers. But under pressure, it is much easier to reduce the denominator to show greater returns. C.K. Prahalad says, 'Denominator management is an accountant's shortcut to assess productivity'. Thus, we tend to go for an easier option, sparking a cost-cutting mania within the company. When the business goes haywire, the top brass sucks all the decision making back up to the top.

In the hour of reckoning, it is the pillars of faith that begin to shake. Our faith shifts from the numerator to denominator. The head honcho morphs into a butcher: chop, chop, chop and the head counts drop to alarming levels. Downsizing has become a crazy mantra in the corporate world. Business leaders should learn to 'smart size' rather than downsize operations: this takes care of both the numerator and the denominator.

❦ Balanced Business Scorecard ❧

Robert S. Kaplan and David P. Norton made a very sharp-eyed observation while developing their unique 'Balanced Business Scorecard'. Managing is nothing but balancing your inner focus and outer focus, on the one hand, and Present and Future, on the other.

We need to adopt a balanced approach in everything we do. Like the dials in the cockpit of a plane, complex information about the company must be available to managers at a glance. Process orientation should be measured in a balanced manner and not merely through financial measures that can be misleading. Executives must understand that traditional financial accounting measures like ROI and earning per share (EPS) can give misleading signals for continuous improvement and innovative activities. Companies are remembered not for attaining a better ROI or EPS.

What you measure is what you get. Business leaders must understand that their company's measurement system affects the behaviour of their managers and employees. If they are groomed to measure the growth in terms of financial measures only, they will give results by sacrificing values. A balanced measurement system shows how the results have been achieved, and where we have gone astray. Did the cost of setups fall because of shorter setup times or bigger batch sizes? Or, was it because the employees invested their emotions and took a vow to set a new record? The financial measures do not take into account the emotional investments that have been made by the employees.

A balanced measurement system acts like a mirror. It reflects whether the company has improved financial measures at the cost of innovation, learning, customer satisfaction, or internal process. It unveils the financial jugglery—or just plain fudging! There is of course an extreme view: Forget the financial measures; improve operational measures like cycle time and defect rates and the financial results will follow. In simple words, it means that you need to take care of the process, and the results are bound to be good.

However, extreme views are the anti-thesis to cosmic principles. Whenever any process takes an extreme position, it is bound to retreat! Let us not go so far as to say that companies ought to dump their financial yardsticks for measuring performance. Business leaders should not have to choose between financial and operational measures: Do not rely on one set of measures to the exclusion of the others. Tai Chi embraces both—Yin and Yang. Extreme views do not jell with Tai Chi.

A balanced perception stems from self-questioning:

How do we look at our shareholders?
How do customers see us?

What must we excel at?

Can we continue to improve and create value?

Financial measures, customers' perception, internal processes and innovative and learning perspectives ensure a cosmic balance.

1. How do we look at our shareholders?

We measure growth of our businesses in terms of turnover, ROI, manpower cost, net worth, earnings per share, value addition, sundry debtors, inventories, bank interest and other financial parameters. I am not opposed to such measurements, but feel they show only one side of the picture. Don't bow and scrape for financial gains. If you over rely on Yang, you are deprived of Yin; it is such a simple and universal principle.

2. How do customers see us?

The Customer is God! However, in today's heretic world of business, God finds a secondary position to the Boss. So, it is better to see your customer as your Boss.

The Japanese treat their customers virtually as Gods. It is the only place where customers are allowed to decide the tariff in a grand hotel—of course, as an experimental pursuit.

I reproduce an excerpt from *Paper News*:

'Experience with about 500 guests have shown the effect is about the same as a 10 per cent discount,' said a hotel spokesman who identified herself only by her surname, Kondo. 'But the novelty draws even more

> *Tokyo: How much is a room for the night? A meal in the hotel restaurant? A drink in the bar? A Japanese hotel owner said, he will leave that up to the guest, and he still expects to make profit. This new system began on 1st October 1997 in the restaurants and bars at the hotel Nagoya Castle in Nagoya, 270 kilometres west of Tokyo.*
>
> —**Paper News**

customers than an ordinary discount would,' she added. Patrons get a bill showing the suggested price, with space next to it in which the customers write the amount they are going to pay. However, the customers have an option. On entering the restaurant, customers are asked whether they want to use the new system or pay the standard prices. If all goes as planned, the new system will determine the room rates for the next year keeping in view the customer's choice to pay.

Gone are the days where values were given the supreme place in day-to-day life. In India, guests were regarded as the blessings of God. The number of guests visiting one's house was taken as a barometer to assess one's dignity. In olden days 'Sarais' (motels) were built where rent-free shelter was provided to the travellers.

India has a rich heritage. Chanakya's *Artha Shastra* is considered as one of the best treatises on economics and business management. It is only in the 1980s that companies started talking about 'customer satisfaction' and customer care. However, Mahatma Gandhi, India's greatest leader, had alerted the business world in the 1940s to respect the customer.

A customer is the most important visitor on our premises. He is not dependent on us, we are dependent on him. He is not an interruption on our work. He is the purpose of it. He is not an outsider in our business. He is part of it. We are not doing him a favour by serving him. He is doing us a favour by giving us an opportunity to do so.

—Mahatma Gandhi

A customer looks for timely delivery, a quality product, competitive cost, aesthetic designs, quick response, trouble-free service and, above all, a show of courtesy.

143

The customer does not stop buying from your company because he finds a better product elsewhere. He stops buying from you when he feels ignored by your marketing people. 'Customer complaints offer the opportunity to regain the trust a customer may have lost, and identify areas that need improvement,' says Sunder Hemrajani. You can retain your customer not just by your intellect but also through your emotional strength. To retain your customers and expand your market share, you need to not only invest in customer service but also make an emotional investment to champion the cause of the customer. Courtesy and complete honesty are the best emotional investments a company can possibly make. 'To be number one in delivering value to customers is a typical mission statement,' says Jack Welch while sharing the secrets of his success.

3. What must we excel at?

Process, designs, systems, skills, quality, technology, machinery, materials management, housekeeping, industrial relations, HRD, and a host of such activities constitute the 'internal process' with which your customer is not bothered. But you have got to take care of your internal process. It is essential that you must set your house in order and excel in order to offer the best services to your customer. Many believe that excellence in everything we do as excellence as a goal is often the precursor of great growth. Each skill, each process and each system affords an opportunity to strive for excellence. If an organisation aims to attain excellence in every sphere, profits will automatically follow.

4. Can we continue to improve and create value for customer?

Learning and creativity are inescapable needs for a balanced growth of your organisation. Learning? It's what you breathe in! Creativity? It's what you breathe out!

Think! When was the last time you did something creative?

'Don't' look elsewhere to see what everyone thinks. Think for yourself,' says Jack Welch. The best way to get a good idea is to generate a lot of ideas. Think of something different. First shape your idea softly, think in terms of feasibility, and then bake it to harden the idea.

The cosmos has given you many options. Find the path that leads to success. It is not necessarily a path that others have traversed earlier. Discovery consists of looking at the same thing as everyone else but thinking something different. One must come out of his mental block first—the knot that you see in the issue as a problem lies, in fact, in your own stomach.

Take a holistic view, counterbalance your actions, and then measure the growth of your company in terms of financial measures, customer-satisfaction, internal process and learning and creativity.

⚘ Tai Chi—A Symbol of Balance ⚘

Tai Chi is the symbol of balance. Another dimension of the balanced Tai Chi is success and failure. Failures are not bad; they are natural. We should learn to welcome a wake-up call that snaps us out of deep slumber. We fail because we must succeed; even the best must fail otherwise they would not try harder and they would not grow.

Mistakes are taken as an opportunity to learn; in a fast-changing global economy, more and more companies will encounter failures; many of them will be those that have only tasted success so far.

145

Times have changed; the focus needs to change as well. Organisations need to keep their feet firmly on the ground as the howling winds of change buffet them. They must witness action in inaction; observe inaction in action. They must learn to take a holistic view of their business. They must also be clear about what they want to achieve and how they want to get there. They must maintain balance even as they move forward.

Bear one thing in mid: the tortoise can tell you more about the roads than the hare.

Part III

Wisdom from Ancient India

The Bhagvad Gita, one of the classics of Hinduism, essentially related to the Upanishads in content, and is variously dated between the 3rd century BC and the 4th century AD. It is the highest expression of philosophical Hinduism. It is a chapter of the immense Indian epic, the Mahabharata, the saga of the war between the Pandavas and the Kauravas.

Ancient Indian texts include the goldmines of the Vedas and Upanishads. The power of the mind has a distinct place in Hindu philosophy especially in the two great religions, Buddhism and Hinduism.

8

Buddha's Cosmic Truths

*The things of the universe are not sliced off
from one another with a hatchet;
Neither the hot from the cold
Nor the cold from the hot.*

—An old saying

Cosmic truth is a continuum. It cannot be sliced into nano, pico or atto seconds. Unfortunately, man always strives to bring some semblance of order into what he sees as a chaotic world. So, he starts by dicing up his world into components; he hangs labels on them and pigeonholes the lot.

The trouble with this approach is that the cosmic world doesn't allow itself to be pigeonholed quite so easily. There is a large amount of vagueness that exists and it is difficult to categorise these ineffable elements because we comprehend so little, and yet we sense that they do exist. Let us take a question: What is melody? Do you produce melody just by hitting the keys on a piano? Or does it include the infinitesmal sounds of silence that nestle between the octaves? Melody includes the space between the musical notes.

The great note sounds muted; the great image has no form, says a sage. Greatness is vague! Clarity comes from vagueness.

Sadly, we live in a world that is impatient with anything that cannot be easily identified and labelled. It is tragic that we prefer to be precisely wrong than vaguely right!

When we say something is fuzzy, we mean it is unclear and is, therefore, unacceptable or spurious. However, we need to realise that vagueness is a strength and not a weakness, even in management matters! It creates greater space and openness so that other elements can emerge. It often gives vent to thoughts that are buried. Unfortunately, our mindset is not attuned to haziness or fogginess. Clarity, even if it is a mirage, appeals to our minds.

To prove that vagueness is a virtue, Lotfi Zadeh spent almost two decades to conceive and one decade to convince people about what he called fuzzy logic. Fuzzy logic—as opposed to binary logic—is a multi-valued logic. Classical logic holds that everything can be expressed in binary terms: 0 or 1, black or white, yes or no. Like Boolean algebra, everything is in one set or another, but not in both—either it is right or wrong, it can't be right as well as wrong. Contrary to this principle, fuzzy logic allows for values between 0 and 1, the shades of gray. 'Fuzzy logic is used for understanding the hidden assumptions, with an expert system; logical inferences can be drawn even from imprecise relationships,' explains Zadeh. But it needs a new mindset.

Today, fuzzy logic is the principle that drives automatic washing machines. When Zadeh floated the concept, he was derided for trying to foist a theory that militated against accepted principles. Like all of us Zadeh had always believed

150

in precision. Yet, the more he examined complexity, the more he started to question his beliefs. Manifestation started its cosmic dance and the truth dawned on him. He describes how it was all revealed to him: 'This was something that was bothering me. We need a radically different kind of mathematics, the mathematics of fuzzy or cloudy quantities which are not describable in terms of probability distributions.'

Lotfi Zadeh brought the concept of fuzzy logic into our homes through washing machines and other consumer appliances. Why fuzzy? Zadeh found the name most descriptive. Clarity cannot be segmented; it cannot be divided and pigeonholed.

> *Why Fuzzy Logic? Even with a negative connotation, it is most illustrative. Vagueness is hazy at the edges; in haze lies clarity.*
>
> **—Lotfi Zadeh**

It is not the going out of port, but the coming in that determines the success of voyage: Henry Ward Beecher highlighted the fact that the success of fuzzy logic lies in its application. In 1985, Lotfi Zadeh made a prophecy: he said that in a matter of two to five years, most expert systems would use fuzzy logic! He was proved right. Today, it is used to automatically optimise the operation of a washing machine by sensing the load size, fabric mix and quality of detergent. It is also used to control elevators, operate household appliances, cameras, automobile systems and smart weapons.

Fuzzy logic is the gateway to tomorrow's business world. Its application in business management will be the real turning point. What the business leaders of tomorrow require is a fuzzy mindset.

Management is not just a numbers game. You need to inject a bit of fuzziness into the picture to achieve clarity.

❦ Intellect of And ❧

Business leaders have always followed an exclusivist approach to deal with situations or find solutions. When considering a problem, they adopt an either/or approach: they look for mutually exclusive solutions. They tend to see everything in black and white: they are blind to the grays that lie in between. Increasingly, they will need to adopt an inclusivist approach; they will have to learn to appreciate the power of 'and'.

Binary logic—the exclusivist 'zero or one' approach—needs to be seen in a wider perspective. We cannot see everything in terms of black and white. More important and real are the various shades of gray—the nuances that lie beneath the surface.

Aristotle, whose reflective contributions to human thought are inexpressible, has unwittingly caused an indeterminate deprivation to society and, in turn, to the world of business management by strongly advocating the Either/Or logic—this or that. This has crippled man by making him unable to appreciate the intellectual vastness of the inclusivist 'and'.

'Aristotelian logic is simply concerned with the formal properties of an argument, not its factual accuracy,' explained Zadeh. The Aristotelian logic espouses three laws which are basic to all logical thought: the law of identity (A is A), the law of contradiction (A cannot be both A and not-A), and the law of the excluded middle (A must either be A or not-A).

'When the only tool you have is a hammer, everything begins to look like a nail,' says Lotfi Zadeh striking a witty blow at Aristotelian logic. 'For this reason, the binary logic could breathe hard for eons beyond its lifetime because there was nothing else to fill the gap.'

Digital logic is binary; the central idea is simple. At the bottom of binary logic rests a 'true/false' dualism. Fuzzy logic, on the other hand, works on a different plane!

The polar opposites—Yin and Yang—do not oppose but harmonise by waning and waxing as a continuum and not as mutually exclusive forces that keep crossing the Rubicon. Fuzzy logic is akin to such a continuum and kindred to the intellect of And.

Visionary companies do not agonise over either/or choices. The so-called rational mind cannot easily accept a paradox; it cannot live in peace with two seemingly contradictory forces or ideas at the same time. But the test of intelligence lies in handling the paradoxical situations proficiently.

F. Scott Fitzgerald rightly says: 'The test of a first-rate intelligence is the ability to hold two conflicting ideas in the mind at the same time, and still retain the ability to function.'

It is hard to get people to break out of their current world-view while continuing to operate within it. Nevertheless it is not impossible. In business management thinking, as also in life, one is often asked whether it is possible to improve Today while creating a new Tomorrow. Again, one must build first and foremost for the long term while simultaneously trying to meet the highly demanding short-term demands. Attempting to improve the Present while designing the Future is difficult, but not impossible. One must allow the Past and the Future to co-exist in the Present.

While all of this may seem contradictory, we need to expand our world-view to include differing streams of thought. We have been taught to see things in either black or white. We don't see the seven colours coalesce into a ray of light from the sun. We don't see the unity of the seven colours in the spectrum. We tend to see things as stand-alone entities.

Unfortunately, 'either/or' divides. It is not holistic. 'And' joins. When you put together the snapshots, you learn to create a big picture.

◁ The Truth is Hazy ▷

The cosmos is indivisible; true knowledge is a continuum.

The edges of truth are always hazy. Let me examine this proposition a little closely. Let us assume that you have a pile of sand in front of you; you start removing one grain of sand at a time from that pile. At which point does it cease to be a pile of sand? Can you tell?

The answer is: No one knows.

We must appreciate that precision and vagueness are the features of language. Carefully read the following famous oracle and try to solve it:

The Theseus' ship was the Athenians' pride once;

As the planks rotted, they replaced them with new ones.
Initially, the first plank was replaced;
Then, the second one was replaced;

Everyone agreed, it was the same Theseus' ship;
Likewise, the Athenians replaced every plank of the ship.
Was it, then, a different ship?
At which point did it cease to be Theseus' ship?

If you order your driver to 'turn right', will he do so in a jiffy?

> *When I come back from Japan, I always find me in a hot pan. For us in America, ambiguity is a matter of fuss. There in Japan, I notice, I have to be roundabout—everything is subtlety and nuance… It's like a winter's foggy day of France. 'About'. 'I think'. 'Well—more or less' are the phrases, suffixed to 'exactness'.*
>
> **—An American Annalist**

No. He will wait until the first intersection, and then turn right. Thus, this simple directive carries a hidden assumption: Go straight until you reach a corner, and then turn right. 'Turn right' in fact means to do so when it is possible to do so.

Alas! In the world of management, such hidden assumptions—what I term prudence—are imperfectly understood. When rules and systems are applied without understanding the hidden assumptions, they play havoc and we curse the systems while defending our imperfect applications.

Fuzzy logic is based on hidden assumptions. It requires listeners to 'defuzzify'.

Fuzzy logic took root in Japan. The Japanese were the first to seize upon fuzzy logic because vagueness is more central to their lives and they become aware of it more quickly. Moreover, they are highly pragmatic. 'We didn't even know fuzzy logic was important and the Japanese had been using it for years,' says Federico Fagin, who worked along with Bart Kosko, the follower of Lotfi Zadeh who first scientifically proved fuzzy logic.

But there's no need to be astonished! The Japanese practise vagueness. They make use of ambiguities in everyday speech. They tend to make indistinct sentences even when they know the exact answer. Daniel McNeill and Paul Freiberg, the authors of *Fuzzy Logic,* describe this in an interesting manner. 'If asked, "How many yen do you have in your wallet?" a Japanese may say, "About 10,000," even if he knows he has exactly 10,000. Thus, when speaking English, the Japanese say "I think" more often than native speakers. The Japanese sentences commonly trail off into a but or however, leaving the listener to infer the reservation. The term *maa* means "well, more or less", and speakers employ it when they disagree with the listener but don't want to say so outright.' Such habitual vagueness requires listeners to defuzzify more.

Seeing the invisible is as important as hearing the unheard. Zen philosophy, which is laced with fuzzy logic, believes space is not empty—it is full of nothingness.

The Ryoanji rock garden in Kyoto, perhaps the most famous in the world, has 15 rocks on a field of raked white gravel. Yet no observer ever sees all 15 rocks at once. As one Japanese philosopher once said no one sees everything. The Japanese practise seeing the invisible in their gardens where beds of pebbles and huge rocks attract the attention of the visitors. The Japanese are trained to pay attention to the space around them.

'Buddha was the first Fuzzy Theorist,' claims Bart Kosko. The Japanese as well the Chinese have embraced Buddhism.

Twenty-five centuries have passed since Gautama blossomed into the Buddha—the enlightened one. Buddha gave the agonised world a message of peace and happiness that was so inspiring that today one-fifth of mankind follows him. Recognising the potential of high spiritual success in everyone, he taught a totally pragmatic way of life, based on ethics, mental culture and wisdom. I shall only broach upon one aspect out of his multifarious virtuous teachings and practices— fuzzy logic, which will bring the future to our doorstep!

The Buddhist sects of Japan and China are based on the practice of meditation rather than adherence to a particular scriptural doctrine. Its foundation in China was established by the legendary Bodhidharma (5th century AD), who taught wall-gazing. Yogacara, or the consciousness school of Buddhism, held consciousness as real but not its objects.

Wall-gazing is a modern management technique to inspire creativity. 'Reward the person who doesn't work', says an HRD-ian. After an uneasy pause, he adds, 'Hey—wait a minute...!' And finally he reveals the hidden assumption: 'But, be sure that he often looks at the wall, aimlessly blurring his vision. And believe me, this person will fashion an image out of the ashes for your company and bring the future to your doorstep!' Allow your creative brains to accept what Bodhidharma taught as wall-gazing.

'He that will not apply new remedies must expect new evils; for time is the greatest innovator,' said Francis Bacon. Similarly, Einstein's vagueness was the cause of his success, not the laws of mathematics.

> *As far as the laws of mathematics refer to reality, they are not certain; they do not refer to reality.*
>
> —**Albert Einstein**

Zen teaching of sudden enlightenment, or satori, goes back to Hui-neng, an illiterate master belonging to the 7th century AD who defined enlightenment as the direct seeing of one's original nature i.e. Buddha. The golden age of Zen (8th–9th century AD) developed a unique style of oral instructions, including non-rational elements such as the koan, a subject given for meditation, usually in the form of paradoxical statements to test the enlightenment of the students of Zen. Here I would like to clarify that the usage of koans first started in Hinduism in India and later Buddhist monks used the technique to kindle awakening.

Here is a sample:

1. *Oh, West is West and East is East;*
   And never shall the 'twain meet!
2. *The heavens are as low as earth below the mountains;*
   The mountains are on the same level as the marshes;
   Why? The hovering clouds form below mountains,
   And on the mountains, can lie high the marshes!

157

Opposites in a continuum require each other:

3. *Difficult and easy complete each other;*
    Long and short form each other;
    High and low fulfil each other;
    A 'set' and a 'complement' make each other.

The Chinese and Japanese mystics have picked koans—
those seemingly nonsensical riddles—from Zen Buddhism to
transmit their teachings.

'These koans establish an important parallel to modern
physics,'observes Capra in his *Tao of Physics*.

4. *Leaves falling;*
    Lie on one another;
    The rain beats the rain.

'Eastern mysticism has developed several different ways
of dealing with the paradoxical aspects of reality,' writes Capra.
'Whereas they are bypassed in Hinduism through the use of
mythical language, Buddhism and Taoism tend to emphasize
the paradoxes rather than conceal them.'

5. *We were parted many thousand of kalpas ago, yet we have not*
    been separated even for a moment. We are facing each other
    all day, yet we have never met.'

Daito—a Zen master (when he met Emperor Godaigo).

6. *You can make the sound of two hands clapping. Now what is*
    the sound of one hand?
7. *What was your original face—the one you had before your*
    parents gave birth to you?
8. *The great square has no corners...*

All koans have more or less typically designed solutions that a competent Zen master recognises. Solving a koan is not easy—it demands concentration and total involvement. Koans can only be understood but cannot be explained through the figure of language.

❧ Aristotle Out; Buddha In ❧

Vagueness stems from a continuum; infinity is extremely vague! The cosmos, which has been expanding, is getting fuzzier with the passage of time.

Vagueness is cosmic and it, therefore, ought to be a strength and not a weakness.

Hui Shi, a zen follower who studied Lao Tzu and Chuang Tzu, once said, 'Going to the state of Yue today, one arrives there yesterday. Time is relative. Today is the yesterday of tomorrow, as yesterday is the yesterday of today.' The koan almost anticipates Einstein's Theory of Relativity.

Bart Kosko, who is crowned as an American Samurai, is deeply inspired by Lotfi Zadeh's fuzzy logic. How Bart was baptised is a moment of truth—the spell cast by Zadeh when Peter Cheeseman had challenged Zadeh's fuzzy logic and ridiculed him before luminaries. I quote the parable from *Fuzzy Logic* authored by Daniel McNeill and Paul Freiberg:

> In 1985, Bart Kosko sat in the packed hall at a conference at UCLA. On stage were Peter Cheeseman, Lotfi Zadeh, Judea Pearl, and other luminaries. With the flair of a standup comic, Cheeseman gave a once-over of Bayesian probability, lightly taunted Zadeh, and issued a challenge: $50 to anyone who could solve any problem Bayesian inference could not. By then he had completely won the crowd over. Zadeh rose to speak soon after, and Kosko watched in disbelief as he ignored the blazing gauntlet. Audience enthusiasm turned to stone.

'I really felt a cold chill in my spine,' Kosko says. 'It was the first time that I fundamentally thought fuzzy logic was a tremendous mistake. I really thought the old vessel simply couldn't hold water. And when the push came to a shove, when you finally got out of the fuzzy ghetto, you got pushed right back into it. Even the Grand Master couldn't hold his own against an upstart.'

At this moment of truth, Kosko decided to fathom fuzzy logic to its depth, to determine once and for all if it had substance. If it existed, I would pursue it out to the end. If not, I would flay it so savagely that I'd make Cheeseman look like nothing.

Unlike Zadeh, who took over two decades for convincing the people, Bart Kosko is powerful and brutally frank. "Kosko is a singular individual, brilliant, brash, self-disciplined, competitive, and highly controversial within the fuzzy community." The American Sumarai throws up the challenge:

My theorems are false if, and only if, $2 = 3$. So you don't have to like it. You just have to take it... The fact is that what Einstein did with 'gravity' was to eliminate it. That's what we do here: eliminate 'probability'... What makes society turn is science, and the language of science is math, and the structure of math is logic, and the bedrock of logic is Aristotle, and that is what goes out with fuzzy logic.

Who gets out is Aristotle; who gets in is Buddha!

Traditional logic has forced us to create categories which, when examined in the larger scheme of things, are nothing more than lines drawn in the sand. Even today, the human beings and business managers make detailed plans that are like building sandcastles on the beaches holding steadfast to binary logic, unaware of the mighty tides and the violent winds that have already started rocking the foundations.

One may wonder: where are the thoughts of the Buddha? All that I have mentioned above are a part of Buddha's wisdom that has been adopted as fuzzy logic today.

160

To understand fuzzy logic one must know clearly that it is anything but logic. Zadeh added the word logic to the word 'fuzzy' only to ensure its acceptability and not to make it more comprehensible.

9

Learning from the Bhagvad Gita

Vasudaiva Kutumbam

Vasudaiva Kutumbam, proclaims the Bhagvad Gita. The world is a large family! The phrase also appears in the *Panchatantra*, the book of parables. The ancient epic talked about a 'borderless world' long before Kenichi Ohmae turned it into a shibboleth for the new-age economy where people live and work in an interlinked world.

The world has chosen to go in a direction in the new age that was mapped out long before in Hindu scripture. The world is turning into a global village—or a *Vasudaiva Kutumbam*—that cuts across political borders by building and merging the political segments into regional blocs.

Today, the Internet has turned the entire globe into a small village or a family. The way we work has changed dramatically. Electronic networks have created a radically different world of business that binds us into a single networked family; distances have vanished and new bonds are being forged.

The Bhagvad Gita, one of the classics of Hinduism that is essentially related to the Upanishads in content, is variously dated between the 3rd century BC and the 4th century AD. It is the highest expression of Hindu philosophy and encapsulates the essence of the Mahabharata, the great Indian epic that depicts the war between the Pandavas and the Kauravas—the Good and the Evil. The epic is in the form of a dialogue between Krishna, the charioteer, and his disciple Arjuna, who is caught in an ethical dilemma over going to battle with his cousins, the Kauravas, to reclaim the kingdom.

The Bhagvad Gita is pantheistic. God is in all things; all things are in God.

> *He who sees Me everywhere and sees everything in Me, he never gets separated from Me, nor do I get separated from him.*
> **—Bhagvad Gita (VI–300)**

God is the pinnacle of all things—the radiant sun of the lights, the shining intellect of beings, the ocean of waters, the Himalayas of mountain ranges, the Ganges of rivers...

Without beginning, middle or end, of infinite power,
Of infinite arms, whose eyes are the moon and the sun,
I see thee, whose face is a flaming fire,
Burning this whole universe with Thy radiance.

(XI–19)

Something that is infinite, without a beginning or an end, cannot be described through finite words, nor can the infinite picture be captured on a finite canvas. Lao Tzu said much the same thing in the 6th century BC: 'The Tao that can be told is not the eternal Tao.'

163

✎ The Creation Hymn ✐

I begin with the Creation Hymn from the Rig Veda which gives us a glimpse of what the authors envisaged as the beginning of the world:

'There was neither "non-existence" nor "existence" then; there was neither the realm of space nor the sky which is beyond. What stirred? Where? In whose protection? Was there water, bottomlessly deep? There was neither death nor immortality then. There was neither a distinguishing sign of night nor of day. That one breathed, windless, by its own impulse. Other than that there was nothing beyond.'

'Darkness was hidden by darkness in the beginning; with no distinguishing sign, all this was water. The life force that was covered with emptiness, that one arose through the power of heat.'

'Who really knows? Who will here proclaim it? Whence was it produced? Whence is this Creation? The "Devas" came afterwards, with the creation of this universe. Who then know whence it (the cosmos) has arisen?' (10.129)

✎ The Creator! ✐

Man's search for the creator is never ending. There are no conclusive answers and we have all chosen to believe in some philosophy and have formulated at our own conception about the theory of creation itself. We all want to get to the source or root of this existence which, for want of a better expression, we call the Ultimate Truth, and which, if it exists, might be so pure that the feeble human intellect will not be able to grasp it. There is a restless urge in human nature to gain a vision of this Ultimate Truth. Perhaps, this urge has prompted

Man to 'condition' the Ultimate Truth, by giving form to something that is essentially formless. The desire to envision the Ultimate Truth led to a personification of the Creator, thereby opening the doors to image worship through a symbolic representation of gods and goddesses.

There are two ways to catch a glimpse of reality. One is by qualifying the Absolute with attributes; the other is by depriving Him of all attributes. 'It was the other process that was particularly followed by the Upanishads—the process of negations, "Neti, Neti",' writes Abdul Kalam Azad. 'Such a process undoubtedly affords a very advanced view of transcendentalism; but it ends in nullification, and denies us the consolation of positive belief.' It is an opinion. Faith is much deeper than thoughts; faith begets faith.

The creation story of cosmos is a perfect mystery. Even the scientists do not seem to agree on a single assumption. Carl Sagan, a physicist who was famous for his attempt to popularise science through a best-selling book *Cosmos* that was later turned into a hugely successful television documentary, was humble enough to admit that the various creation stories in different religions were worthy of respect.

Understanding our origin is significant and relevant for broader and quality perception of the whole. Ecology has already become a part of business management and corporate managers realise the worth of 'eco-systems' in managing businesses with a holistic approach.

⋐ Business Lessons from the Gita ⋑

So, what does the Bhagvad Gita say to the corporate manager? Like all great religious classics, it is filled with questions as well as answers. It provides solutions to the many ills that plague modern society. It is pregnant with deep philosophy for high-end applications. One may find its philosophical flight beyond the understanding of a common man.

> *He who sees 'inaction' in 'action'*
> *And 'action' in 'inaction', He is a*
> *man of established wisdom*
> *And a true performer of all actions.*
> —**Bhagvad Gita (IV–18)**

The Bhagvad Gita sees truth and good in all things. It is an exposition of the fundamental beliefs of Hinduism. The basic principle of the Gita is *karma,* or action; it defines the entire process of human life in the context of *karma.* It is governed by the simple logic that what we do is what confronts us later in life. This is a principle that has a lot in common with the biblical exhortation: 'Do unto others what you would have them do unto you'.

A business leader needs to develop an intuitive eye that can see 'action' in 'inaction' and 'inaction' in 'action'. The repetitive use of the words 'action' and 'inaction' may seem to be part of some elaborate word play, but it is not. Let me try and explain.

I will borrow from Einstein the concept of 'frame of reference' and try to explain this. 'Action' or 'motion' has relevance with the 'coordinate system'. There is a marked difference when the seer and the seen are in the same 'coordinate system' (CS) and when they are in two different 'coordinate systems'—what appears to be 'motion' could appear 'motionless'. As I have explained earlier, in a moving train, my co-passenger is 'motionless' with respect to me, but a person sitting in another halted train will find both my co-passenger and me in 'motion'. And if his train also moves and picks up the speed of my train and if both trains run parallel to each other, all three of us will become 'motionless' again.

166

However, the meaning hidden in the Bhagvad Gita is far deeper than what I have tried to explain superficially. The entire cosmos is motionless as well as full of motion; those who have the insight will understand the truth.

Moreover, 'manifestation' is in the likeness of 'inaction'. Those with intellectual impulses and intuitive wisdom will allow things to manifest for they see 'action' in 'inaction'. This goes well with the art of Wu Wei that I have discussed earlier. True knowledge is everywhere. Problems arise when we try to give them names or titles and try to dissect the truth.

A business leader with intuitive wisdom does not jump into action when he can find the solution through 'manifestation'. On the other hand, an impulsive heroic business leader jumps into the fray, thereby pre-empting cosmic forces and earn results that are not good for him, his business, and his people.

The Lord is aware of the restrictive understanding that human beings possess. It is because of this that He cautions humankind to understand perfectly the meaning of 'action' and 'inaction':

> *What is "action"?*
> *What is "inaction"?*
> *As to this, even the wise are confused.*
> *Therefore, I shall teach thee such action,*
> *By knowing which thou shalt be liberated from evil.*
> *Verily, the true nature of action should be known,*
> *As also of forbidden action and of inaction;*
> *It is hard to understand the course of action.*

(IV–16, 17)

Besides 'action' and 'inaction', there is a clear reference to permissible and prohibited 'actions' and 'inactions'.

167

Are actions good or evil in themselves, or should they be judged by their results? If the latter is accepted, then the question arises, 'How is it possible for us to foresee the results?' If the former is accepted, then another question will arise: 'Who will judge which action is good and which evil, and what are the criteria for judgement?'

The answer is not simple. As a sage says, 'The scriptures differ among themselves and even the sages differ among themselves.' Certain aspects of knowledge have to be ignited by pondering over and discovering the truth.

⚘ Inaction ⚘

Even the sages differ...

Lao Tzu, the Old Master, has also spoken about 'inaction' with a different mystic undertone—he used the word 'stillness' for 'inaction':

> *The "stillness" in stillness is not the real stillness.*
> *Only when there is stillness in movement*
> *Can the spiritual rhythm appear*
> *Which pervades heaven and earth.*

The connotation of the words 'action' and 'inaction', as used in the Bhagvad Gita, has a bottomless depth. I confess my attempts to describe it are at best shallow; it needs a sage to grasp such infinite designs of intent. 'When God threw me, a pebble, into this wondrous lake I disturbed its surface with countless circles,' says the Lebanese sage Kahlil Gibran in all humility. 'But when I reached the depths, I became still.' Yet, I am on the surface; how can I understand and explain the meaning of inaction?'

An intangible cannot be grasped by a logical mind. You have to develop intuitive wisdom to begin a hazy study of truth. This is a region where even digital logic dares not tread; it is where fuzzy logic comes. It is a game of nuances.

Business management is also a game of nuances—no one can really say what is right and what is wrong. We live in a world of uncertainties and imperfection. One may try and make grand predictions about the Future. However, the fact is that the Future is unknown and unknowable.

◖ Process Orientation ◗

Here is another intellectual inspiration:

> *To action alone have you a right;*
> *And never at all to its fruits.*
> *Let not the fruits of action be your motive;*
> *Neither let there be in you*
> *Any attachment to inaction.*

—Bhagvad Gita

This explains the 'process orientation' that is followed by the Japanese and most of the Southeast Asian countries. The only difference between the Japanese and the Western management practices is that between 'process orientation' and 'result orientation'. Unlike the Western entrepreneurs, the Japanese perfect their processes and obtain the best yields. If you take care of the processes, the results are bound to be good.

Unfortunately, without understanding the core difference between Western and Eastern approaches, managers in the East are scrambling to ape the West. I do not object to this. My concern is whether people fully understand what they are doing. The East seems to be in a mad rush to embrace Western thoughts and ideas while rejecting the richness of their own heritage.

You will find the same concept in the *Gitapodesh*. Take care of your actions, meaning 'process', and never consider that you have control over the fruits, meaning 'results'. You ought not to make the results your objective: take care of processes, and the results will follow. Finally, there is a rider that makes the process of action complete without any sluggishness or idleness: never let there be any attachment to 'inaction'.

Keep your eyes focused on the ball, not the scoreboard. The purpose of the game is to play your best; you just need to look up at the scoreboard once in a while. If you totally concentrate on the scoreboard, then you obviously will not be able to focus on the ball, and will lose your wicket.

What does this mean for your business? Profit—what we call the bottom-line—cannot be the *raison d'etre* for any organisation. We exist and exert for a greater objective than just making money. Our actions should keep that 'purpose of being' in focus at all times rather than eye the fruits, i.e., profit.

Here are some notable quotes from the Bhagvad Gita, which do not require explanation; they substantiate what has been said already.

Perform thou action that is (religiously) required;
For action is better than inaction.
And even the maintenance of the body for thee
Cannot succeed without action.

(III–8)

Except action for the purpose of worship,
This world is bound by actions;

170

Action for that purpose, son of Kunti,
Perform thou, free from attachment (to its fruits).

(III–9)

Therefore, unattached ever
Perform action that must be done;
For performing action without attachment
Man attains the highest.

(III–19)

For Me, son of Pritha, there is nothing to be done
In the three worlds whatsoever,
Nothing unattained to be attained;
And yet I still continue in action.

(III–22)

These marvellous bits of advice in the Bhagvad Gita encapsulate the secret formula for success through 'process orientation'—a precept that the Japanese imbibed so well. The roots of what we call 'BPR'—business process reengineering—can be traced right back to the Hindu scriptures.

≋ Humility—A Leadership Trait ≋

Humility is one of the best attributes of leadership.

> *A sense of humility is a quality I have observed in every leader who I have deeply admired. I have seen Winston Churchill with humble tears of gratitude on his cheeks as he thanked the people for their help to Britain and the Allied cause. My own conviction is that every leader should have enough humility to accept publicly, the responsibility for the mistakes of the subordinates he has himself selected and, likewise, to give them credit publicly for their triumphs.*
>
> **—Dwight Eisenhower, former President of the US**

'Be humble,' says the Bhagvad Gita, 'be harmless, have no pretensions, be upright, forbearing, serve in true obedience...'

The leadership in the next millennium will come from the ranks of servants. Referring to the servant leader who would be tomorrow's leaders, Plato wrote in the 4th century BC: 'Those having torches will pass them on to others.'

A good leader gives his people the pleasant feeling that they have done all the work by themselves. Stay in the background and watch things move in the right direction. Let your people steal your ideas. How subtly you allow them to steal depends on the quality of your leadership. When your people own your vision, they will achieve miracles.

✎ The Power of Intellect ✎

The power of the mind has a distinct place in Hindu philosophy. Buddhism and Hinduism are the two great religions that give more prominence to 'the power of mind' than any other religion.

> *The mind is said to be twofold:*
> *The pure and also the impure;*
> *Impure, by connection with desire;*
> *Pure, by severing the connection with desire.*
>
> —Maitri Upanishad

However, the Bhagvad Gita emphasises the role of intellect but in connection to desire. This is extremely important in business today where actions are often not motivated by our intellect but our desire. Whenever we approach a situation, we look at what our need in that situation is. It is when we are able to look at situations dispassionately that we are able to make the right decision. There is an inherent balance in the right decision between our desire and our intellect. One does not need to kill desire; one needs to understand its true nature and then contextualise it to a situation.

It is then that there is the handshake of the mind and the heart—the intellect and emotion.

Beyond the senses is the Mind;
Beyond the mind is the Intellect;
Higher than intellect is the Great Atma;
Higher than the Great Atma is the Unmanifest;
Beyond the Unmanifest is the Person,
All pervading, and imperceptible.

—Katha Upanishad

I have used the word 'handshake' purposely. The Upanishads envisaged a real handshake of the human mind with Supreme Truth. Transcendentalism is the essence of Hindu philosophy: it prescribes how one should control the mind, dip into tranquillity and become aware of the Self.

'Transcendentalism' is the core philosophy in Maharishi Mahesh Yogi's University in India, where students are taught business management through the Vedas or the Vedic principles, which tackles the rot at the root.

⚘ Knowledge is Blissful ⚘

There is always a gap between man's imagination and man's attainment that can only be traversed by his longing. How should one pursue such longing? By understanding your actions in the light of wisdom!

173

Him the sages call wise
Whose understandings are devoid
Of desire for results and of plans,
Whose actions are burned by the fire of wisdom!
                                              —Bhagvad Gita: IV–19

Once the actions flow from your wisdom, you begin to pursue your strategic vision and then strategic planning takes a backseat.

The Bhagvad Gita kindles the awakening. It helps hold the body and the soul together. Your obligation in any lifetime is to discover the Self!

Today, we have gone crazy with the enormous information available on the Internet. We have become hungry for information but have also become confused because of the overload. While this craze continues, we ourselves don't know the beginning or the end of this revolution. We have forgotten the difference between useful information and pointless information. The line between the public and private lives is also blurring. Where is all this leading us? There has to be a balance while seeking knowledge.

Any knowledge that does not bring us the supreme bliss and freedom is not worth acquiring. We stuff our minds with knowledge of so many facts and things gained from all and sundry, or reading all kinds of books. The brain becomes a repository of learning about all the ephemeral and passing phases of life. Naturally, such a man becomes a restless being—unbalanced, confused and erratic in his behaviour and conduct. Seek, therefore, to know the true source of your life—God. That is why you are here.

—Swami Ramdas

Today, the amount of knowledge available over the Internet is phenomenal and incomparable. But does it lead us

174

anywhere? Can we obtain the gist of what we are looking for? There is an information overload on the Net; there is a lot of this 'raw material' swirling about in cyber space and what we need to do is choose, pick, mend, reconfigure and reshape all of it to fashion a new aspect of knowledge or understanding.

The information available on the Internet is 'data'; pick up what you need and then create a new information base. It is time to deploy 'content managers' who can browse Internet and cull the required bits from the available 'raw material' to construct a new knowledge bank.

⒃ Vedic Corporate Philosophy ⒥

The Vedas are the oldest scriptures of Hinduism and accepted by Hindus as the most authoritative statement of the essential truths of Hinduism. It is the literature of the Aryans (who invaded the Indus Valley in 1500 BC).

According to the *Columbia Encyclopedia*, the four Vedas—the Rig-Veda, Sama-Veda, Yajur-Veda and the Atharva-Veda—were compiled between 1000 and 500 BC. The Upanishads are words of mysticism and speculation. Vedic writings express the idea of a single underlying truth embodied in *Brahman*, the absolute Self.

Prince Dara Shikoh, the oldest brother of Emperor Aurangzeb, was immensely attracted to the Vedas. Dara was a learned person who became a Sufi and acquired extensive knowledge of the Vedas and other religious systems and their holy texts. From the age of 25, he gradually extended his interest to understand Vedic wisdom. Prince Dara Shikoh made a study of the Vedas, the Upanishads and other Hindu philosophical and religious writing. A proclamation in the

Qur'an stating that no nation has been left without prophetic guidance, emanating finally from the supreme power, convinced Dara Shikoh that the Vedantic writings embodied such 'hidden scriptures'.

'Prince Dara Shikoh,' writes V. Shankar Chari in his article 'The Mingler of Two Oceans', 'went on to express the view that the Upanishads were, in fact, the ultimate source of all monotheism, including that of Islam... Dara was inspired mainly by the Advaita interpretation of Vedanta, propounded by Adi Shankaracharya, in 8th century.'

Prince Dara Shikoh, with the assistance of Brahmin acharyas and pandits, had 52 of the Upanishads translated into Persian in a work entitled, *Sir-u-Akbar*. He also undertook the mission to translate the Yoga-Vashista and the Bhagvad Gita. Prince Dara also produced a highly significant study called the *Majma Ulbahrayn* or '*The Mingling of the Two Oceans*', where he argued that the central doctrines of Hinduism and Islam bear the same monotheistic identity. Prince Dara Shikoh was accused of blasphemy and beheaded. Some feel it was a political murder; blasphemy was just an excuse to serve the cause.

To my mind, Dara Shikoh was an intoxicated soul who chose to walk the road less taken. He had the urge to discover the underlying truth in two oceans of great religions—and paid the price for it. He used to seek out the company of leading Hindu pundits and mystics of his day and made probing inquiries into their doctrines and concepts. His search was probably for a greater truth. It was in a time where religious systems were in their own water-tight compartments.

Let the change-makers be aware of the unrelenting truth—eventually most of them will have to bear the Cross. This has happened; is happening at present, and will continue to happen.

The world needs a Jesus to bear the cross in each epoch!

No pain, no palm;
No thorns, no throne;
No gall, no glory;
No Cross, no crown.

A change-maker is often destined to bear the cross or drink hemlock; we must understand this, but it should not deter us.

Religion is not for the worthless, unintelligent and the abnormal. It is meant for the most level-headed and balanced men of virtue. Cowards cannot progress in spiritual life. The prerequisites of business management are no different. A coward has no place in a boardroom. Great leaders create vision, articulate vision, passionately own it, and drive it to completion; they are never deflected from their purpose by the fear of having to drink hemlock or bearing a cross. They enjoy the voiceless joy of perfection and re-alignment that they try to bring about by managing change.

♚ Karma ♛

The philosophy of karma needs to be understood with the brilliance of intellectual impulse than through conventional wisdom. It is far deeper than one can think. Unfortunately, the law of karma is grossly misunderstood as the 'Law of Destiny'; it goes beyond destiny. The philosophy of 'cause' and 'effect' does not hinge on linear progression. The same cause may produce different effects! Again, the effects resulting from causes may emerge after varying time lags. Sometimes the fruition takes place within the 'lifetime' itself; sometime it extends beyond the temporal life. The causes caused collectively can have a common effect for the group of people or the society. There's a divine difference between 'Life' and 'Lifetime'. The former is eternal for it has life beyond lifetime—call it the Hereafter.

Swami Chinmayananda describes karma in his discourse on 'Kenopanisad': 'The law of Karma is based upon the final conclusion that this life is not an end in itself but is just one of the little incidents in the Eternal Existence of each one of us... We think that life means the period spent by us between our birth and our death, and what we see and experience around during this interval is life. When life is viewed in its nearer perspective, we find that it is illogical, unrhythmic, etc. In detachment, we will have to move away from our present life to view the whole Life and understand it as such... You must understand that there is a rhythm in the Universe, in that the planets "move" regularly, the stars "ride" their appointed paths, etc. Everywhere, there is the "Law of Rhythm".'

'Process orientation' is nothing but the 'Law of Rhythm' of business management. Perfection in 'process' needs no intervention—things just happen. 'Manifestation' needs no intervention.

'Cause' and 'Effect', or the Law of Karma, is appropriately relevant in business management. What we preach in discourses in India, the Japanese practise in management. Kaoru Ishikawa, professor at the University of Tokyo, was the first to understand the meaning of theory of karma—cause and effect—and to express it as a part of a formal discipline of quality management. The diagram that is assigned against his name—the Ishikawa diagram—shows causes and effects. The common name given to the Ishikawa diagram is 'Fishbone diagram'.

Fishbone diagram

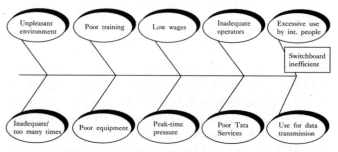

'Switchboard inefficient' is an 'effect' or a 'symptom'
The 'causes' for this 'effect' could be many as described above.

—Adapted from Kaoru Ishikawa's Fishbone diagram

If someone cares to see the fishbone diagram thought-fully, he will discover that the 'causes' and 'effects' are not on a one-to-one basis. A few causes may give rise to a good number of effects. We only try to beat the symptoms rather than go deeper to the roots to find the root cause. If there are a 100 problems, the Ishikawa diagram helps plot the causes, which may be just five or six in number. In simple words, by discovering the root-causes—a few in number—and correcting them, you can resolve hundreds of problems. You do not need to find a hundred solutions to a hundred problems.

Again, what do we really mean by problems in management affairs? What we term as 'problems' today are nothing but the 'solutions' that we discovered yesterday. What I wish to stress upon is that even the 'solution to problems' is not beyond the pale of Karma or the 'cause and effect' philosophy.

If we were to look at the business environment purely from this perspective then the future is not really a mystery. The past modified in the present alone is the future. In this context, I had said earlier that it is possible for the past and the future to co-exist. The present is but a product of the past; the future is but the product of the present. What you sow, so you reap! But some sort of mid-course correction modifies the future. Today, when speed is the deciding factor, mid-course correction has assumed a significant place in business management. It is possible to modify the future.

Like the other Holy Scriptures, the Upanishads do not directly and openly express or explain; they only give us 'indicative meanings'. Likewise, the management systems should not be rigid like laws—they should be 'indicative' rather than 'restrictive'.

No action is complete unless its reaction manifests. As the Romans believe, the Goddess of Nemesis plays her role. The karma philosophy is no longer confined to the scriptures; it has become the corporate philosophy for most of the value-based commercial organisations. What is karma in Hindu philosophy, and Nemesis in western philosophy is known as 'the universal law of energy response' in Tao philosophy. Today, the new-age corporate world is leaning towards the philosophy of karma and dharma. The corporate pharaohs have understood that 'build to last' is akin to 'build on values'.

✎ Walk the Talk ✍

The Bhagvad Gita needs to be understood in its appropriate context. Each of its hymns provides us with an insight into how one needs to act in that appropriate situation. The corporate world is probably the best place to practise what the Bhagvad Gita preaches!

Yoga Vasishta prescribed the precepts to his disciple Rama: Knowledge without practice is superior to practice without knowledge. Practice with knowledge is superior to knowledge without practice.

'Business practice with business knowledge' is better than 'business knowledge without business practice'.

> *He understands It not, who comprehends It not; and he understands It not, who feels he has comprehended It. It is the unknown to the Master of True Knowledge but to the ignorant It is the known.*
>
> **—Kenopanisad–Chapter II**

We boast about what we know not. What we claim, we know not. What we know is naught. In the same tune and with the same melody, Yung-Chia Ta Shih, a Chinese philosopher, sings the cosmic song:

It is when you hunt for It
That you lose It;
You cannot take hold of It.
But equally, you cannot get rid of It.
And while you can do neither,
It goes on Its own way.

The cosmic song is a fact; if you believe, it stays; if you don't believe, it doesn't stay with you. But it Is.

The fact is, a truth that does not need to be dressed up.

10

Panchatantra—*Wisdom for All Ages*

By virtues raised to lofty heights;
By those same virtues the noble fall!

—Visnu Sarma (from the *Panchatantra*)

The *Panchatantra* is one of the best books of management I have ever read. Visnu Sarma was one of the several names used by Visnugupta Chanakya (350–275 BC) who has also authored the *Arthashastra*. The *Panchatantra*, which was compiled in the 4th century AD, has been spun out of the tales and the bits of sage advice from Visnu Sarma.

How did this great epic come into being? That in itself is an interesting story.

৺ A Legend ৶

Chanakya was the principal advisor and strategist to Chandragupta Maurya, one of the most powerful kings of ancient India. The legend goes that at the age of 80, Chanakya was asked to teach three very refractory princes about the art of governance in six months. It was a huge challenge for the genius in such a tight timeframe. The *Panchatantra* is the result of the challenge that Chanakya undertook. He found 'storytelling' to be the best medium to educate the crown princes in the limited time that was allotted to him. He adopted the simple mode and completed the mission successfully.

Storytelling has its origin in pre-historical societies. It was the medium of entertainment and imparting knowledge in a simple manner without making the recipients conscious about the inputs that each parable held. Each story had a moral and some wisdom that would touch the hearts of listeners and awaken their minds.

The *Panchatantra* is not a book of ethics or values. It is a book that teaches you when to be ethical and when not to be virtuous towards some people. It does not teach immorality but it does make one aware of how to deal with immorality. The *Panchatantra* says one needs to keep a watchful eye on the weathercock. One must be aware of the practical situations and nature of people in life to remain virtuous. Even if you are a mighty king, you will fall if you do not understand the meanness of the meanest.

The *Panchatantra* is considered by wise men as an excellent means of awakening the young minds. No other work appears to have travelled so far and wide. The Fables of Bidpai', 'The Arabian Nights', and 'La Fontaine's Fables' may be the various popular streams that sprang from this fountainhead.

The book begins with a challenge:

Whoever always reads this work;
Whoever listens to it told;

He will never face defeat, no,
Not even from the Lord of Gods, Himself.

While accepting the challenge of grooming the three crown princes in six months, Visnu Sarma told the king: 'My lord, I do not sell my learning, not even for the gift of a hundred land-grants. Now hear me speak; I speak the simple, unvarnished truth. I have no craving for wealth, my lord. I am now 80 years of age, and my senses have turned away from their objects. But I shall do what you ask of me. If I do not teach your sons in such a manner that in six months time they do not have complete mastery over all the wide expanse of political and practical wisdom, then let my name be thrown away and forgotten. So let this day be noted and set down. In six months' time, your sons will possess unsurpassed knowledge of all branches of practical wisdom. Hear! This is my lion-roar.' (Chandra Rajan: *Visnu Sarma—The Panchatantra*).

Visnu Sarma completed five books of stories entitled 'Estrangement of Friends', 'Winning of Friends', 'Of Crows and Owls', 'Loss of Gains', and 'Rash Deeds'. The collection of five books is known as the *Panchatantra*.

The *Panchatantra's* wise teachings can be adopted as an HRD tool to develop new-age managers. Each quotation in the book can stand as a corporate mantra for the manager. For example:

By virtues raised to lofty heights;
By those same virtues the noble fall!

It has a mantra that grants wisdom against bookish knowledge.

With mere book learning men remain fools;
The man who acts using his knowledge, he is wise.

184

Then there is the mantra to see through deception and ulterior motives:

Honey flows freely in her speech;
Deadly poison lurks in her heart.

Proponents of business may be surprised to learn that it even contains a mantra that cautions the reader about moneymaking:

A trouble to acquire; a trouble to protect;
A trouble if it's lost; a trouble if it's spent;
Money is nothing but trouble;
Alas! From beginning to end!

There is also a mantra that highlights corporate vices:

What are the vices in ordinary men,
Those very vices are virtues in kings!

The singular quality of the *Panchatantra* is its duality. It stands for values, virtue and wisdom and yet it teaches how to be aware of the evildoers and thwart their evil gameplans. Chanakya advises that one ought not to be good to those who do not deserve grace. This is where the *Panchatantra* stands out as a book of practical wisdom. The only parallel seems to be Machiavelli's thoughts that match some of the negative strategies prescribed in the *Panchatantra*.

Chanakya says you need not 'mistrust' everyone, but you must be watch-

> *The weak, if wary and mistrustful,*
> *can easily withstand the strongest;*
> *The strong who are foolish and trustful,*
> *may be overthrown by the weakest.*
>
> **Estrangement of Friends; 1:87**

ful. It is foolish to trust mean people. 'Trust begets trust'— that is a virtuous thought. One must also understand the price that one would have to pay if one simply trusts without understanding the culture and people properly.

Not everyone can become like Buddha and win over a hardened criminal with the power of his love and compassion for the weaker soul. So, it is wise to be cautious. Trust begets trust: if you want this precept to work, you must acquire Buddha's piety, patience, prudence and persistence to deal with evil people. There are no short-cuts in such matters.

A lie is always bad. But to lie to your superior or boss can be suicidal at times. There is no right way to do a

> *Even the smallest lie spoken before a king*
> *has the gravest consequences;*
> *the ruin of speaker's parents and teachers,*
> *and that of the gods as well.*
> **Estrangement of Friends; 1:90**

wrong thing! The *Panchatantra* cautions you not to lie to your superiors for it will have far-reaching consequences.

❦ The King and his Team: Lessons from the *Panchatantra* ❧

One of the most important lessons that the *Panchatantra* teaches us is the value of teamwork. Visnu Sarma advises the princes that they must learn to build a strong team. We rarely realise that the strength of a chain lies in its weakest link. Even if the chain has 99 strong links, just one weak link is enough to cause damage. If the leader creates a strong team of stars, he can pursue his vision, plans and strategies with the support of his competent team.

Even an amateur sailor can show his craftsmanship when the sea is calm. The real test of the sailors' skills can be gauged

> A king is held firm by ministers,
> who are tested and true, straight, resourceful,
> accomplished and endowed with inner strength,
> as a temple is well-supported by pillars
> straight, strong, well-polished and firmly-grounded
> Wisdom shows herself in action;
> a minister's in forging friendships;
> physician's in healing life-threatening illness.
> Who is not wise when everything goes right!
>
> **Estrangement of Friends; 1:95-96**

when the sea is turbulent. When you are successful, everyone wants to remain close to you. In bad times, even your shadow deserts you. What distances people is your inability to protect their livelihood.

❦ Downsizing is Dreadful ❧

An important lesson that the *Panchatantra* teaches us is that downsizing is dreadful as it threatens the livelihood of the people around you. The *Panchatantra* cautions the king never to take away the bread from his loyal people, for they will turn hostile when they feel insecure. Management gurus have tom-tommed the virtues of downsizing; but it has far-reaching consequences that cannot immediately be visualised. This has to be seen in the larger context of society. Wisdom dawned

> Even retainers of noble birth
> and unimpeachable loyalty,
> who are held in high honour at court,
> are certain to leave the loyalty of a
> king who breaks the thread of their
> livelihood.
>
> **Estrangement of Friends; 1:111**

on one of the pioneers of BPR. Thomas H. Davenport who said, 'Companies that embrace re-engineering as the silver bullet are now looking for ways to rebuild the organization's torn social fabric.'

'Those who survive downsizing suffer as much as those who lose their jobs,' observes Richard Barrette in his book *Liberating the Corporate Soul*. 'They find themselves living in a climate of fear. As fear increases, personal productivity and creativity decline. The stress becomes intolerable and the best people—those with strong employability—leave.' Therefore, the *Panchatantra advises* against hurting people's livelihood as it could have bad consequences for both the king and kingdom.

Man management is all about managing relationships. Sometimes relationships create a dilemma. A manager must learn how to manage a paradoxical situation in life and business. The only way is to maintain perfect balance when dealing with contradictory or

> *Look after the ruler's interests,*
> *and you earn the people's hatred;*
> *work then for people's interests,*
> *you are shown the door by the prince.*
> **Estrangement of Friends; 1:100**

conflicting interests. Sometimes the interests of the management and employees may be in conflict. A good manager must know how to balance his role with the top management and the unions in such a way that both find a solution that is mutually satisfying. It is a tough task but not impossible.

Here is another mantra to understand your people:

> *One without ambition does not hold office;*
> *One fallen out of love does not care to adorn himself;*
> *One who lacks learning displays no eloquence;*
> *One who is blunt in speech is never a cheat.*

People build organisations. People create wealth. People are the lifeblood of any organisation. They are the real strength behind the organisation and the leader. The *Panchatantra* explains a unique relationship between the 'prosperity of the people' and the 'prosperity of the leader and the organisation'. The prosperity of an organisation and the leader depends crucially on the prosperity of people. If someone tries to win his prosperity by ruining his people, he must be ready to face his own ruin.

> *A king is a lamp, wealth, the oil*
> *gathered from people.*
> *Who has ever perceived him as shining*
> *lit by in-dwelling virtues radiant!*
>
> *Gold, grain and gems and drinks of various sorts*
> *And whatever else kings enjoy*
> *All come from the people.*
>
> *Great monarchs prosper greatly,*
> *working for the people's good.*
> *It's only in the people's ruin,*
> *they find their own ruin, without a doubt.*

A man of wisdom alone has the divine ability to distinguish between allies and bedfellows. People in power are usually surrounded by a wall of sycophants. Those who lack wisdom cannot penetrate it and see beyond. They cannot see the loyal and committed people who are outside this dense wall of hangers-on. This creates double trouble: the best people are outside, the worst are inside. When you depend excessively on this coterie, you become a prey to your own indulgence. The second law of thermodynamics applies to both the animate and inanimate worlds; people, systems and institutions can go into terminal decline in a variety of ways.

> *A king is ruined by bad advice;*
> *an ascetic by company;*

189

a child by fond indulgence;
a Brahman by lack of learning;
a noble line by evil sons;
virtuous conduct by serving the base;
friendship from want of regard;
investment by mismanagement;
affection from long absence;
and a woman by drink;
a farm too from neglect;
wealth through misdirected charity.

The wise man can tell the difference between milk and phenyl. Both look white, but one gives you life, the other death. Visnu Sarma also advises:

He is true friend who stands by you in bad times
even if he be of another race.
The whole world is your best friend in happy times;
such is the way of the world.

He is a true friend who when times are bad is there for you;
he is a father who feeds and protects you;
he is a friend too in whom you place your trust;
she is a wife in whom you find repose.

The man of wisdom understands people with one glance:

A wise person takes a man's true measure
at one shrewd glance,
as an expert jeweller gauges the true weight
of metal by simply holding it on his palm.

And when wisdom is lost:

Friends appear foes; foes appear friends,
and all to gain their own ends;
A few are farsighted enough,

to tell the difference.
Better take a walk with a snake,
or share your home with rogues or foes;
Never put your trust in evil friends,
false, fickle and foolish!

What the *Panchatantra* says about alliances is simple and pertinent:

Alliance with villains is like earthen pots
easily broken, difficult to mend;
Alliance with virtuous, like golden pots
difficult to break, easy to mend.

Starting from the tip, sugarcane juice
grows sweeter by degrees, node after node;
So does friendship of the upright; the reverse
Is true in the case of those perverse.

On the contrary:

Never form an alliance with a foe;
Even an alliance well contracted, approved.
Water though boiling hot
Will do no less than put the fire out.

As a shrewd manager:

Fear danger while it's still to come;
Once you've to face with danger,
Strike hard, with no hesitation.

Remember that there are certain things that don't work. So never try to plant pumpkins on the pathways.

A cry in the wilderness;
rubbing perfume on a corpse;

191

planting lotuses on dry ground;
incessant rain over salt-marshes;
adoring the faces of the blind—
like these is speaking good sense to fools.

Visnu Sarma spells out his advice on a variety of issues
with brutal honesty and admirable bluntness. It is like an
extremely wise, experienced and seasoned strategist talking to
new and middle-level managers. His advice is not extreme for
he advises on a variety of situations that we may encounter
both in our personal and professional lives. He counsels us to
always judge the situation and act accordingly. He advocates
no extreme measures and yet asks the reader not to hesitate
to take harsh measures when these are warranted.

According to him, a leader with no sense of timing and
direction can take you on a reckless journey.

He who has no sense of time and place;
and of what is right and proper;
who does not know a thing beyond himself;
who acts without due deliberation;
He is a fool who reaps no reward.

When one reads the *Panchantantra*, one is struck by
the fact that the author always places the individual at the
centre of all conflicts. He is constantly telling us to decide.
He gives us advice but the decision to heed any of it is entirely
ours. He advocates introspection and calls it a boon though
it is difficult to practise. He believes self-introspection is
necessary to succeed.

Self-examination comes hard;
from not knowing how to, or lack
of discernment in carrying it out.

> But whoever has this knowledge,
> never sinks under misery's blows.

Visnu Sarma also tells us to balance and control our thinking. He says there is a distinct difference between thinking and worrying. In distress, we mostly worry and are unable to think cogently to determine how we should deal with a crisis. Worrying about the past, excessive excitement about the present and anxiety about the future only dissipate your energies.

> The wise do not grieve
> for what is dead, or lost, or past.
> Between the wise and the fools,
> just this is the difference.

And here is a thought that Zen masters call the art of Wu Wei:

> What is not to be can never be:
> what is to be comes effortlessly;
> what lies right in the palm of your hand
> is lost if you are not destined for it!

Visnu Sarma speaks strongly about virtues and the need to do the right thing. According to him, the righteous path can never lead you astray in the long run. A man of virtue can never fall:

> All of a sudden a noble man may fall;
> But he will bounce back like a ball,
> But the coward who falls will stay
> On the ground, like a lump of clay.

However, he cautions even people of virtue about the dangers of being inflexible. He feels they must know when to be soft when to be hard!

193

When times are good, noble hearts
are tender as lotus blossoms.
When times are bad they become hard
as the solid rock of the Great Mountain.

No penance equals patience;
No joy equals contentment;
No giving is like friendship;
No virtue equals compassion.

These words of wisdom appropriately relate to every aspect of life including business management. Managers can learn how to face different situations, when to act and when to watch; when to hurry and when to slow down the pace; when to be soft and when to be hard. Life is not a static philosophy; it is an action-packed adventure. Vision gives direction, values show the righteous path and wisdom takes you to the destination. 'Wisdom' without 'action' is barren.

Visnu Sarma also warns us against those with massive egos and maladjusted personalities. They are unfit to be managers. It does not help at all if you withdraw or sulk. As a manager, you cannot afford to be a silent spectator. Similarly, conformists or time-servers are no managers:

Even if his opinion is unsolicited,
A minister should speak his mind at such times;
And when his advice is specially sought
It should be for the good of the king.

As for him who when asked for advice
refrains from speaking what is right
and in the royal interest as well,
who offers soothing words instead, regard
him as an enemy in minister's guise.

The *Panchatantra* is replete with such corporate mantras that the new-age manager can profit from while managing people and situations.

🌾 The Enemy 🌿

How should one face a powerful enemy? The *Panchatantra* suggests some sure-fire methods to deal with such situations. Be cautious with the enemy if he is a person of determination and knows how to choose his time. It suggests a range of options: 'Start negotiations, or hostilities, begin a retreat or make a stand, seek alliance or sow discord in his ranks'. But the best option is to forge an alliance for...

> ...*He who gains a firm alliance*
> *with the victor of many wars*
> *will soon find his other foes come to heel,*
> *awed into submission by his allies' power.*
>
> *Desire to make peace even with your equals;*
> *For victory is never a certainty;*
> *Better not take risks,*
> *Counsels the sage, Brahspati...*
>
> *Victory is ever uncertain, even*
> *When warriors are evenly matched.*
> *Try first the other expedients*
> *Before you opt for hostilities.*
>
> *Blinded by wounded pride,*
> *reluctant to sue for peace,*
> *a man may be destroyed even by an equal;*
> *unable to make a stand*
> *he comes apart*
> *like an unbaked clay pot.*

195

I know of no test that lays down
you ought to fight a powerful foe.
A rain cloud never moves ahead
if contrary winds prevail.

Today, the world of business has turned into a battlefield as corporates fight to grab marketshare and occupy consumer mindspace. Companies stop at nothing to thwart competition. Nevertheless, the important thing to remember is that war is not a 'win-win' game; it is either a 'lose-lose' or 'win-lose' situation. Corporate wisdom lies in forging alliances and collaborations. He who beats competition meets greater competition. Try to rise above competition. In war, success is always uncertain. Healthy competition is not akin to war. 'Live, and let live—that should be the motive for there is enough in this world for everyone. There is enough to meet your needs but not your greed.

When one resorts to underhand tactics to beat the competition, it is the first sign that one neither has the ability to innovate and come up with new products nor the gumption to devise new marketing strategies. Some corporates get round the problem by either forging business alliances or going in for mergers and acquisitions. More and more organisations are trying to leverage their strengths through mergers. This has a downside in that it leads to the creation of monopolies; but it conversely has an upside in that it helps fulfil consumer expectations.

While strongly recommending alliances, Visnu Sarma also lays down clear do's and don'ts. Be careful while forging an alliance with a 'former enemy' and a person devoid of truth and justice who comes professing amity:

At no cost should peace be proposed
with one devoid of truth and justice;

however binding the agreement you make,
inborn viciousness will in no time change his course.

◈ Take with a Pinch of Salt ◈

Here are some negative strategies to deal with situations. I
don't subscribe to them as they go against the spirituality and
value-based management that I profess. However, it is better
to know them and be aware of the negative aspects.

Like the tortoise a wise man will retreat
into his shell and suffer cruel blows;
when the time is ripe he will rear up
ready to strike like a deadly serpent.

What glory can a monarch whose kingdom
is not drenched with blood of foes
and tears of their wailing wives
truly boast of!

Foes crumble before a king
who wields like death a cruel rod.
But foes are all quick to fall upon
a king by compassion ruled.

Towards an enemy powerful and evil
always harbour deep distrust;
now offering peace, then again making war,
adopting a policy of duplicity.

Kill a foe when he is down
before he grows in strength;
once he gains his fullest vigour
he will become invincible.

One should understand the harsh ground realities. In
life and business one can ill-afford to discount the value of

money—the bottom line. I quote a very important verse on the 'power of money'. It is better to be aware of this even though money isn't everything in life. Nevertheless, it is a means to an end: the end often being comfort, mobility and the provision of such other necessities of life to the people whom we care for.

Nothing in this world there is
that wealth cannot accomplish;
so, let the sole aim be
of men of sense, to make money...

A man's strengths might be grounded in justice,
but if he has no money in his purse,
he might provide good and faithful service,
yet his employer hates his guts;
his close kin leave him all at once,
high and dry; and his sons,
his own flesh-and-blood forsake him too;
the wife though nobly-born
grows cold and pays him no honour;
good friends shun his very sight;
virtues do not glow forth bright,
and miseries wax and grow space.

✎ Golden Tips ✎

This is a selection of some of the most pertinent extracts from the *Panchatantra*. They could serve as the guideposts to our lives. They represent the best and the worst of the human spirit. They provide rich advice to those who wish to learn the simple but irrefutable truths in order to live with dignity and achieve a modicum of success in this world.

At home in his own world a crocodile
can seize and hold a lordly elephant;
but once dislodged from his habitat
even a dog can beat him hollow.

A lone tree firmly rooted,
and mighty, is yet no match
even for a moderate wind;
Whereas trees closely packed in groves,
firmly rooted, stand tall
even when swift winds trip into them,
because they stand together.

Likewise a lone man
heroic in the extreme
is regarded easy prey
by foes who soon hem him in.

The right moment comes once only
for him who waits for it eagerly.
To find the moment once again,
to do the thing you wish to do,
that is by no means easy.

Never denounce anyone publicly:

A person with sense and good feeling
should never defame others in public
and make statements that cause distress,
even if they happen to be true.

Never underestimate the collective power of the people:

You should not put your strength against a mob;
it is hard to win against the masses;
The little red ants kill and eat the great snake
in spite of all his twisting and twitching.

199

The future belongs to those who make preparations to welcome it:

> *He rejoices who carefully prepares*
> *for events yet to come.*
> *He grieves who is caught unawares*
> *by events when they come.*

The goddess of glory blinds. Glory sticks with no one! It is restless in the extreme, as fickle as the wandering clouds, and as unreliable as an alliance with a woman of easy virtue. We often forget that glory is evanescent; it is a shimmer in the golden clouds at sunset. It is as fragile as the bubbles that float on water. One should not be enamoured with such transient phenomenon.

The *Panchatantra* contains both prose and poetry. The prose part of the *Panchatantra* is in the form of stories. With the aid of these tales, Visnu Sarma (Chanakya) instructed the crown princes and fulfilled his commitment to groom them within the limited timeframe of six months. I have mostly quoted from the verses. In fact, the *Panchatantra* is a work known in Sanskrit as 'Champu', written in a combination of verse and prose. This book of wisdom is considered as a book of strategy that combines both the positive and negative aspects of human life.

Part IV

Learning from Judaism, Christianity and Islam

Prophet Abraham is in many ways the patriarch of several faiths. Religions such as Judaism, Christianity and Islam originate from his spiritual faith.

All the great religions of the world have originated from the continent of Asia—Zoroastrianism, Judaism, Christianity and Islam came from the deserts of South West Asia; Hinduism, Buddhism, Jainism and Sikhism were born in India, South Asia; Taoism and Confucianism emerged in China and East Asia.

11

Revisiting the Torah and the Gospel—Ethics and Integrity

He who walks with integrity walks securely.

—10:9 Proverbs (Old Testament)

Integrity is the nervous system of ethical business management. It is a portmanteau word that encapsulates a range of expressions and emotions: physical, intellectual, emotional and spiritual integrity.

Integrity is the gateway to success in business management. When you give your best physical labour to the organisation, you walk with 'physical integrity'. When you use your brainpower to add value to the product, processes and the customer, you are harnessing your 'intellectual integrity'. Your emotional investment in the organisation and in the people is your emotional integrity. Reducing the gap between your competence and commitment is both your 'intellectual integrity' and 'emotional integrity'. Putting your heart and soul in the work and performing management meditation is your 'spiritual integrity'. In your daily prayers, when you ask the Lord to grant His mercy to your organisation and its people, this reflects your spiritual integrity at the deepest level.

Integrity and humility, though seemingly different, have the common origin—nobility! And kindness is the seed of nobility.

> *Show kindness to those who live on earth, so that your Lord may show kindness unto you.*
>
> **—Jesus Christ**

It would be interesting to find out what the religious scriptures such as the Torah (Torait), The Psalms (Zubur) and the Gospel (Injeel) have to say about values that apply to the world of business. However, first let us examine their genesis. The Torah was bestowed upon Prophet Moses—the Hebrew lawgiver—during the 13th century BC. Many of the Psalms are ascribed to Prophet David—the Hebrew king during the 10th century BC. The Gospel is the collection of the revelations of God to Jesus Christ—the second person in the Trinity as per the Christian belief—that marks the beginning of Christian calendar. The three holy books—Torah, The Psalms and Gospel—are part of the Bible that includes the Old Testament and the New Testament.

≌ Corporate Values and Virtues ⧓

The Bible talks of kindness, humilty, sacrifice and forgiveness. These values are perhaps not much practised in the business world. Our ability to show kindness, make sacrifices and forgive mistakes has been greatly diminished in an era where the increasing demand from consumers for reliable products and services allow little room for error.

However, businesses are run by people and there will be errors at all levels: in decision making, in devising products and services, and in dealing with clients and consumers. Corporates need to be able to balance the demands of the marketplace with the need to nurture the human resources within the organisation. The corporates that succeed will be able to nurture the talent within the organisation and this will be possible only when they adopt the best practices in the realm of human resource development. This will entail the need to foster human values—and that is where the spiritual teachings come in. In the corporate world, it will be increasingly necessary for managers to show kindness, display, humility, make sacrifices and be able to forgive the mistakes made by their juniors.

✉ Humility in Leadership ✍

Biblical accounts tell us that Christ was always humble before his people and always believed in humility and participation. He even washed the feet of his apostles. He never believed in the hierarchical superiority. To my mind, he was a better manager of men than most of the high-paid executives I encounter today. He treated everyone with respect that it won him their unquestioned loyalty.

Christ once said: 'Let the greatest among you become the youngest, and the leader is one who serves.' Ponder over this statement. It will help you

> *Let the greatest among you become the youngest, and the leader is one who serves.*
> **—Jesus Christ**

understand the true traits of a leader and give you an insight into organisational structures and business practices like bottom-up management, empowerment, and hierarchy-less organisations.

Once Prophet Mohammed described the traits of some of the prophets and angels. Michael: 'A carrier of God's pleasure and forgiveness'. Abraham: 'Sweeter to his people than honey itself.' Jesus: 'If you punish them they are only Your servants; and if You forgive them, You are the All-wise and Almighty.' Noah: 'O God, spare not one of the unbelievers.' Moses: 'O God, destroy their wealth and confirm them in their error that they may not believe until they receive the painful punishment.' Likewise, the leadership beliefs in business management differ from manager to manager. But all of us know: 'forgiveness' is nobler than the inability to pardon.

Christ had countered the then prevalent religious hypocrisy and lack of morality that blinded the wisdom of the Jews at that time.

The sayings of Jesus Christ need to be seen in the context of the circumstances that prevailed at the time. Christ had appeared during a period of history when the Jewish morality had reached its lowest ebb, and when the purity of life had given way to outward ritual that passed for devotion to God. The inspired utterances of Christ have a natural figurative charm. Whenever Christ said, 'Love your enemies', his meaning was certainly not that one should become a devoted lover of his enemies. On the other hand, he meant that instead of exciting in oneself feelings of anger, hatred or revenge, one should develop the feeling of togetherness. This is an exceptional lesson for managers. In an era of cut-throat competition, where each one of our peers represents a threat, we often forget that we alone cannot get the work done. Clearly, the business organisation that will succeed in the new age will be one that is able to foster teamwork.

Business management is no longer about beating competition through fair or foul means. Now, it's all about co-operation and collaboration with your competitors. Co-existence and interdependence are clearly foreseen. How long will you beat the opponent? How long will you blunt your competitors' potential? How long will you play games with those who are trying to gain a competitive edge over you? One can change the business scenario by putting this wisdom of cooperation into practice—decide the segments, collaborate and increase the market share instead of fighting with each other to grab a greater slice of a market pie that is presumed to be finite. The future will witness more collaboration and competition will recede. 'Grow; and let grow'—that is the credo that businesses need to adopt to derive better dividends than devising devious stratagems to outfox your opponents in the anxious desire to beat off competition. It will no longer be enough to beat your competitor with fair means!

Christ always sermonised that one should develop the feeling of forgiveness or forbearance.

Forgiveness or forbearance is the sine qua non in the world of business. It creates space and scope for growth in the heart and the mind. It is quite easy to punish and condemn an employee but it is our belief in human potential that allows us to give people a second chance. HRD is all about making people realise their errors and then providing them assistance to help them improve. Similarly, the aim of all religions is to inculcate in man a sense of loathing towards sinful behaviour and not the person who commits a sin; managers or business leaders must also learn to draw this subtle distinction. Christianity teaches us to hate the sin and not the sinner! We should condemn errors, misconduct or faults and not the doer.

A manager is like an expert surgeon who cuts out the malignant tumour and saves the patient. If the patient dies on the operation table, what acclaim does the surgeon deserve? This simple wisdom eludes today's cut-throat corporate world.

Forgiveness and tolerance send out clear a message within an organisation that it is the error that deserves condemnation and not the person who commits it.

'The righteous man walks in his integrity; His children are blessed after him.' Likewise, the CEOs and managers who have integrity shall leave behind a string of honest and committed people who will continue to carry on the good work and ensure that the organisation shall neither decay with the 'second principle' of thermodynamics nor rot with entropy. Several Indian and global organisations have had noble forebears who have passed on a fine tradition of integrity. To name a few: Cadbury, IBM, Hewlett Packard, Tatas, Godrej, and Wipro.

> *The path of the just is like the shining sun, That shines ever brighter unto the perfect day.*
>
> *The way of the wicked is like darkness; They do not know what makes them stumble.*
>
> —Torah

❦ Life-cycle of a Corporation ❧

'Few large corporations live even half as long as a person,' says Peter M. Senge in his book *The Fifth Discipline*. 'In 1983, a Royal Dutch/ Shell survey found that one third of the firms in the Fortune 500 in 1970 had vanished.' But there

> *When wisdom enters your heart, And knowledge is pleasant to your soul, Discretion will preserve you; Understanding will keep you, To deliver you from the way of evil, From the man who speaks perverse things, From those who leave the paths of uprightness.*
>
> —Torah

208

are companies who survived for more than a 100 years. They are visionary companies who are consciously aware of their purpose for being and they know what they stand for. 'We are in business of preserving and improving human life. All of our actions must be measured by our success in achieving this goal,' says a vision statement articulated by Merck, the pharmaceutical giant. Values and virtues make the commercial organisations timeless and deathless!

Confidence in business matters comes from following the path you believe to be right and living by values you hold true. Articulate your vision, hone it and carry it passionately till the mission is completed. Once your management concepts are clear, you need not fear the winds of change or the violent market trends. Those who follow the straight path in business management never stumble. One must always remember: there is no right way to do the wrong things. Once you follow the right path, you are bound to do only the right things.

In the way of righteousness is life,
And in its pathway there is no death.

The parable about British Airways is revealing. BA's old nickname was 'Bloody Awful', until the British Airways turned to a righteous path and held steadfast to values. Today BA stands for 'Beatitude At-heights'. British Airways employs scores of trained 'problem solvers'. They go by different names: 'hunters', 'trouble shooters' and 'resolvers'.

The airline has now learnt how to pamper its customers. Since it took the righteous path, it has survived and how! BA is one of the finest examples of a corporate that makes a complete makeover by stressing on values.

❦ Knowledge ❧

There is gold and a multitude of rubies,
But the lips of knowledge are a precious jewel.

Those who believe too much in material gains must know that the rupee or the dollar that come from different sources do not have the same worth even though they may have the same economic value. What matters is where you earn your rupee from.

Apart from values and virtues what will be critical for business is knowledge. Tomorrow's businesses will be guided by those who not only acquire knowledge but also understand its true nature. These management monks, as I call them, will be those who will contextualise knowledge in each situation and not use it mindlessly as solutions arising out of trends or fads. Critical knowledge will be the cornerstone for resolving difficult situations. 'The heart of the prudent acquires knowledge, and the ear of the wise seeks knowledge.'

Those who do not share the joy of their knowledge with others cause more damage to the organisation or society than those who do wrong. Life is a participative process of learning. One must learn and share his or her knowledge with others. Those who know must contribute. If they do not, the guilt is unpardonable. Chanakya puts this across succinctly: 'More harm is caused to society by the inaction of good men than the misdeeds of evil men.' The fact that you have knowledge is a responsibility in itself.

Pride, ego and arrogance are three corporate vices that lead to decadence within the organisation. Success without humility makes a head swell with arrogance. It is almost a disease that can afflict the most promising managers and warrants treatment. To stay healthy, keep your success in your heart and the failures in the mind. Solomon's wisdom has a universal applicability. It is quite relevant to today's corporate world that is going astray.

> *A man's pride will bring him low,*
> *But the humble in spirit will retain honour.*
> —**Proverbs 29:23 (Old Testament)**

Be courageous; be courteous, be competent; be committed—they are the 4 C's that are the keys to success. The weak faint at the hour of reckoning. The corporate world routinely goes through such pe-

> *If you faint in the day of adversity,*
> *Your strength is small.*
> —**Proverbs 24:10 (Old Testament)**

riod of crises. Cowardice has no place in business: First, a coward lacks courage and faints at the first sign of adversity. In tomorrow's world of business, each moment will throw up a challenge and timorous managers will fail all the time. This is why business managers have embraced the concept of an 'Adversity Quotient'. Second, the coward has no place in the new world of business that will embrace spiritual values. Only the value-based organisations will survive. You need a great deal of courage to build values and practice virtues. A coward certainly will have no place in such an organisation.

Today, some organisations do not believe in values. They believe that might is right and that all's fair in love and war. They see business as a form of war and consider their competitors as their enemies. I call this a business perversion. Nike's strategic vision is a unique blend of

> *Do not rejoice when your enemy falls,*
> *And do not let your heart be glad when he stumbles.*
> —**Proverbs 24:17 (Old Testament)**

211

positive and negative values—'To experience the emotion of competition by winning and crushing competitors'. In the pursuit of this strategic vision, Nike finds nothing wrong with crushing its competitors. This is a view that runs counter to Solomon's wisdom: 'Don't rejoice when your enemy falls'. In the anxiety to beat the competition, we should not try to beat the competitors. In doing so, we might make some gains for the company, but we shall cause a great damage to society. Let there be a fair opportunity and a level playing field so that one can thrive amidst competition and satisfy 'customer's need'.

Flattery is another contagious corporate vice. People flatter to serve the egos of the corporate pharaohs. In doing so, they don't even experience the feeling of guilt. Flattery kills the conscience of managers. I always tell my managers never to be conformists. I tell

> *A lying tongue hates those who are crushed by it,*
> *And a flattering mouth works ruins.*
> **—Proverbs 26:28 (Old Testament)**

them, 'Don't become a time-server.' I also tell them, 'Be true to your souls.'

'Say yes and survive, after all the boss is always right'; that is a fallacy. However, this is not entirely the fault of managers and executives. Unfortunately, we groom managers to pay more attention to what the people above want from them. Our social, family and education systems teach our children to conform. Coupled with this is the huge premium that we place on success in our society. Success at all costs is the message we seem to give to each successive generation.

Everyone looks up and waits to hear what the boss says! Everyone likes to play safe and do what he is asked to do. No one wants to bear the cross by speaking the truth or giving negative feedback. People in an organisation learn and adapt to the environment. 'After all we don't lose anything,' they wrongly assume. They lose their individuality and their self-respect. Most importantly they lose their self-confidence and the distinctiveness of their character in the anxiety to serve. Once this happens, you have done yourself incalculable harm.

The king would like to hear what pleases his ears. The Boss is also a human being and we must bear this in our minds at all times. Managers are not hired to backbite and practise sycophancy. Your job is not to 'kiss the one above you and kick the one who follows you'.

> *He who rebukes a man will find more favour afterwards*
> *Than he who flatters with the tongue.*
> —**Proverbs 28:23 (Old Testament)**

The patriarchal environment is best described in a funny poster that shows a chimpanzee in the chair with a chart in the backdrop with the production curve sloping downwards. The caption reads: The Boss is always right. Sycophancy sows the seed of decadence in organisations—the flatterer ruins an entity! I've seen too many of these corporate ruins. Appeasement and flattery spread a net for your feet—beware of the sycophants.

⚜ Injelititis! ⚜

When the jealous people work against the intelligent and competent people to gain some mileage, it incubates a deadly disease within an organisation. Parkinson has given this disease a name—Injelititis! He explained this corporate disease in terms of the following equation:

$$I3 + J5 = Injelititis$$

When an overall 'incompetence' (I3) jells with rampant 'jealousy' (J5) against the 'intelligence' and 'competent' managers, the deadly organisational disease of Injelititis sets in. Incompetence overlaid by jealousy secretes a toxic substance—Injelitence. This toxic substance creates the disease Injelititis.

Jealousy is disastrous! One of the verses of Torah says that one can withstand cruelty and brutality, but not jealousy.

Wrath is cruel and anger a torrent,
But who is able to stand before jealousy?

'Jealousy' plays havoc in business organisations. Parkinson's Injelititis is no fiction; it is based on his lifetime study and meticulous analysis. One must be careful with those who have a jealous mind and an envious soul for no one can withstand their jealousy and ill-will.

'What is your prime objective as a trade unionist,' I once asked a trade union leader. 'Get more,' he smiled. This is an attitude that has wrecked today's corporate scenario. Water doesn't quench the thirst of mother earth; enough is never enough. Those who believe that by paying enough they can motivate and inspire must learn from Solomon's wisdom quoted in the box alongside.

There are three things that are never satisfied,
Four things never say, "It is enough";
The grave,
The barren womb,
The earth that is not satisfied with water,
And fire that never says, "It is enough."

—Proverbs 30:15&16 (Old Testament)

214

Jealousy and greed are the signs of death that undermine corporate prosperity.

However, it is incorrect to stand in judgement on those who feel jealous. After all, we all feel jealous once in a while. If it is not at work, it can strike in other aspects of life. It is easy to ask someone to avoid jealousy. Instead we must learn to introspect and understand it, and then tackle it. Jealousy is usually a result of the limitations within ourselves. As we introspect, we realise these limitations and learn to address them or deal with them. Sometimes, we must accept these limitations and learn to live with them. This level of introspection is a sign of tremendous growth and maturity. As one makes a habit of introspecting whenever jealousy strikes, one discovers oneself, self-awareness increases and we grow. As we grow, one shows more grace and a greater ability and competence. One learns to be prudent and judicious. People respect you for these qualities and often give you greater responsibility.

🖙 Corporate Sagacity 🖎

There're three things, which are majestic in pace,
Yes, four which are stately in walk:
A lion, which is mighty among beasts
And does not turn away from any;
A greyhound,
A male goat also,
And a king whose troops are with him!
          —Proverbs 30:29-31 (Old Testament)

Like the loyal troops with the king, competent and committed people confer a majestic status to an organisation. It is not the size, but the capability that matters. A man with a few loyal friends is much better off than one with many acquaintances who show no genuine fondness or affection. But we continue to look at size as a determinant of success. A manager wants a larger team not necessarily a competent or a committed one. Skills are more important than the number of hands that work. It is interesting to note what the Old Testament says with regard to size.

> *There're four things which are little on the earth,*
> *But they are exceedingly wise:*
> *The ants are a people not strong,*
> *Yet they prepare their food in the summer;*
> *The rock badgers are a feeble folk,*
> *Yet they make their homes in the crags;*
> *The locusts have no king,*
> *Yet they all advance in ranks;*
> *The spider skillfully grasps with its hands,*
> *And it is in kings' palaces.*
>
> **—Proverbs 30:24-28 (Old Testament)**

Unfortunately, human beings are often more barbarous than beasts and are feebler than tiny insects. We wrongly assume that the line that divides humanity with brutal behaviour is not all that thin. We forget what the Torah reveals unto us: 'In His own image God created man.' God has breathed His soul in Adam—the ancestral father of the humankind. Each one of us is spiritually potent. The Chinese consider every man a *Chu-Goku*, meaning the centre of the universe. Ken Blanchard rightly says, 'We are not human beings having a spiritual experience. We are spiritual beings having a human experience.'

Mark your identity as a human being and live by the values that you believe in.

In closing, I remember the first psalm of Zubur, the revelations that came unto Prophet David:

Blessed is the man
who walks not in the counsel of the ungodly,
Nor stands in the path of sinners,
Nor sits in the seat of the scornful;
But his delight is in the law of the Lord,
And in His law he meditates day and night.
He shall be like a tree
Planted by the rivers of water,
That brings forth its fruit in its season,
And whatever he does shall prosper.

The Holy Scriptures represent a collection of organised beliefs from a certain school of thought. What we learn from them depends on one's appetite. The Ganges goes on flowing; it is for the thirsty to come and take water from it.

While we may not all agree with the religious tone of this extract, we all must endeavour to understand the spirit behind it. The purpose of our existence is to do what we believe is right and not live by what the others say. While one may not believe in any religion, it is always important to understand the varied ways of thinking and looking at life.

12

Islamic Corporate Governance

O my Lord! Give unto me more knowledge.

—Qur'anic verse (20:114)

The Qur'an has explicit views on knowledge, wisdom and the way business should be conducted. It charts a whole business system, balances commercial interests and the larger interest of society. It stresses the need to create a balance between profit and social responsibility.

'To be fond of learning is to be near to knowledge,' said Confucius in the 6th century BC in China. Prophet Mohammed—who was unlettered—said in the 6th century AD: 'Seek knowledge from the cradle to the grave.'

The Qur'an tells us that knowledge is virtue and learning is worship. It

> *Read! In the name of thy Lord and Cherisher, who created man... Proclaim the glory of your Lord who is the most bountiful. He taught man the use of his pen; taught him what he did not know.*
>
> **—(Surah 96: 1-5)**

is wrong to believe that knowledge is the source of power only in this information age. Knowledge has always been powerful. The age-old adage says, 'Knowledge is Power'. It took considerable time for the world of business to understand and acknowledge the power of knowledge.

The Qur'an lays great emphasis on knowledge, virtue, wisdom, and the straight path that leads to the creation of a virtuous society. Today, most of the nation states are trying to create a 'gracious society'. The Qur'an also lays emphasis on 'science' and 'learning'. It repeatedly warns the readers not merely to parrot the text, but read it with greater understanding so that they can practise its teachings. The very beginning of Qur'anic revelations to Prophet Mohammed was with the word, 'Iqra', meaning 'Read'.

Thus, the first revelation extolled the power of the pen and shook the unlettered—the Prophet. The distinction of the Qur'an is that it begins to glorify the power of the pen.

The Prophet, an unlettered person, had always preached the virtues of seeking 'knowledge'. Many people will not believe Prophet Mohammed's passion for science, especially since they regard science as a natural foe of religion. Islam charts out a whole set of rules to govern business and business systems. It is a road map that shows how a good Muslim should conduct business and undertake monetary transactions. Nothing could be more revealing than the famous words of the Prophet: 'Seek for science, even in China.' He strongly believed that the search for knowledge was a strict duty for every human being. Learning is at the core of Islam; most of people do not know that *Iqra* was the first word that God spoke unto Mohammed through the archangel.

☙ Wisdom and Knowledge ❧

Today, business thinkers and corporation regard knowledge as a form of capital. Never in the history of the corporate world has so much emphasis been laid on knowledge as in the past couple of decades. But have we really understood the meaning of knowledge? The scraps of information that we download from the Internet isn't knowledge; it is just the raw material. We can at best call it information or an accumulation of data, but it should not be construed as knowledge.

We intuitively understand the statement: 'Knowledge is power'; what we need to now acknowledge is: 'Knowledge is virtue'.

Beyond a point, knowledge without wisdom is useless. In fact, wisdom is the seed of knowledge. It takes time to grow in wisdom; as we grow in knowledge, the focus on pure knowledge decreases. We learn to look at the macro picture and see the role of knowledge as an enabler and not an end in itself. However, every man of knowledge is not blessed with wisdom; we all know this. So, what is the worth of knowledge without wisdom? It is not mere knowledge but wisdom that makes knowledge worthwhile. In the absence of wisdom, knowledge can even cause harm. Knowledge can become a virtue only when it is pursued with wisdom. 'The highest in God's view is the most virtuous,' proclaims the holy Qur'an.

Wisdom and virtue are appropriately relevant to business matters; they lead us down the path of success. God has granted wisdom to the

> *Verily Allah is the Guide to those who believe, to the Straight Path.*
>
> **—(Surah Al-Hajj: 54)**

blessed ones: 'He granted wisdom to whom He pleaseth; and he to whom wisdom is granted receiveth indeed a benefit overflowing; but none will grasp the message but men of understanding' (Surah 2:269). Every scripture says this. If a manager has to grow in wisdom, he has to practise virtue.

The 'straight path' is considered to be at the core of the Qur'an and is the central tenet of Islamic merchandise law. The Qur'an always guarded the followers against dishonesty and usury in business. The path of honesty is the only path of business.

The 'straight path' was the guiding force for people long before Islam came into existence. Lao Tzu's Tao or Buddha's mid-path preached the virtues of taking the straight path, which in Arabic is called '*Siratul Mustaqueem*'. Following the universal integral way of life means practising selflessness and extending virtues to the world unconditionally. 'All true guidance is intangible because the universal integral way is beyond the limits of the mind. The universal way is neither religious nor worldly,' says Lao Tzu. In the realm of universal life, or what the Old Master calls the 'River of Timelessness', the 'universal law of energy response' provides blessings to those who follow the universal integral way.

You could construe the cosmic pathway as Tao, the universal integral way, the virtuous path, Buddha's mid-path, or *Siratul-mustaqueem*—it does not matter which way you choose to follow. Both in life and business one must follow the straight path—and that is the central tenet of Islamic corporate governance.

Let us first scan the business environment of Mecca before the spread of Islam.

ᛰ Business Environment ᛈ

To understand the appropriate context of Islamic views on business, we must examine it historically. Mecca stands in a plain surrounded by mountains on all sides. Gifted with a number of springs, it became a natural halt for two caravan routes—one going South to Yemen and the other going north to Palestine. Due to the gift of Nature, Mecca became an important trading centre. Mecca's traders excelled in business and the others found it difficult to compete with them. Besides the natural surroundings, their competence in business contributed further to the growth of Mecca as a major trading centre.

It was in this dynamic, vibrant and competitive business environment that Prophet Mohammed was born. He was an orphan. He grew up under the patronage of his grand father Abdul Muttalib. After his death, his uncle Abu Talib, a renowned trader, became his patron. During those days, it was very risky to take a trading caravan from one place to the other through the desert because of the threat to life and material. It was because of this that Abu Talib was hesitant to take young Mohammed along with the trading caravans. It was only after Mohammed's strong insistence that his uncle later allowed him to go on these trading journeys. He started his business venture with the trade trip to al-Sham, the territory presently known as Lebanon, Syria, Palestine and Jordan. Young Mohammed turned out to be excellent in trading—the key value that he followed was 'honesty'. This brought prosperity to his uncle's business.

Attracted with Mohammed's business acumen and honesty, a rich and noble tradeswoman, Khadijah, offered to let him manage her business. Mohammed's keen business sense and honesty enabled him to make great gains for his employer, more than anyone had done before. Later, after his marriage to Khadijah, Mohammed contributed to the management of his wife's large business interests. He, therefore, had ample opportunities to learn and observe the various business practices adopted by others—both honest and dishonest conduct of businessmen. 'It is not surprising, therefore, that Mohammed later on established a wide-ranging and practical Islamic code of business ethics based upon Allah's revelations,' explains the author of *Islam and Business*, Nik Mohamed Affandi Bin Nik Yusoff.

Islam considers business as the most widespread and beneficial of all human economic activities. It strongly condemns the practice of earning income from dubious means or non-economic activities like gambling and speculation or, for that matter, any game of chance.

In Islam, the word profit has a much larger meaning that goes beyond the boundaries of economics. 'Doing good deeds' is very much like conducting a profitable business. In this way Islam provides a wide scope of opportunities to Muslims to gain profit by doing good deeds to other mortals. Such ethical activities and honesty in business bring prosperity and happiness to the performer and to mankind.

❦ Ad-Deen ❧

Islam is 'ad-Deen', i.e., it is a whole way of life covering both the needs—the worldly needs and the needs to prepare for the 'Hereafter'. Islam teaches a method of living a pious but socially and economically productive life. Thus, the concept of ad-Deen provides for both material well-being and spiritual pursuits. To strengthen the concept of ad-Deen—a balanced fusion of the spirituality and material aspects of life—Islam introduces the concepts of *fard' ain* and *fard kifayah*. The Arabic word f*ard* stands for 'compulsory obligation' that cannot be avoided or compromised in any circumstances. So,

> *The best among you are those who do not ignore the Hereafter for the worldly and also do not ignore the worldly for the Hereafter.*
>
> —**Prophet Mohammed**

the two codes which have been made compulsory for every Muslim are: f*ard' ain*, meaning individual's obligations to perform his religious duties towards God such as the mandatory five daily prayers, fasting during the month of Ramadan, and charity to poor, and *fard kifayah*, meaning the individual's obligation to perform good deeds towards humankind. The purpose of life is to maintain a perfect balance between worldly needs and spiritual obligations. If you carry out one and not the other, the code of ad-Deen is not fulfilled. One cannot be carried out at the expense of the other. Islam makes this absolutely clear but most of the Muslims who construe their religion in a narrow sense of only praying and fasting, do not understand this *meezan* (perfect balance) obligated by Islam without any compromise.

The Prophet said: 'A Muslim who likes to do good deeds in this world will be fully recognised in the Hereafter and will be given special preference to go to Heaven.' Note the emphasis that is laid upon 'good deeds' for earning a place in Heaven. He also cautioned the worshippers saying, 'A Muslim will not go to heaven if his neighbours do not experience peace from him.' He further makes it clear saying, 'But seek, with which Allah has bestowed on you, the Home of the Hereafter, nor forget your portion in this world.'

Both those who serve the needs of other men but ignore their spiritual duties, and those who fail to serve the needs of other men while following the spiritual obligations are at fault. Faith is considered insufficient in Islam. So are actions without faith. When I say 'actions', I mean those of a worldly nature such as earning an honest living, maintaining warm and sincere relations with others, and sharing one's knowledge and wealth with others.

As seen above, Islam encompasses all aspects of human life and it, therefore, devotes substantial attention to the economic system—and one of the major components of such system, business management. Business as a worldly activity is also an act of piety towards the Almighty and, therefore, has to be carried out with utmost honesty and with the objective of serving the society.

✢ The Islamic Economic System ✣

The Islamic economic system is premised on the basic faith of a Muslim:

All wealth is a trust, as well as a test, from Allah. Absolute ownership of all material things is reserved for Allah alone. The rich as His trustees will, therefore, have to pass His tests by ensuring that some of their wealth is used for the good of community and mankind. One can see the roots of the modern concept of corporate social responsibility (CSR) right here.

Nothing belongs to the human being who apparently owns the wealth, neither in material form nor in the form of his children and grandchildren. Both wealth and children belong to the Almighty. We as human beings are only trustees of His wealth. A Sufi has therefore said, 'Children are not born to us, they are born through us!'

225

The Islamic economic system stands for an 'exploitation-free' economy in a compassionate society. Islam encourages social and economic relations with people irrespective of their religion. The Islamic economic system also

> *Truly Allah likes to see his servants striving to earn an honest income.*
> —**Prophet Mohammed**

encompasses non-Muslims provided they do not pose a threat to the Muslims.

Every man should strive to attain economic well-being and self-sufficiency in income within the confines of Islam's moral norms and values. Large economic freedom is given to individuals, subject again to the confines of Islamic norms and values and the common good of the society. It prescribes that the high standards of Islamic morality must prevail in all economic activities. Both exploitation and undue profit is strictly prohibited in Islamic economic order. The strong sense of honesty and fair business practices is ingrained in all followers of the faith.

The major objectives of an Islamic economic system can be encapsulated thus:

No individual or community should be deprived of the basic necessities of life. Wealth should not be concentrated in the hands of a few individuals. Wealth should not be left idle but used as productively as possible. A proper balance should be maintained between materialism and spiritualism, and between economic and humanitarian objectives. Equal opportunities should be created for all to earn their legitimate income based on their potential and respective capabilities. Imposing social, moral and spiritual constraints on production should be considered as one of the important economic activities. The purpose of economic activity is to seek Allah's blessings for self and to serve mankind.

To ensure that an Islamic economic system operates fairly and justly, Islam imposes three constraints.

> *The best of men are those who are more useful to others.*
> **(Part of Ahl Sunnah)**

Although businessmen are entitled to profits, Islam does not accept profit maximisation as the sole or even the most important objective of business. Although Islam strongly believes in a market economy, it does not believe that mankind is perfect and, therefore, behaves rationally all the time. Therefore, the market economy should be regulated at certain times in order to protect and promote the interest of the whole community. The payment of wages is the most important factor of business activity as it involves human resource. Thus, wages must be fixed not only on the basis of capabilities and contribution, but also in consideration to certain basic necessities of life.

If someone studies the Islamic economic system closely, he will realise that it takes the best from capitalism and Marxist socialism, and then adds certain elements that are special to Islam. Purposefully, Islamic economic freedom is constrained by the greater interest of the whole community. Islam requires Muslims to achieve a proper balance between materialism and spiritualism even through the economic system.

The Islamic economic system provides a perfect balance between economic and human objectives.

✉ Demand and Supply ✉

The Prophet recommended a 'demand and supply' market, but with certain prescriptions to avoid exploitation. He did not encourage a broker's or middleman's intervention to usurp a trader's profit. During the Prophet's time, it was a common practice for people from the town to sell on behalf of those from desert. The Prophet discouraged this practice. He felt such brokerage was bad, both for the trader and the buyer. It had a twin advantage: it would help the traders get a reasonable profit for their efforts and goods; the town people would also benefit by being able to buy at a lower price.

In *Islam and Business*, Nik Mohamed Affandi Bin Nik Yusoff quotes two of the Prophet's statements that establish Islamic principles with regard to the market economy.

It is prohibited for even the government to compel businessmen to sell their goods at prices not acceptable to them or which denies them a reasonable profit. A situation where demand rises but supply remains static, and prices therefore increase is to be regarded as Allah's Will. To compel the businessman to sell at the previous price, thus denying him a high profit is therefore prohibited.

Having provided traders the opportunity to make reasonable profits, Islam simultaneous prohibits creating artificial shortages or hoarding. Islam firmly forbids any form of price manipulation. The Prophet regarded Allah as the fixer of price through the forces of supply and demand. So if anyone tries to manipulate prices, he will be going against Allah's Will. The Prophet has therefore warned: 'If anyone withholds goods until the price rises, he is a sinner. The man who hoards goods is evil. If prices fall, he is grieved and if they rise he is happy.'

Islam also forbids monopoly that conflicts directly with a market economy, free trade and open competition. The Prophet said: 'Whoever monopolise food for 40 days, they are therefore removed from Allah, and Allah is removed from them.'

In Islam, a free market is considered essential. Even the government is not permitted to fix prices, except under certain conditions. When prices of certain goods rose to a high level during Prophet's time, people asked him to fix prices. The Prophet refused to intervene. The Islamic economic system favours a free trade, prescribing certain norms and prescribing certain excesses, which are harmful both for traders and consumers.

> *Allah is the One Who fixes price, Who withholds, Who gives lavishly, and Who provides, and I hope that when I meet Him, none of you will have a claim against me for any injustice with regard to blood or property.*
>
> **—Prophet Mohammed**

Today, Free Trade Agreements (FTAs) do not create a free market in a real sense. The FTAs impose restrictions designed to protect the interests of the western world that has emerged as a strong economic power. The West is able to dictate terms to poor countries and adopt a course of action that will only further its economic interests. This may sound exaggerated, but in reality FTAs provide restrictions that are in effect more binding. An FTA can force a country to remove restrictions on pornography, for instance, because it is a billion-dollar industry in the West. I understand that Singapore was under such pressure while signing the FTA with America. While this may be acceptable in some cultural contexts, other cultures may find it repugnant. The adoption of free market principles should not require a nation to abandon its cultural ethos. Many are of the opinion that Asian countries today face a cultural invasion from the West that has an insidious purpose of creating a market for western businesses that deal in cosmetics, pornography, and pop music.

≝ Islamic View on Interest or *Riba* ≝

Riba is an Arabic word for usury. Some translate the word *riba* to mean 'interest'. But 'usury' is better since it captures the essence of the word. *Riba* is strictly prohibited in Islamic economic order. Making money through usury is considered to be a ghastly sin. The person who earns profits from usury is compared to a vampire that sucks human blood. A Muslim is not supposed to drink water from the house where income is earned through usury.

Most interestingly, the followers of Judaism and Christianity, who encourage the practice of usury today, were cautioned in clear terms in their respective scriptures not to indulge in it.

Perhaps the best known constraint placed by the Qur'an on Muslim businessmen is the prohibition of *Riba* (usury). Although Muslims universally accept prohibition of *Riba*, there is a growing debate over what constitutes *Riba*. For instance, does *Riba* cover interest earned by commercial banks? This is a moot point. Some scholars suggest that one should go with the spirit and not the words. *Riba* was prohibited due to the 'exploitation' factor. Since in commercial banking there is neither any force nor any exploitation, it should not be considered as *Riba*. However, there are other scholars who believe that earning interest from commercial banking is akin to earning through usury and, therefore, sinful.

It will be relevant to discuss two types of Riba:

Riba al-Nassiah refers to 'loan-based interest', where the lender takes 'interest' in addition to the principal amount from the borrowers. This type of *Riba* is prohibited without any iota of doubt. The Qur'an clearly prohibits this type of *Riba*.

Riba al-Buyu or *Riba al-Fadi* refers to trade-based interest. This type of *Riba* was relevant during the days of barter trade. Prophet Mohammed had prohibited exchange of bad quality commodities with good quality ones. The rationale was to prevent dishonest and unjust business transactions by exploiting a position or authority. It is possible that a trader may be forced to accept lower quality stuff from a per-

> *A time will come when people will devour usury, and call it trade.*
> —**Prophet Mohammed**

son of authority in a barter deal. To avoid such type of exploitation, the Prophet had proscribed trade-based *Riba*. Dishonesty, bribery, cheating, and usurping are but a few forms of *Riba al-Buyu* or *Riba al Fadi*, which are prohibited by the prophet.

Among the various prophecies made by Prophet Mohammed some relate to 'usury' as a well-accepted norm in the economy during the last age before doomsday. He had very clearly indicated that before the Last Day (Doomsday), the world economy would be so thoroughly corrupted by usury that even those who would like to avoid taking interest would be polluted. As we all know today, it is virtually impossible to live a life free from bank interest.

As mentioned earlier, there remains no doubt about the prohibition of *Riba* in the Islamic economic order, but the question whether transactions with conventional banks, accepting and giving interest, fall within the meaning of *Riba* is subject to debate.

✎ Prohibition of Gambling ✎

Maisir is prohibited. The Arabic equivalent of gambling is *Maisir*, which means 'getting something too easily' or 'getting a profit without working for it'. Islam therefore prohibits any business transaction that has any gambling element or highly speculative activities. It prohibits gambling not only through playing cards and bidding at race courses or in casinos, but also any transaction where money is earned by making wild speculation. Nik Mohamed Affandi Bin Nik Yusoff in his book *Islam and Business*, argues, 'Buying listed shares on a stock exchange on a very short-term basis and based on rumours and a feeling of being lucky could be regarded as speculating or gambling.' Therefore, genuine investors ought to buy shares largely based on the company's fundamental strengths, especially its current and potential earnings.

✎ Human Relations ✎

Human assets are considered significant in the Islamic economy. In today's environment, the greatest lie that companies perpetuate is to say: 'Human Resource is our greatest asset'. If that is really so, why is it that at the first sign of a downturn, the axe falls on what we once claimed to be our greatest assets. As an HR person by profession, I refuse to accept the concept of downsizing which is often given a veneer of respectability by giving it a false name: rightsizing. The solution does not lie in downsizing your human asset; the solution lies in upsizing your business. Most of the time we work as 'denominator' managers forgetting the numerator part of the equation. Let me take you through the concept of HR in Islam.

The first and foremost obligation cast upon the employer is to pay reasonable wages in time. The Prophet had once said: 'Pay the worker his wages even before his sweat dries up.' Timely payment of wages is the first obligation of an employer in Islamic business ethics.

Islam believes in equality and provides that a happy and comfortable life is the right of every human being, poor or rich, employer or employee. The Prophet emphasised: 'Hope for others what you hope for yourself...' An employer has therefore to be always fair to his employees. One of the aspects of fairness is the wage that he pays to his people. In Islam, salary is not based solely on a worker's contribution to production, but more importantly on his

> *It is most important for you to provide food and clothing to your assistants... For your worker there must be satisfaction with their basic requirements.*
>
> **—Prophet Mohammed**

basic needs. Even if an employer's income does not warrant it, he is still required to try to pay his employees sufficient wages to enable them to have the basic necessities of life. One may call this as the Islamic principle of minimum wages.

'For those employers who can afford it, Islam requires them to pay their workers a wage that enables them to live a reasonably comfortable life. This can be considered as a just wage,' writes Mohamed Affandi in *Islam and Business*. 'A model employer in Islam is one whose standard of living is not too different from that of his workers. This is the principle of ideal wage.'

> *Your employees are your brothers whom Allah has made your subordinates. So he, who has his brothers under him, let him feed them with what he feeds himself and clothe him with what he clothes himself...*
>
> *Do not overburden your unskilled female employee in her pursuit of living, because if you do so, she may resort to immorality; and do not overburden a male subordinate, for if you do so, he may resort to stealing. Be considerate with them. It is incumbent upon you to provide them good and lawful food.*
>
> **—Prophet Mohammed**

The provision of employment by those who can afford it is mandatory to protect society from immodesty and corruption. Paying them wages, which help them lead a good healthy life, is one of the important principles of Islamic Corporate Governance. 'Although it is difficult for the employers to achieve the objective of an ideal wage, every Muslim employer should at least try his utmost to ensure that his employees are able to share his increasing profit and wealth through salary increase, better bonus payment, better facilities and even through a share option scheme,' suggests the author of *Islam and Business*. Surprising as it may sound, one of the oldest religions in the world gave us the concept of share options.

Favouritism and nepotism run counter to Islamic principles. Islam stands for 'meritocracy' in recruitment, placement and career development. The Prophet said: 'If you give a job to someone who is not knowledgeable, just wait for the destruction.' Therefore, an employer is obliged to ensure that recruitment and promotion is based on merit. Justice and fairness are the two central tenets of Islamic corporate governance.

After suggesting the guidelines for employers, Islam lays down clear guidelines for workers as well. It requires employees to sincerely and fully reciprocate by giving their best when carrying out their responsibilities.

> *Whoever is appointed to manage the affairs of the Muslim community, and he appoints someone based on nepotism, he will therefore be condemned by Allah, and his compulsory and voluntary obligations will not be accepted until he is admitted to hell.*
>
> **—Prophet Mohammed**

The Prophet consistently said, 'A worker is the guardian of his employer's property... Allah loves that when anyone does

234

a job, he does it perfectly... An employee who excels in his devotion to Allah and also renders to his master what is due to him of duty, sincerity and obedience, for him there is a double reward with Allah.'

Islam also instructs workers to give their best in terms of production and services. They must earn their wages from the sweat of their brow. Any earning, even through wages, is not lawful if it is not earned through sincerity, dedication and commitment. Allah warns in the Qur'an: '... but you shall certainly be called to account for all your actions.' The Prophet said: 'He whom we have appointed for a job and have provided with livelihood, then whatever he appropriates beyond this is ill-gotten.'

Having provided a code of conduct for employers and employees, there remains little reason for workers to form unions to pursue their demands. This, of course, works on the premise that both the employer and the employee scrupulously follow these guidelines. Workers should refrain from forming unions in order to pressure responsible employers to agree to their unreasonable demands. The Prophet cautions the workers against frequently making demands unless necessary.

At the core of this belief lies industrial harmony, which can be achieved by following the principles of mutual concern and caring. When productivity rises, the employer will make more money. So, when employers share the gains with the workers, they will be motivated to produce more and get more. This then forms the bedrock for a prosperous and extremely harmonious company which will, in turn, contribute to the cause of prosperity for the entire society.

The Prophet said, 'Allah will always assist His followers as long as they assist their fellow human beings.'

The Power of Simplicity

We forget simple principles in our day-to-day business and therefore lose focus—we concentrate on what doesn't add value to the product or the customer, and make simple things difficult in the process. Do not make a hue and cry about darkness, just light a candle and it will solve the problem.

Be simple! Be simple in management systems and business practices. We have made business management quite complicated. It is time to 'uncomplicate' things. Jack Welch's KISS—Keep It Simple, Stupid—is the need of the hour. The Prophet said this long ago: 'Simplicity, too, is a part of faith.'

Today, the certainty of Kaizen offers a better payback and steadier contribution to the bottom line than the uncertainty of innovation. A drop makes an ocean. Islamic principles subscribe to the concept of Kaizen. 'Even the smallest good deed will suffice,' said the Prophet. What he preached and practised can be termed as 'Value-Kaizen'!

Walk the Talk

No amount of preaching proves effective if it is not supported and supplemented by action. 'Wisdom without action hath its seat in the mouth; but by means of action, it becometh fixed in the heart,' says Shekel Hakodesh.

A parable goes like this...

Once, an old lady went to Prophet Mohammed along with her grandson and requested the Prophet to counsel the young boy not to eat too many dates as it was not good for his health. The Prophet asked her to come back along with her grandson after a month. Next month when the old lady and her grandson visited him, the Prophet counselled the boy

236

not to consume so many dates. The old lady was astonished. 'Such a simple piece of advice could have been given by you last month itself,' she told the Prophet. To this the Prophet replied that till last month he himself was fond of dates and enjoyed eating them as much. He first gave up eating dates before counselling the child.

'Walk the talk' is a simple concept that is found in the thoughts and writings of many great men. Confucius had said: 'Action without thought is labour lost; thought without action is perilous.' No amount of preaching proves effective if it is not supported and supplemented by a demonstration.

To create change one must be able to demonstrate. It is only then that a piece of advice or instruction hits home. It is in many akin to inspiration. Guiding people is not enough. We need to change ourselves to serve as a beacon to the people whom we lead.

◎ Leading with Virtue ◎

Once a companion asked the Prophet what virtue was? 'That which brings peace to your mind and tranquillity to your soul,' replied the Prophet. And what was vice, he was asked. 'That which makes your heart flutter and which throws your soul into perturbation,' replied the Prophet.

Virtuous leadership is perhaps what is required in the next millennium! In the cut-throat world of business, we might be tempted to dismiss such a concept. But the truth is that as individuals we all have an innate sense of right and wrong. Our inner self or our soul is disturbed when we have deviated from the right path. When we speak of virtuous leadership, we are discussing the inner balance that must exist when we make decisions. The Qur'an lays emphasis on three traits that

237

a leader must possess: 'When he is overcome by anger, his anger should not drive him to falsehood. When he is happy, his happiness should not take him beyond the bounds of what is right. When he has power, he should not stake a claim to something which is not his.'

Virtuous leadership ends when a leader forces his people to work for an unjust cause. The Qur'an compares such a leader with a man who catches hold of the tail of a camel that is falling into a well. We all know of many managers and CEOs falling from place of dignity into the pits, 'holding the tail of the camel', in their attempt to support their people even when they were wrong or pursuing unjust causes.

If power blinds the leader, he loses the sensibility to draw a distinction between sycophancy and intellectual integrity of his people. A good leader knows how to see through the opaque 'human-wall' that surrounds him when he is in power, and

> *When you see sycophants, throw dust in their faces.*
> —**Prophet Mohammed**

locates the ones who are quietly engaged doing good things for the company without bothering to take a shine to the boss.

The Qur'an also advises leaders on people management. It says that you should not make a commitment to your people that you cannot fulfil. 'If you commit something to your people's care, be sure to return it to them,' advises the Prophet. 'Never betray anyone's trust, not even if the person concerned has failed to stand by his commitment to you.'

❦ Leadership Traits ❧

The concept of leadership is deeply rooted in Islam. The Qur'an tells us that even the smallest enterprise needs a leader to succeed. Once the Prophet advised his companions that whenever they moved in a group of three or more, they should choose one of them as the leader who shall guide them. To quote the Holy Prophet, 'Even if a group of people in a jungle numbers only three, it is still incumbent upon them to choose a leader.'

The Qur'an talks of faith and trust in one's people. The Prophet was proud of his companions and always reposed faith in their competence. 'My companions are like stars; whichever of them you follow will guide you,' he said. He always used to advise his companions: 'None of you should complain to me of another. I would like to come to you with a clear heart.'

Prophet Mohammed also followed the servant leadership model. Abdullah ibn Masud describes how during the battle of Badr, one camel was shared by Prophet and two of his companions. One person used to ride and the other two walked, lest cruelty was caused to the animal. When it was the Prophet's turn to walk, the companion mounted the camel would say to him, 'Mount the camel. We will walk in your place.' The Prophet would reply, 'Neither of you is stronger than I am, nor am I less eager for rewards (from God) than you.'

When one examines the stories and anecdotes about Prophet Mohammed, it becomes clear that he was not in favour of building power centres. He believed in 'companionship' rather than 'followership'. 'True, he was the Prophet of God, but he consistently refused to adopt any of the appearances of power, authority, kingship, or temporal sovereignty,' writes Haykal in *The Life of Muhammad*. He used to caution them who would bend before him to show respect: 'Do not stand up for me as the Persians do in aggrandizement of one another.' He always used to sit at the edge of the space rather than in the centre.

Collaboration will be the leadership style of tomorrow. Good leaders of tomorrow will tend to see people as colleagues, companions or partners, but certainly not as followers, let alone 'subordinates'. When a position is exploited to abuse

> *Your position never gives you the right to command. It only imposes on you the duty of so living your life that others can receive your orders without being humiliated.*
>
> **—Dag Hammarskjöld**
> **Former UN Secretary General**

power, juniors are treated as subordinates who are expected to follow the boss blindly. They are questioned and upbraided publicly at meetings and orders are given causing them humiliation—and that is the beginning of the end. The 'power centres' that we build to manage businesses are as durable as the sandcastles that children build on beaches which are washed away with the morning tide.

'The price of greatness is responsibility,' wrote Winston Churchill, 'position is really secondary.' One should acquire greatness only by paying its price, i.e., by assuming responsibility. This goes well with the Islamic way of leadership that Prophet Mohammed preached and practised.

The Prophet never gave others tasks that were beyond their capabilities. He created space to allow the human mind to ponder. He would set the targets that one could try and achieve.

'Despite his great intelligence and outstanding ability, he listened well and attentively to anyone who spoke to him, never turning his face away from his interlocutor.' Haykal described 'listening' and 'modesty' as two virtuous leadership traits of the Prophet that were second only to 'truthfulness', the trait that made Mohammed's leadership style divinely distinct from others.

'Whosoever addressed him, Muhammad was never satisfied to lend his ear alone but turned to him with all his being,' says Haykal. He used to speak little and listen more. He was inclined only to serious conversation though he was not averse to a 'sense of humour'. 'His anger and fury were always sublimated, and his magnanimity, candidness, and loyalty knew no bounds. He loved to do the good, and was charitable, hospitable, and friendly, as well as resolved and strong willed.'

The Qur'an also underscores the need for humility and dignity in a leader. 'Do not treat people with scorn, nor walk proudly on earth: Allah does not love the arrogant and the vainglorious.' It cautions mankind to desist from arrogance and harshness—and speak in humility. 'Lower thy voice—moderate thy pace, for the harshest of sounds without doubt is the braying of the ass.' (31:19)

Most importantly, it advises on the value of making the right decisions in the long run and the need to avoid hostility as far as possible.

The Qur'an teaches us to avoid hostility; the world

> *The use of kind words*
> *And indulgence to others*
> *Are better than charity*
> *Or the loss that one may*
> *Suffer in doing so.*
>
> —Qur'anic verse 2:263)

of business is moving away from competition to collaboration. Surah Al-'Asr which contains just three *ayats*, makes loud and clear unto us that people will be at a loss unless they have faith and do good works, and 'exhort each other to justice and to fortitude.'

◈ Life Skills in Islam ◈

Many view Islam as a strict and authoritarian way of life, but at the core of its philosophy lies its concern for the human being and its ability to go astray. The strict yet simple everyday routine that Islam ordains serves to create an understanding and respect for ideas such as time management, virtue, and emotional and spiritual well-being.

Time is one of the most important resources in life and business. The popular saying 'Time is money' has held true ever since it was first uttered.

Time is of cardinal importance in Islam. 'Don't vilify Time for Time is God,' said the Prophet. 'We are nearer to him (man) than (his) jugular vein,' says God (Surah 16: Qaf). Prayers are offered in accordance with the time-cycles of day. The morning prayers, long before the sun rises, elongate the day for doing good work. It creates a sense of purpose in those who follow this schedule.

Time is capital in today's business world; 'Productivity' can be increased by reducing the 'throughput' time. Commitment to customer satisfaction makes no sense unless you are able to maintain the delivery schedules. The time cycle is of primary importance in value engineering.

Today speed in business matters is determined by two outer limits: 'Look before you leap' and 'Leap, then look'. Tom Peters brings home the importance of speed saying that today's business must follow the maxim: 'Leap, then look!' While we may choose to follow whatever suits us, the point is that this pace will only hot up with the passage of time. On the one hand, complexities will increase manifold and, on the other, we shall witness a hectic pace that we have never witnessed in the past. The only way to survive and thrive in today's business is by holding steadfast to the cosmic principle—don't vilify Time for Time is God.

✒ Purification of the Soul ☙

The concept of fasting is one of the pillars of Islam. Fasting is common to all religions in one form or the other. It is believed that fasting purifies the soul.

'Everything has a cleansing agent,' says the Qur'an. 'And fasting is the cleansing agent for the body. Fasting is more a matter of patience than of anything else.'

A leader must know how to overpower one's desires by practising 'self-restraint', which is divine and holy.

> *O, you who believe in Us!*
> *Fasting is prescribed to you*
> *As it was prescribed to those before,*
> *So that you may learn*
> *Self-restraint. (Surah 2:183)*

Tapping spiritual energy is ever so important today. Unfortunately, the corporate world has been able to tap only the physical and intellectual energies of people; emotional and spiritual energies remain untapped. The secret of success in business lies in 'How to tap the untapped energy?' One needs to burn his body by thirst and hunger to kindle the candle of emotionality and spirituality in his or her self.

Nay, one must experience the thirst and hunger to know its meaning. There is one more benefit—hunger and thirst toughens your body and strengthens your soul.

We celebrate a 'Quality' month to build and develop quality awareness. Shouldn't there also be a month specially marked to develop emotional and spiritual strengths? Ramadan is earmarked precisely for this purpose!

'Zakat' means charity or giving the poor the due that belongs to them. Zakat is another important pillar of Islam, which is part of the socio-economic value system. It conveys something more than what the word charity encapsulates. Give away to others. If everyone amasses wealth, then social equilibrium will be unbalanced. History is replete with tales of how the have-nots have clashed with the haves just to claim a few privileges that are denied to them. You have no right to eat and have a sound sleep if your neighbour is hungry. It is this sense of 'caring for others' that makes us humans and not brutes. Otherwise, like the seagulls, one could spend an entire lifetime figuring out how to get more food from the shore. When words elude me, I sometimes turn to Richard Bach: 'A mile from shore a fishing boat chummed the water, and the word for Breakfast Flock flashed through the air, till a crowd of a thousand seagulls came to dodge and fight for bits of food. It was another busy day beginning!'

There should be much more to living. There must be a reason to live. 'Giving' provides the reason to life!

Proper distribution of wealth is the sign of prosperity and health of the economy: what can be better than a voluntary gesture in building such an economy? Business prospers when the 'purchasing power' is more extensively distributed. Zakat is one of the most important practices in developing a new social order of tomorrow's gracious society.

Zakat builds socio-economical values but it also fosters the ethical value of Giving! The cosmic principle is simple: You receive from the world that which you give to the world. Giving is an art and a passion. 'What you give' is no doubt important. But the act of giving with passion makes it holy and humane. Prophet Mohammed always used to say that give with such a passion that when your right-hand gives, the left-hand does not see the act of giving.

One can acquire corporate wisdom from the words of a great Sufi: 'You owe more than gold to him who serves you. Give him of your heart or serve him.' Salary and incentives are no substitute to the contribution of your people who have performed for the sake of your company by joining their mind, heart and soul.

Islam and its philosophy represents a huge realm of ideas. This chapter has only culled out what the author felt would be relevant to the reader. One can keep studying and learning from the Qur'an. The important part is to understand the emphasis that this religious philosophy places on truth, honesty and discipline and human well-being. It enshrines the concepts of virtuous leadership, collaboration and commitment.

While closing this chapter, let me emphasise that 'patience' and 'faith' are two important factors in Islamic business governance. The Qur'an proclaims: 'Surely with every hardship comes ease.' (Surah 94:5-6) Neither the dark night remains forever nor does the bright daylight. Success comes to those who dare and act. Dare and act fearlessly following the right path.

'With hardship comes ease'—that will serve as the dictum for the new age. No pain; no gain.

13

Sufi Sagacity

To come empty-handed to the door of friends
is like going to the mill without wheat.

—Rumi

How does one describe what Sufism is and identify who is a sufi? In Arabic and Persian, there are many terms for sufis—Fakir, Dervish, Majzub. A number of classical definitions of Sufism abound; Seyyed Hossein Nasr one of the foremost scholars of Islam, defines it as the inner esoteric dimension of Islam. However, in simple terms, many stalwarts of sufism have described it as 'being with god' or 'abandoning oneself to god'. It would mean complete and absolute surrender to God in each moment. The sign of a true sufi is that he feels poor when he has wealth, is humble when he has power, and hides when he has fame. The sign of the false sufi is that he struts like a rich man before the world when he is poor, behaves like a tyrant to conceal his deep-seated insecurities, and tries to attain fame to leap out of obscurity. These are also the signs that will help you distinguish between a true leader and a false one. At the core of sufism lies the search for truth and love.

Kahlil Gibran (1883-1931), Jalal al-Din Rumi (1207-73), Omar Khayyam (1048-1122), Al-Arabi (1165-1240), Shirazi (1571-1640), Mansur al-Hallj (d-922), Hafiz, Amir Khusraw, Dara Shikoh (1615-59), Ghous-e-Pak, Hazarat Nizamuddin, Muinuddin Chishti (1142-1236), Jalaluddin Ganji, Hafiz, Ghazli (1058-1111), Baba Farid, Kabir Das (1440-1518), Bibi Rabiah of Basra (717-801), Bibi Jamal Khatun (d-1647), Sant Tukaram (14th century), Jeevan Das Dadu (disciple of Kabir), and Guru Nanak (1469-1539) are some of the great sufis that the world has known.

Iran, Afghanistan, Syria, Iraq, Lebanon and India are fertile lands where sufism flourished. Some of the religions and faiths have born out of sufism. Sikhism is one such faith that sprang from the sagacity of Guru Nanak.

Sufism, Bhakti, and Mysticism are three names that belong to the same spiritual practice. Their purpose is to establish a direct link with God without looking for a go-between or a specific way of meditation. The sufis or mystics are the enlightened beings who are capable of establishing bonds with God directly.

The sufis are known to speak the truth in plain words. Yet, the people do not understand the truth because they don't take sufis seriously due to their deceptive appearance. Lao Tzu, the old master, captures this in simple but powerful words: 'My words are easy to understand and easy to perform; Yet no man under the heaven knows them or practises them. My words have ancient beginnings; my actions are disciplined. Because men do not understand, they have no knowledge of me. Those that know me are few; those that abuse me are honoured. Therefore, the sage wears rough clothing and holds the jewel in his heart.'

247

Perhaps the most common epithets for the sufis were drawn from the vocabulary of love and intimate affection. Sufis are known as the lovers of God. Intoxicated with divine love, they grow into divine madness. They know the inner truth. They discover the universe within. They are humble in their knowledge. They understand their limitations. They strongly believe that they do not know the entire truth. Their knowledge is limited by the extent that God has chosen to reveal to them.

As we study the tenets of sufism, we realise that at the core of it lies an understanding of self and surrender to God. The advocates of sufism tell us over and over again to understand the self and acknowledge one's limitations in life. A human being is guided by five sensory perceptions. Beyond this, a common man cannot see. The sufis, who know more than common men, also do not have perfect insight. They too work within their limitations.

The corporate world can learn a lot from the sagacity of the sufis. Kahlil Gibran was one such great sufi whose sagacity can be translated into management thoughts and practices. His sagacity is ageless and timeless. 'We were fluttering, wandering, longing creatures a thousand years before the sea and the wind in the forest gave us words. Now, how can we express the ancient of days in us with only the sounds of our yesterdays?'

The thoughts of someone like Kahlil Gibran are not easy to understand. They should be absorbed slowly and mulled over. Although Kahlil Gibran belongs to the 20th century, people know little about him; however his sagacity is universally known and his writings quoted.

To understand the real breadth of Gibran's writing let us examine what he says on a wide variety of topics.

On poetry: 'A poet is a dethroned king sitting among the ashes of his palace trying to fashion an image out of the ashes...Poetry is not an opinion expressed. It is a song that rises from a bleeding wound or a smiling mouth.'

On philosophy: 'The philosopher's soul dwells in his head, the poet's soul in his heart; the singer's soul lingers about his throat, but the soul of the dancer abides in her body...'

On daydreaming: 'A man dreamed a dream, and when he woke he went to his soothsayer and desired that his dream be made plain unto him. And the soothsayer said to the man, "Come to me with dream that you behold in your wakefulness and I will tell you their meaning. But the dreams of your sleep belong neither to my wisdom nor to your imagination."'

On madness: 'They deem me mad because I will not sell my days for gold. And I deem them mad because they think my days have a price!'

On strategy: 'It is wiser for the lame not to break his crutches upon the head of his enemy.'

On a virtuous man: 'A shy failure is nobler than an immodest success.'

Managers can glean a message from each one of his thoughts. Each of his lines or couplets conveys a deep thought. In my understanding, *The Great Works of Kahlil Gibran* is a book of wisdom that appropriately suits business leaders and corporate managers.

Some see Kahlil Gibran as a mystic. To my mind, besides all this, he was a great management guru. This becomes apparent when one reads Gibran who talks eloquently of the need to create happiness in all aspects of life. The notion meshes well with the true purpose of business, which is to create happiness for all the stakeholders—the employees, customers, vendors, associates, shareholders, and the society which is the prime stakeholder whom we often seem to forget.

The sufis believe that you cannot motivate anyone. It is a fallacy to believe that one can motivate others. The switch that sparks understanding is not outside; it lies within every human being. One is motivated only when one becomes aware. This is particularly relevant for business managers: it is only when you are able to create awareness and inspire people that you can achieve miracles.

It is important to make each employee realise the importance of their tasks and their responsibility towards it. Every employee of the company must vow to add value to the customer.

A scholar becomes a wise man only when he attains wisdom; knowledge is not enough. A poet with passion attains the position of a prophet as he can sing songs about life. The green field transforms a scholar

> *There lies a green field between the scholar and the poet; should the scholar cross it, he becomes a wise man; should the poet cross it, he becomes a prophet.*
>
> —**Kahlil Gibran**

into a wise man and a poet into a prophet. Likewise, there lies a green field between practising managers and business leaders. If the practising manager crosses the field, he becomes an intrapreneur; if the business leader crosses it, he becomes a management monk.

Business leaders who have brilliance and competence, commitment and guts, knowledge and the desire to succeed will turn into colossal failures if they lack wisdom and virtue. That is why some organisations have started to focus on ethics and the need to inculcate a sense of self-awareness among their managers. The Sufis work by their instincts. In much the same way, 'intuitive wisdom' is gaining currency in today's business world.

Sufism stands for and supports passion, compassion, caring and giving. These virtues lead not only to happiness in people but can also be seen as a gateway to greater productivity. Take care of your people. 'You owe more than gold to him who serves you. Give him of your heart or serve him.' The concept of humility in leadership is deeply ingrained in sufi sagacity. 'I admire the man who reveals his mind to me; I honour him who unveils his dreams. But why am I shy, and even a little ashamed before him who serves me?'

'Giving' is the most powerful virtue of sufism. Let me quote Kahlil Gibran's sagacity on 'giving' and 'caring'. 'Generosity is not in giving him that which he needs more than you do, but it is in giving him that which you need more than he does!'

'Generosity is giving more than you can, and pride is taking less than you need.'

Kahlil Gibran says: 'Only those beneath me can envy or hate me. I have never been envied nor hated; I am above no one. Only those above can praise or belittle me. I have never been praised nor belittled; I am below no one.' This clearly points to the need to manage your people well; don't compete with your seniors or juniors. The truly great man is he who would master no one, and who would be mastered by none. This also points to a more fundamental level of self-awareness where a manager or a leader understands their true role in the context of their teams.

'Don't envy for the silence of the envious is too noisy,' advises Kahlil Gibran. 'I have learnt silence from the talkative, tolerance from the intolerant, and kindness from the unkind; yet strange, I am ungrateful to these teachers!' says the great Sufi whose thoughts are unparalleled. We can always learn from wrong people 'what not to learn'.

Whenever I speak to people about silence, they wonder how it applies to business. After all, business is all about communicating with people. Nevertheless, I suggest that they try this exercise from which I have learnt a great deal. In all my workshops, I ask the participants to close their eyes and spend three to five minutes in total silence. There may be noise all around them, but they are not allowed to speak a word. They seem transformed as people at the end of this exercise. Calmer, more honest and at peace with themselves.

'Silence' is the seat of Sufism. Eloquence that lies in tranquillity speaks louder than words. 'Give me silence and I will out-dare the night,' says the Sufi. 'Only when you drink from the river of silence shall you indeed sing. And when you have reached the mountaintop, then you shall begin to climb. And when the earth shall claim your limbs, then shall you truly dance.' What we call excellence in management is the beginning, not the end. Silence is a life skill we must learn to acquire and appreciate. It brings us closer to ourselves, creates self-awareness and then fosters better understanding of our environment and the people who inhabit it.

◁ Tranquillity ▷

From silence rises tranquillity, balance, understanding and a true sense of self. 'If your heart is a volcano how shall you expect flowers to bloom in your hands!' asks Kahlil Gibran. You can attain tranquillity only after going down to the deepest depth. Tranquillity is the sign of maturity and wisdom.

One can learn and adopt sufi thoughts to achieve management excellence. I quote below some of Gibran's thoughts which are relevant for different aspects of leadership:

Reward the deserved and the rightful?
Fame is the shadow of passion standing in the light.
If you reveal your secrets to the wind, you should not blame the wind for revealing them to the trees.

He who listens to truth is not less than he who utters truth.
Trickery succeeds sometimes, but it always commits suicide.

It is indeed misery if I stretch an empty hand to men and receive nothing; but it is hopelessness if I stretch a full hand and find no one to receive.

'Every thought I have imprisoned in expression I must free by my deeds.'

The sage has many sayings; it will need volumes to cover them all. *The Great Works of Kahlil Gibran* is a thick volume of over a 1,000 pages. I have read his work many times and tried my best to practise the wisdom it offers during my active corporate life.

⛭ Corporate Mysticism ⛭

The central tenet of sufism is 'direct contact with God'. There is no intermediary. Anything between them is taken as 'barriers'. The Sufi's way of worship is to override these barriers—which is also the central tenet of business management. So, can we learn and acquire sufi wisdom to hone our management practices? Business leaders must overcome bureaucratic inertia; they must tear down institutional barriers. Just as a sufi establishes direct contact with God, corporates need to come closer to the customer by demolishing all the vertical barriers that stand between the entrepreneur and the customer.

Mysticism is encouraged in Greek, Christianity, Judaism, Buddhism, Hinduism, Islamic world and Taoism. Although mysticism is linked with religion, the term itself is used very broadly in English, extending it to magic and occultism. Here, I refer to pure spirituality. Sufism is a pure and positive side of spirituality. I wish to stretch it further in a positive direction encompassing business principles and business practices, especially the ones that relate to values, virtues and wisdom.

The ancient mystic philosophy is based on the later doctrines of Plato. Rejecting dualism, Plato saw reality as oneness based on hierarchical orders containing all the various levels and the kinds of existences. Today, Stephen Hawking and others are trying to prove the cosmic connectivity through the 'String Theory'. Management perception is also changing with our changing understanding of science. Today what we call a 'big picture' is nothing but universality in our approach.

> *All things in this creation exist within you, and all things in you exist in creation; there is no border between you and the closest things, and there is no distance between you and the farthest things, and all things, from the lowest to the loftiest, from the smallest to the greatest, are within you as equal things. In one atom are found all the elements of the earth; in one motion of the mind are found the motions of all the laws of existence; in one drop of water are found the secrets of all the endless oceans; in one aspect of you are found all the aspects of existence.*
>
> —**Kahlil Gibran**

In business management, we must learn how to find oneness in dualism. In building inter-personal relationships we must learn to be together, yet maintain distances. Team-building and inter-personal relationships need no other business lessons. We should work as a team, but no member should lose his or her identity.

The constituency of a global manager is the future. Kahlil Gibran finds tomorrow in the soul of a child: 'You may house their bodies but not their souls, for their souls dwell in the house of tomorrow, which you cannot visit, not even in your dreams. You may strive to be like them, but seek not to make them like you. For life goes not backward nor tarries with yesterday.'

Someone once asked me: 'When we can see our past, why not the future?' The only way to see the future is to collaborate with it. Young managers and entrepreneurs across the globe represent the future. Their thoughts and ideas will determine the course of the future. Drawing on the wisdom from the sufis, we must encourage young professionals to unleash their creative thoughts and put them into business practice. We must learn to trust our juniors and talented young. We must not try to turn them into our clones; we should be receptive to their ideas and dreams.

To become a good student of management, one need not go through the 'so-called' management tomes. Business management can as well be learnt from sufis, saints, sages and monks. It is precisely for this reason that some of the premier management schools adopt sufi thoughts in their curricula. Kahlil Gibran's great work *The Prophet* is one of the recommended books for management students in Jamshedpur-based Xavier Labour Relations Institute (XLRI), one of India's premier management institutes.

❦ An Understanding of Self ❧

To discover our latent human potential one needs a sufi's insight and a sage's seat of passion:

> *They say to me in their awakening, "You and the world you live in are but a grain of sand upon the infinite shore of an infinite sea." And in my dream I say to them, "I am the infinite sea, and all worlds are but grains of sand upon my shore".*

It was but yesterday I thought myself a fragment quivering without rhythm in the sphere of life. Now I know that I am the sphere, and all life in rhythmic fragments moves within me.

Here is one more to discover the power of nature to empower ourselves:

I am forever walking upon these shores, Betwixt the sand and the foam. The high tide will erase my footprints, And the wind will blow away the foam. But the sea and the shore will remain forever!

Only once have I been mute. It was when a man asked me, "Who are you?"

—Kahlil Gibran

And try to fathom this to discover the powerhouse of human potential:

The Sphinx spoke only once, and the Sphinx said, "A grain of sand is a desert, and a desert is a grain of sand; and now let us all be silent again." I heard the Sphinx, but I did not understand.

We are often caught in paradoxical situations and the knowledge we have derived while pursuing our MBA and PhD degrees do not show us the way. We want to catch up with the Future, while dwelling in the Past and not even understanding our Present. How should we proceed? Gibran finds 'action' in 'inaction' and 'inaction' in 'action'. He allows the Past and the Future to coexist in the Present...

My house says to me, "Do not leave me, for here dwells your Past." And the road says to me, "Come and follow me, for I am your Future."
And I say to both my house and the road, "I have no Past, nor have I a Future. If I stay here, there is a 'going' in my 'staying'; and if I go there, there is a 'staying' in my 'going'. Only love and death change all things."

256

Both, the Present and the Future are important. Understand your Today and then alone will you be able to visualise the Tomorrow. Let Today and Tomorrow co-exist.

❦ Dreams Unlimited ❧

The philosophy and the sayings of the sufis go well beyond poetry. However, the world of business may see them as a mere collection of sayings—a compilation of trite homilies that are disconnected from the rough and tumble of the corporate world.

Fantasy finds no place in business management. People are ridiculed for daydreaming or building castles in the air. People are laughed at for counting the chickens before they hatched. But the power of fantasy must be understood. In order to create, one must first dream. In fact, fantasy is the blueprint through which you can convert your dreams into reality.

One must dare to dream the impossible or the inconceivable. It is the daydreamer or the wall-gazer who will fashion the

> *Trust the dreams, for in them is hidden the gate to the eternity.*
> —**Kahlil Gibran**

future of your company, and not the one who barks for silence.

A manager must develop an eagle's eye to look beyond what other birds cannot see. Experience and an understanding of the larger picture will help a manager to hone his intuition and be able to envision the future. Intuitive wisdom is the soul of Sufism. The sage says:

Once I saw the face of a woman,
and I beheld all her children not yet born.

257

*And a woman looked upon my face
and she knew all my forefathers,
dead before she was born!*

A manager should have the capability to understand and make the right moves at the right time. The only way he can do so is through collaboration and connectedness with the world. No longer can a manager behave like a patriarch boss who believes in supervision and control. A patriarchal leader is like the dog that barks for silence:

'The full moon rose in glory upon the town, and all the dogs of that town began to bark at the moon. Only one dog did not bark, and he said to them in grave voice, "Awake not stillness from her sleep, nor bring you the moon to the earth with your barking." Then all the dogs ceased barking, in awful silence. But the dog who had spoken to them continued barking for silence, the rest of the night.' How many of us stop barking as a manager even when things are moving the right direction! We bark because we believe that we have been hired to bark.

Managers also need to stop sermonising. These sermons are like lullabies that put your people to sleep. We often sing lullabies to our children that we ourselves may sleep! The spectrum between barking and singing lullabies is too wide. Locate the right spot in the bandwidth; it may not necessarily be the midpoint.

The trouble with heroic managers is that they disturb business harmony in their anxiety to create vibrations, waves, and ripples for the self. Those with profundity encourage their people at the right time.

One needs to be truthful not only in what he says but also in his actions. Encourage your people to be truthful at all times.

Humility is the pre-requisite, both for a leader and sage. 'I am ignorant of absolute truth. But I am humble before my ignorance and therein lies my honour and my reward.' The true leader is able to 'hear the unheard' and 'see the unseen'. 'If you can see only what light reveals and hear only what sound announces, then in truth you do not see nor do you hear,' says the sage. So, listen to what is left unsaid. One common mistake that managers do is that they wait for someone to lodge a complaint and only then react to solve his or her problem. What they don't understand is that the 'most sacred tears never seek our eyes'.

One more masterly tip for the new-age managers from Gibran: 'The reality of the other person is not in what he reveals to you, but in what he cannot reveal to you. Therefore, if you would understand him, listen not to what he says but rather to what he does not say.'

A leader also needs to be realistic. You see but your shadow when you turn your back to the sun. You should not shy away from the reality. What you thought was a solution yesterday might reappear tomorrow as a bigger problem. Today's problems are yesterday's solutions, says Peter Senge. Kahlil Gibran puts this in his angelic words: 'We choose our joys and our sorrows long before we experience them... We often borrow from our tomorrows to pay debts to our yesterdays.' The law of Nemesis and Karma does work. No action is complete unless the reaction of the action takes place. If you sow the seeds of values and virtue, you will reap the harvest of profit that will profit your life. But if you earn money by dubious means, you will still make profit but that profit will not profit your life.

When a company falls sick, it also sickens the mind of the management. When it comes to the crunch, we lose our values, wisdom and virtue. We forget the simple wisdom that there is no right way to do a wrong thing. In rectifying the errors committed in the past, we unwittingly jeopardise the future. In this way, we create an unending vicious circle.

⟨ Long For ⟩

'Longing for...' is the first and the foremost objective of business management.

Every company has this seed; people assume wrongly that a company exists simply to make money. It exists for a purpose. Find a purpose, and the means will follow.

The significance of man is not in what he attains, but rather in what he longs to attain. Purpose is the reason for a company's existence. Purpose and strategies are distinctly different in business management and we should never confuse between them. One might achieve the goal through business strategies but a purpose cannot be fulfilled. In their book *Built to Last*, James C. Collins and Jerry I. Porras compare purpose with a star: 'It is like a guiding star on the horizon—forever pursued but never reached!'

A business organisation is no exception. To discover its greater self, it needs to long for something. If corporate managers fill their heart with such sufi sagacity, the corporate world will change.

Carry your cross, and drink hemlock but never compromise with the human values; never go for puny gains. Broaden the bandwidth of your perspective and widen the horizon of your thoughts.

🍃 Sufi Poetry 🍃

Of all the sufi contributions, the best known and most appreciated is the legacy of sufi poetry. It is deep and meaningful. However, sufi poetry was

> *Poetry is wisdom that enhances the heart.*
> *Wisdom is poetry that sings in the mind.*
> *If we could enchant man's heart and at the same time sing in his mind,*
> *Then in truth he would live in the shadow of God.*
>
> **—Kahlil Gibran**

first interpreted in terms of universal romantic norms. For that reason Omar Khayyam's poetry was grossly misunderstood.

'Throughout the nineteenth century, scholarly debates continued over the interpretation of great poets like Hafiz and Rumi,' says Carl W. Ernst in the Ph.D. thesis written on 'sufism'. The sufi poet writes of his aching love for the beloved (God) and often goes into a trance-like state. One of the best known sufi poets was Rumi, whose poetry is heart-wrendingly beautiful.

'Water in the boat is the ruin of the boat; but water under the boat is its support,' says Rumi. As corporate managers we must understand that no business principle or business initiative can be taken in absolute terms to be good or bad. It becomes useful and harmful as per the circumstance. So, it is time to stop looking for sure-fire cures. What works in a particular situation will create a disaster in another situation.

Rumi also says: 'When self-interest appears, virtue hides; A hundred veils rise between the heart and the eye.' In this one line he identifies the root cause of all human error. The root cause is greed or self-interest. I often tell the participants at my workshops that in a group picture one should never try to locate himself first. Once you do, the appearance of the group photo will depend on your appearance in the group. However, if the larger picture is good, so is your appearance.

'When ten lamps are present in one place, each differs in form from another; yet you can't distinguish whose radiance is whose when you focus on the light.' Similarly, when works as part of a team, there is no division in team performance; no individual exists. Corporates talk about teamwork but they create warped performance management systems that reward individuals for the work that was performed by the team.

Be alive to the power of thought! Nothing in this world is more powerful than an 'idea' whose time has come. 'By a single thought that comes into the mind; in one moment a hundred worlds are overturned,' say Sufis.

A manager must create happiness within to create happiness among people. A leader who is frustrated will only generate frustration among his people. The leader who is happy cultivates happiness all around and creates a sense of goodwill.

Anger is a vice and not a virtue. A manager may show anger as a strategy once in a while, but he should never become angry. Showing anger and becoming are two different things; one should never confuse the two.

The first is strategy, and the second is habit. On one occasion, a group of saints from a spiritual organisation called 'Brahma Kumaris' came to an industrialist and asked for some donation. When the industrialist asked his secretary to bring the cheque book, one of the saints told him that they did not want money in donation. Then in the same breath she clarified, they wanted him to donate one of his vices to the Ashram. Wisdom dawned; the industrialist understood the deeper meaning. He donated his anger for he had a fiery temper. Whenever he used to get angry, he used to behave like a beast with his people, though he was a man of wisdom and a kind-hearted person. But after he donated his anger to the Ashram, his people never saw him become angry.

A true leader works for his or her followers. His or her thoughts and feelings resonate with those of the people who work with him. When one lives for others one seeks immense pleasure in serving others. A leader or a manager must live for his or her people and the organisation.

⚘ Bear in Mind... ⚘

What you achieve is secondary to what you long for. The cosmic principles of management are no different—like life, business management is a journey.

If you cannot slow down the pace of time, keep pace with time. If you cannot slow down the pace of the business world, you have to match pace with it. But while doing this, you must not lose sight of who you are and what you want to achieve. When humility blends with willpower you have a powerful combination that will ensure success. The new-age manager must acquire the humility of a sage and the willpower of a warrior.

Part V

The Wrap Up

Socrates, Plato and Aristotle are the flowers of the fragrance of the Greek philosophy. However, one of the greatest Greek philosophers, Heraclitus, is largely unknown; the west has forgotten him. Instead, Aristotle and Plato's thoughts became the cornerstone of western philosophy. This chapter contains pearls of wisdom from the Lao Tzu of Greece—Heraclitus. Socrates, Plato and Aristotle also find place in this chapter.

14

Pearls of Wisdom from the Greeks

You cannot step into the same river twice

—Heraclitus

In the above mentioned words, the great Greek philosopher Heraclitus put the essence of change. No book, no discussion, no workshop on 'change management' would be complete without visiting this quotation in some form.

The first section of this book begins with 'Chinese Vista' and in it the 'Art of Wu Wei' discusses the dynamics of change. As this book ends, we once again visit the forces of 'change management'. It was Heraclitus who first proclaimed: Everything is temporary except change.

But what do we really understand from this aphorism: 'You can't step into the same river twice'? Why not? Surely, we can step into the river as many times as we wish to. Isn't that true? No, you cannot.

A flowing river constantly changes its content, shape and course. It may look the same, but it never is the same. The river is like the world. Yesterday's world is not the same as the world today or tomorrow.

There is a protean quality about the corporate world as well. Jack Welch's famous saying explains how yesterday's world is completely different from the world today and why tomorrow's world will not resemble what we have today. Welch said: 'The pace of change in the 1990s makes the 1980s look like a picnic—a walk in the park!'

What worked yesterday will probably not work today; what seems improbable today could just be the solution for tomorrow's travails. It is important to continually update our assumptions about what is 'real' or 'perfect' and find solutions that are appropriate to the problems we encounter. Things may appear to be same as we saw them yesterday, but they are never exactly the same. As one considers this one understands the timeless wisdom in Heraclitus' words.

Today, time is considered to be the fourth dimension of space. It is a view that will hold until someone comes along and knocks the bottom out of Albert Einstein's theory. That seems implausible now: so it is safe to say that we will continue to call space and time as spacetime. By referring to them as discrete terms—space and time—we are splitting what is essentially indivisible. Although space remains static, time changes. Therefore, spacetime changes and it never remains the same. If you can accept this, then you do not need to stretch credulity to believe that you can't step into the river twice—or a pond for that matter. By the time you take the second dip, the spacetime has already changed. Even a pond with stagnant water no longer remains the same. Since time is the fourth dimension of space, with every atto second or its one-billionth part, space changes as well. It cannot remain the same.

There is no one-size-fits-all sort of remedy to problems that you might face in the corporate world. What is effective in one situation fails in another—or even in the same situation the next time round. The reason is simple: what we consider to be 'the same situation' isn't really so. 'Dynamism' is the goddess of worship in the new age.

⚐ Cosmic Patterns ⚑

Heraclitus believed that the cosmos reveals its secrets to us in patterns. 'The cosmos speaks to us in patterns,' he writes. Can the cosmos really speak? Probably.

One can see the unseen or hear the unheard only by going beyond the five sensory perceptions. However, one can hear the cosmos through the five sensory perceptions themselves. We just need to pay attention. Indeed, we need to use all our senses to discover new patterns. To see the pattern, one needs to get into a 'pattern-seeking, pattern-finding' frame of mind. First you notice something. Then, you focus your thinking and try to find something similar to it, occurring again or simultaneously. As Diane Ackerman puts it: 'Once is an instance. Twice may be a co-incidence. But three or more times makes a pattern.'

'Cycles' are very important in management. When the events recur, they form a cyclical pattern. Such a pattern is a cosmic pattern—a true pattern that one can trust.

The storyline of Paulo Coelho's famous book *The Alchemist* is based on such patterns—a recurrence of incidents. While some may call

> *A wonderful harmony arises from joining together the seemingly unconnected.*
>
> **—Heraclitus**

these 'omens', if you closely observe the occurrences, you will find a pattern in them. When the incidents recur, they become an omen. I am afraid I will be misunderstood for talking about omens in management. But what would you call the cycles or cyclical patterns? We give them names and hang labels to create a new vocabulary to make the point. Nowhere is this more true than in business management which has fashioned an argot of its own—and creates neologisms every other day.

⚙ Connect the Unconnected ⚙

Most of us relate 'lateral thinking' and 'divergent thinking' to Edward de Bono. Isn't it amazing that Heraclitus discovered and preached the virtues of 'lateral thinking', which is considered to be the soul of 'creativity', so many years ago! Many of us will be shocked to discover that many of the so-called discoveries in the modern world lie buried in goldmines of ancient wisdom—we don't trawl them enough to uncover the nuggets. Often people discover a few, give them a new burnish and float them as their own theorems. Some of us are honest enough to acknowledge that they sourced it all from the fountainhead of ancient wisdom by writing a book of the kind that I have written.

'It is the connection of previously unconnected ideas that stimulates us to think, that makes us say "Aha!" and see our situation in a fresh way,' says Roger Von Oech in his famous book, *A Whack on the Side of The Head*. 'Indeed, joining together apparently unrelated ideas lies at the heart of the creativity process. It's the basis of invention, poetry, art, crime-detection, humour, and problem solving.'

❧ Sniff Out Opportunities ❧

In todays information age, the amount of information available is boundless. There is a lot of information swirling about in cyberspace and all you need to do is download it. But, do we really find information on the Internet? I feel we make a huge error by mistaking 'raw material of information' for 'Information' *per se.* We need to sift through the raw material and add value to it before we can call

> *If all things turned to smoke, the nose would be the discriminating organ.*
> —**Heraclitus**

it information. The truth is that information is never available readymade: you need to mould all of the raw material into a usable bolus of information that will suit your needs. It is much the same with opportunities in business: they never come readymade, you need to sniff out possibilities and build on them.

Adolf Hitler, much despised though he was, has some advice to give on opportunity. Someone had asked Hitler to reveal his 'secret of success'. 'Jump, whenever an opportunity comes,' said Hitler. 'How do we know when an opportunity comes,' the man asked. 'Keep on jumping,' Hitler replied.

The ability to understand and capitalize on new opportunities also comes from having the ability to fuse ancient thought with current business management practices to develop a balanced understanding in times when everything is in a flux. It will help you recognise business opportunities through intuitive wisdom. While the past has important lessons to teach, it has a critical role to play in the future.

☙ Adversity is a Boon ❧

Heraclitus says, 'That which opposes produces a benefit.' Man is a creature of habit. He may ask for it. But when it happens he resists it as much as he can. It is true we love routines and do not want to try something new, apprehending some adverse consequences. We don't wish to invite problems; if we had our way, we would never welcome them. What we forget is that problems are not guests who come with invitation cards in hand; they will gatecrash your door anyway.

Routines allow you to do things without too much thought: in that sense they can be considered as boons. But they can be banes as well because they prevent us from developing a fresh perspective. It is only when something appears as a hurdle that we look for ways to surmount or get around it. As Kahlil Gibran says, 'Only when a juggler misses catching his ball does he appeal to me.' Likewise, only when we breathe heavily for want of oxygen, does Nature appeal to us!

Sometimes 'adversity' is a huge favour. Against violent winds, the kite goes high into the sky. If there is no wind, you can't fly a kite. Thus, we need opposition of some kind— an occasional jolt to wake us up and shake us out of our staid and boring mental patterns. Let me explain this through a hypothetical situation borrowing Roger Von Oech's logic.

Let us suppose you have a particular routine that allows you to reach a specific objective. One day there is an obstacle in your path. As a result one of the following might happen: (*a*) you use your creative abilities to eliminate the obstacle; (*b*) you go around the obstacle and find another way to reach your objective; (*c*) in the course of the search, you find another objective that is preferable to the original one and that you wouldn't have discovered had you not been forced off the routine path; and (*d*) you question whether you even need to reach your objective. So many options came into your mind because something had gone wrong somewhere; something had not worked out, or something had opposed your line of thinking or practice.

Failure is a part of life. It is only when something fails that something new emerges. Columbus had gone looking for India; he failed. Instead he found America. Viagra, the wonder drug, is again the outcome of a failure. There are many living examples where failures have opened up vistas for new opportunities.

The great 14th century Mongol conqueror Timur (also know as Tamerlane) was once forced to take shelter from his enemies in a ruined castle. He sat alone for several hours in anguish and distress. Wanting to distract his mind from thinking about his hopeless situation, he set his eyes on an ant that was carrying a grain of corn, much heavier than itself, up a high wall. Timur counted the times it tried in vain to accomplish this task. The grain fell 69 times to the ground, but the little insect refused to give up. On the seventieth trip, the ant reached the top. Wisdom dawned upon Timur. The rest is history: Timur became the great 14th century Mongol conqueror.

Thomas Edison, the great American genius and one of the most productive inventors of his times, had a track record of failures to his credit. But he never gave up. Success bowed before his determination to face adversities.

Abraham Lincoln, the sixteenth President of the US, was almost entirely self-educated. He started his career as a storekeeper, surveyor, and postmaster while struggling to study law. His life is exemplary to depict how success comes after a series of failures.

Colonel Sanders' proposal to franchise his grandma's recipe was rejected many times. Wherever he went, his proposal was thrown out. His proposal was rejected 1006 times; he succeeded in the 1007th attempt to fulfil his dreams that led to the creation of Kentucky Fried Chicken (KFC).

What Heraclitus had said more than 2500 years ago has now become reality. 'Adversities' have found a very specific place in today's corporate world. They are trying to measure the power of adversity through what is called AQ—Adversities Quotient.

⊌ Find Meaning in Random ⊌

We believe in order where everything· is meticulously planned and executed. 'Random' is not a good word in today's business vocabulary.

> *The most beautiful order is a heap of sweepings piled up at random.*
> —**Heraclitus**

Heraclitus suggested that one should always try to find the meaning in random ideas. Like Buddha, he believed in vagueness—clarity comes through vagueness. He said one should take advantage of the mind's pattern-recognition abilities. What appears to be without a pattern can form an excellent pattern when you can find some meaning in it. Look at the moving clouds in the sky, or look at the bark of the tree—what shapes do you see? A map, a human figure, a range of mountains or ocean waves? Allow your mind to wander freely and you will discover something fantastic.

Remember, the route of creativity is not an ordered pattern. Its route is random. From the 'heap of sweepings piled up at random', creativity discovers the new patterns.

274

Nitin Nohria has come out with the concept of 'White Space', that explains that most of the business opportunities lie outside the planned or organised area—black space. The power of the word 'random' has finally been recognised today.

'Those who approach life like a child playing a game, moving and pushing pieces, have the kingly power,' says Heraclitus. Sometimes it makes sense to buy a football and start kicking it. All those who succeed are not necessarily the ones who went through rigorous years of planned schooling. 'Unschooled' wisdom is greater than schooled wisdom in terms of purity and originality. Some of the great men like Socrates, Christ, and Prophet Mohammed grew with the unschooled wisdom and became the fountainhead of everything fresh and pure.

What we tend to debunk as a fluke is often really the pathway of creativity. A childlike attitude allows you to play with the issues at hand, to 'push and move'. When you play like a child with various pieces, looking at it in a variety of contexts, you find out what works and what doesn't. As a result of this sort of child-play you may discover many things that you did not know.

⬿ Do the Opposite ⬾

There are always two sides to a coin. One must learn to see both the sides. Learn to shift your point of view and perspectives. Most of the time the context determines the meaning. If you say, 'Make me one with everything' to a spiritual teacher, it means

> *Sea water is both pure and polluted; for fish it's drinkable and life-giving; for humans undrinkable and destructive.*
>
> —**Heraclitus**

one thing. But if you say the same thing to a *bhelpuri* vendor, it means something different.

The two sides of the coin are part of the same coin. They are at opposite sides, but together they make a coin. They are as complementary as Yin and Yang. So, in one sense, they are not really opposed to each other; they need each other. Disease and health appear to be opposite, but if you go deeper into this context, you will understand that both are complementary. They are the two sides of the same coin. 'Disease makes health sweet and good, hunger satiety, and weariness rest,' says Heraclitus. When you face one, try to look at the other. In distress, look for pleasure ahead; in glory, don't forget the misfortunes. When you gain heights be prepared for the fall; and when you fall, don't lose your heart because every dark night is followed by a dawn. Likewise, the concepts of 'beauty' and 'ugly' co-exist. If one ceased to exist, then the other wouldn't have much meaning. Each puts the other in relief. Each is the 'base' from which the other stands out. In fact, we don't really appreciate or understand something until we have experienced or tasted the opposite. A man who has always fed his stomach with rich food wouldn't know the taste of hunger; a person who has never gone thirsty wouldn't know what 'thirst' means.

It is difficult to have a concept of 'up' without one of 'down'. For this reason, Lao Tzu said: 'Going up is coming down.' In the height of glory be humble by remembering that it will not remain forever. I have seen a number of corporate leaders turn arrogant when they assume positions of power.

So, as Heraclitus suggests, 'Do the opposite'. 'The doctor inflicts pain to cure sufferings.' To understand the subtlety of life, discard logic. Roger Von Oech explains this well in his famous book *A Whack at the Side of the Head:* 'Sometimes the best way to reach an objective is to use the reverse of the apparently "logical" approach. For example: 18th century physician Edward Jenner discovered the invaluable medical tool of "vaccination" by inoculating healthy people with a dangerous but usually non-lethal disease (cow pox) to prevent them from contracting a deadly one (small box). Try looking at what you are doing in a reverse manner. By employing a reverse strategy, you might reach the desired objective.' He therefore suggests, 'Cut. If a part of a whole causes the whole to suffer, then remove it.'

'The way up and the way down are one and the same,' believes Heraclitus. Rethink your strategies; revisit your policies. In Heraclitus' worldview, things are continually changing. Thus, the strategy that leads 'up' towards success can ultimately become irrelevant and lead to the 'way down' towards failure. One may acquire a new wisdom that we need to be flexible in what strategies we use and change approaches when necessary. For example, before the pupa becomes a butterfly, it passes through the stages of development in the cocoon. Each needs different processes. What works for the caterpillar, doesn't work for the cocoon and most assuredly won't work for the butterfly.

◄ Life is a Paradox ►

'A thing rests by changing,' says Heraclitus. This thought once again relates to the new age concept of 'dynamic stability' in change management that I have already discussed at length earlier. In Heraclitus' worldview, everything is continually changing, and that it often takes less energy to move on to the next phase of process than fighting to stay in the current position. This thought of Heraclitus matches with Lao Tzu's art of Wu Wei.

Note the resemblance of thoughts between Heraclitus and Lao Tzu—one was born in Greece, the other in China. Heraclitus was born in the year 535 BC and died in 475 BC in Greece. Lao Tzu was a little older. He died in 604 BC. There was no occasion for them to exchange their thoughts. Yet, they spoke of the same truth at two different continents at two different points in time. Truth remains the truth, what changes is time and place. 'Many do not grasp what is right in the palm of their hand,' says Heraclitus. Why does this happen? He explains, 'Truth loves to conceal its true nature.' Heraclitus believed that reality loves to conceal its true nature, that it is intentionally enigmatic. But he also believed that this enigma can be understood if we adopt a creative thinking mindset and look behind the surface-appearances to see the hidden patterns.

Truth has many masks. This is the wisdom of many ancient sufis and saints who believe that the Supreme Truth loves to conceal Itself. So the only way to discover truth is by looking for the 'hidden order', or go beyond the obvious. 'When there is no sun, we can see the evening stars,' says Heraclitus. It is a wonderful paradox.

> *When we're awake, there is one ordered universe, but in sleep each of us turns away from this world to one of our own.*
>
> —**Heraclitus**

Normally, we believe that it is darkness that hides the reality. But, in reality, light also masks reality under its glare. So, both light and darkness can conceal the truth or reality from our vision.

☙ The Fire of Arrogance ❧

'There is a greater need to extinguish arrogance than a blaze of fire.' Heraclitus lays extra emphasis upon 'arrogance' by keeping it above the 'blaze of fire'. A number of CEOs often behave as though they were larger than life. Power consumes them just as fire consumes wood.

'You are not God,' Heraclitus reminds the rulers of his times. Arrogance and ego are the signs of a disease in human beings. A person's high ego indicates that he is suffering from the inner inadequacies. People with low understanding serve their pleasure centres by behaving arrogant and egoistic. 'If happiness consisted in the pleasures of the body, we should call oxen happy.' Heraclitus had never compromised by resorting to low thinking or taking a low approach in life.

⍦ Socrates' Teacher ⍣

Heraclitus was Socrates' spiritual teacher. He was a great missionary. 'Wake up and pay attention to what is happening around you and within you, and then act on what you have found. Do not act and speak like those asleep.'

Heraclitus was almost a contemporary of Lao Tzu, Confucius, and Buddha. Each of them came to create a new awakening amongst the masses. Thales, Pythagoras, Parmenides, and Democritus (known as the Pre-Socratic Group) were older than Heraclitus. They were all the pearls of Greece.

⍦ Socrates' Search for Truth ⍣

Socrates (469–399) was a Greek philosopher whose search for truth forced him to drink hemlock (a poison). Undeterred he drank hemlock but never compromised with his right to seek and preach the truth. Socrates was generally regarded as one

279

of the wisest people of all time. Socrates was the most interesting and influential thinker in the annals of philosophy; his dedication to careful reasoning transformed the entire world.

Although it was not known who was his real teacher, he had been preaching the doctrines of Heraclitus, Parmenides, and Anaxagoras. Socrates himself left no writings and most of our knowledge of him and his teachings comes from the dialogues of his most famous pupil, Plato. His teaching style was unique. It was more through probing and creating awareness. His method of preaching is known today as 'dialogue' or 'dialectic'. He used to draw forth knowledge from his students by pursing a series of questions and examining the implications of his answers. More significantly, Socrates generated a formal dilemma from 'deceptively' simple questions. For instance: 'Is the pious loved by God because it is pious, or is it pious because it is loved by God?'

What is Right? 'Do my parents approve of this action because it is right, or is it right because my parents approve of it?' Yet one more example of his deceptively simple way of cross-examining his pupil to extract the truth from them without revealing to them what is in his mind: 'Does the college forbid this activity because it is wrong, or is it wrong because the college forbids it?' The goal of Socrates' interrogation was to help individuals to achieve genuine self-knowledge, even if it often turned out to be negative in character. The purpose of his cross-examination was not to test others' knowledge but to get 'inside-out' using logical net-picking to expose (rather than to create) an illusion about reality. Even after the jury convicted him, Socrates declined to abandon his pursuits of his truth in all matters.

There are various assumptions about what caused him to drink hemlock. Besides his criticism of political and religious institutions of the times, one of the reasons cited for his death penalty was 'his political associations with an earlier regime'. The Athenian democracy put Socrates on trial charging him with undermining state religion and corrupting young people. Plato has narrated the details about his drinking hemlock in his famous book *Apology*.

The Jury had given Socrates three options. First, he might accept exile from Athens. Second, he might accept 'silence' as his penalty. Third, if he was not willing for either of the two proposals, he might accept to drink hemlock. Socrates would rather die than give up philosophy, and the Jury seemed happy to grant him what he wished.

> *The unexamined life is not worthy of living.*
>
> **—Socrates**

Socrates' disciples came prepared to arrange his escape from the jail. When Socrates didn't agree with them, they argued the merits of their plans. 'Escape would prevent Socrates to fulfil his personal obligations in life,' they argued. They made a case that by agreeing to their plans Socrates would show respect to the wishes of the majority of people. But Socrates dismissed these considerations as irrelevant. 'The only opinion that counts is not that of the majority of people generally, but rather that of the one individual who truly knows. The truth alone deserves to be the basis for decisions about human actions.' He refused to escape from the prison holding steadfast to his logic:

> One must never do wrong, even in response to the evil committed to him by another. It is always wrong to disobey the state.
> Hence, one must never disobey the state.

Since avoiding the sentence of death handed down by the Athenian jury would be an act of disobedience against the state, it followed that Socrates must not escape. Socrates himself was entirely convinced that the arguments held by him were based on truth so he concluded that it would be wrong for him to escape from the prison. As always, of course, his actions conformed to the outcome of his reasoning. Socrates chose to honour his commitment to truth and morality, even though it cost him his life.

✇ Knowing Ignorance ✇

Knowing ignorance is the sign of great wisdom. 'Knowing ignorance is strength; Ignoring knowledge is sickness,' said Lao Tzu in 6th century China. Those who earnestly desire to go deep into the great ocean of knowledge soon realise how shallow a dip they have taken in the bottomless deep sea. Socrates, who is considered the wisest man on the earth, realised his ignorance. He said, 'I am ignorant of absolute truth. But I am humble before my ignorance and therein lies my hour and my reward.' The greatness of the wise man lies in understanding his limitations. Socrates became great with his famous sentence that came from the depth of his heart: 'I know, I know nothing!' This humble realisation can raise one to the height of greatness.

Socrates strongly believed that 'an open awareness of one's own ignorance' is a great wisdom that most of the people lack. This equally applies to management knowledge. 'Everybody is ignorant, only on different subjects,' said Will Rogers. Knowing one's limitations and ignorance is a great wisdom. Swami Vivekananda used to pray: 'Oh God! Give me the courage to change what I can; the serenity to accept what I can't; and the wisdom to know the difference.'

❦ What is Justice? ❧

Socrates' concept of justice has been much acclaimed. But he never defined the word 'Justice'. Book I of *Republic* appeared to be a Socrates' dialogue on the nature of justice. He opened the dialogue by asking his disciples to define justice. The elderly wealthy man, Cephalus, suggested that justice involved nothing more than telling the truth and repaying one's debts. 'Return what belongs to one,' he offered as a simple definition of justice. But Socrates pointed out that in certain circumstances, following these simple rules without exception, could produce disastrous results. He argued, 'Returning a borrowed weapon to an insane friend, for example, would be an instance of following the rule but would not seem to be an instance of just action.' The presentation of a counter-example of this sort tends to show that the proposed definition of justice was incorrect since its application did not correspond with our ordinary notions of justice.

In an effort to avoid such difficulties, another disciple offered a refined definition by proposing, 'Justice means "giving to each what is owned". So, help your friends and harm your enemies.' But Socrates pointed out that the harsh treatment to the enemies was only likely to render them even more unjust than they already were. So, this definition too was not considered as a true reflection of justice in words.

❦ Plato's Concept of Soul ❧

Plato (427–347 BC) was the genius disciple of Socrates. It was Plato who rerecorded the philosophy of Socrates in his books. His book *Apology*, one of the masterpieces, describes the death of Socrates that he invited and accepted to prove that nothing was greater than truth, even the life of a philosopher! In this book, Plato guided the change makers and advised them to pay the price if the truth so demands.

In 407 BC, Plato came into contact with Socrates and then he never looked back. He remained one of the most devoted disciples of Socrates. He himself was a philosopher. So he didn't simply present before us the Socrates' philosophy but also value-added with his own philosophical insights.

Plato believed that every human being had a soul that performs three different functions. For this reason he called them the 'three types of souls'. These three souls correspond to the three classes of citizens within the state, each of them contributing in its own way to the successful operation of the whole.

The Rational Soul: He called the mind or intellect as the rational soul. This part of the soul takes care of the thinking portion within each of us, which discerns what is real and what is false. The rational soul makes the wise decisions in accordance with which human life is most properly lived.

The Spirited Soul: This portion of the soul helps implement the decisions of the rational soul boldly and courageously. 'Doing whatever the intellect has determined to be best' is the function of the spirited soul.

The Appetitive Soul: He called 'emotions' as the appetitive soul. He felt that nothing could be achieved without the support of emotions what he called the 'appetitive soul'.

Plato presented this more graphically, comparing the 'rational soul' to a charioteer whose vehicle is drawn by two horses, one powerful but unruly (desire) and the other disciplined and obedient (will). What we call wisdom is the product of the rational soul. Courage comes from the 'Spirited Soul'. And the 'Appetitive Soul' acts like a moderator. Our emotions moderate the entire process.

During a recent, brief study on the 'human potential powerhouse', I concluded my perspective on the above with four types of human energies—physical, intellectual, emotional and spiritual. Today the corporate world has harnessed only the physical and intellectual energies of people. Though we have jumped to measure emotions through what we call 'EQ', we have not really gainfully utilised the emotional energy of our people. Rather, we consider 'emotions' in a negative sense. What is left fully unutilised is the spiritual energy of our people, what is termed today as 'Spiritual Quotient' (SQ).

✎ Philosopher Kings ✐

Plato was a great political philosopher who arrived at many practical solutions to complex political problems. One of them is his concept of 'Philosopher Kings' that goes well with the practice of 'Scholars' followed in Singapore, or the practice of inducting administrative services experts in India and some other countries as the bureaucratic kings. But it is not a straightforward apple-to-apple comparison.

Plato believed that the highest and best capabilities of human social life could really be achieved, if the right people were put in the chair. 'Since the key to success of the whole is the wisdom of the rulers who make decisions for the entire state,' Plato held, 'the perfect society will occur only when kings become philosophers or philosophers are made the kings.' Plato supported only those with a philosophical temperament who have the wisdom to distinguish between 'what appears to be right' and 'what is right'. Thus, the theory of 'Philosopher Kings' is central to Plato's philosophy—the philosophers who think about such things are not idle-dreamers, but the true realists in any society. 'It is their detachment from the realm of sensory images that renders them capable of making judgments about the most important issues,' believed Plato.

Plato strongly believed that 'philosophers are made, not born'. So, he suggested first examining the education programme and schooling system of the state. Plato supposed that the future philosopher-kings could acquire the knowledge necessary for their functions as decision-makers of the society as a whole. 'The highest goal in all education is knowledge of the Good; that is, not merely an awareness of particular benefits and pleasures, but acquaintance with the Form itself,' said Plato.

In management education 'the knowledge of good' finds no place, or rather it is replaced with the 'knowledge of money'. Moneymaking has become the 'be-all and end-all' of business today. I share the concern of Sir John Harvey-Jones who said, 'It horrifies me that Ethics is only an optional extra in Harvard Business School.' If this is the status of affairs at world's best known business school, what can we expect from the others? How then will the business leaders learn 'the form of the good'?

It is not enough to follow values and virtues. More important is to understand the underlying virtues in values and the hidden values in virtues. The inner illumination can get

> *Just as the sun provides illumination by means of which we are able to perceive everything in the visual world, so the "Form of the Good" provides the ultimate standard by means of which we can comprehend the reality of everything that has value.'*
>
> **—Plato (Republic)**

one external clarity. The philosopher kings are the enlightened ones. People must believe in their wisdom and trust their actions for they have seen the light and they know the truth.

Plato explains this through his famous 'Allegory of the Cave':

Suppose that there is a group of human beings who have lived their entire lives trapped in a subterranean chamber lit by a large fire behind them. Chained in place, these cave dwellers can see nothing but shadows (of their own bodies and of other things) projected on a flat wall in front of them. Some of these people will be content to do no more than notice the play of light and shadow, while the cleverer among them will become highly skilled observers of the patterns that most regularly occur. In both cases, however, they cannot truly comprehend what they see, since they are prevented from grasping its true source and nature.

Now suppose that one of these human beings manages to break the chains, climb through the tortuous passage to the surface, and escape the cave. With eyes accustomed only to the dim light of the former habitation, this individual will at first be blinded by the brightness of the surface world, able to look only upon the shadows and reflections of the real world. But after some time and effort, the former cave-dweller will become able to appreciate the full variety of the newly-discovered world, looking at trees, mountains, and (eventually) the sun itself.

Finally, suppose that this escapee returns to the cave, trying to persuade its inhabitants that there is another, better, more real world than the one in which they have so long been content to dwell. They are unlikely to be impressed by the pleas of this extraordinary individual, especially since their former companion, having travelled to the bright surface world, is now inept and clumsy in the dim realm of the cave. Nevertheless, it would have been in the best interest of these residents of the cave to entrust their lives to the one enlightened member of their company, whose acquaintance with other things is a unique qualification for genuine knowledge.

—**Plato (Republic)**

Plato seriously intended this allegory as a representation of the state of ordinary human existence. We, like the people raised in a cave, are trapped in a world of impermanence and partiality, in the realm of sensible objects, that these things provide. We are unlikely to appreciate the declarations of philosophers, the few among us who, like the escapee, have made the effort to achieve eternal knowledge of the permanent forms. But, like them, it would serve us best if we were to follow this guidance, discipline our own minds, and seek an accurate understanding of the highest objects of human contemplation.'

The allegory explains the status of today's corporate world where most of us behave like the 'people raised in a cave' and don't trust the escapee. Those who talk about the truth are in unbelievably short supply.

I recently conducted a study on the value systems in Singapore, which has earned a reputation for being the least corrupt country and has repeatedly adjudged as the best in governance. One of the conclusions that I made in the study was about the national builders' faith in the ancient wisdom. I found that the wisdom of Lao Tzu, Confucius and Plato had been actually put into practice. This didn't happen by chance. Lee Kuan Yew, the father of the Singapore nation state, is himself a great scholar and a believer in Confucius philosophy. He simply put into practices what he gained from the old sages and monks, of course slightly modifying them as per today's needs. The 'Scholar' system in Singapore is Plato's philosophy of 'Philosopher Kings' in practice.

✑ Aristotle's Universal Method of Reasoning ✑

Aristotle (388–322) was born in Stagria in north Greece. He was a devout disciple of Plato and the honoured teacher of

Alexander the Great. His contribution to political science through his teachings on logic and ethics is noteworthy.

Aristotle's desire was to develop a 'universal method of reasoning' model by means of which it would be possible to learn everything 'there is to know about reality'. The collection of his logical treatises is known as *Organon*.

Unlike Plato, who delighted in abstract thought about a supra-sensible realm of forms, Aristotle was intensely concrete and practical, relying heavily upon sensory observation as a starting-point for philosophical reflection. Interested in every area of human knowledge about the world, Aristotle aimed to unify all of them into a coherent system of thought by developing a common methodology that would serve equally well as the procedure for learning about any discipline.

For Aristotle, logic was the instrument by means of which one could come to know anything in life. He proposed as formal rules for correct reasoning the basic principles of the 'categorical logic' that was universally accepted by western philosophers until the 19th century. Aristotle believed that the 'logical scheme' accurately represents the true nature of reality.

He believed that 'thoughts, language, and reality are all isomorphic, so careful consideration of what we say can help us to understand the way things really are.' He suggested, 'Beginning with simple descriptions of particular things, we can eventually assemble our information in order to achieve a comprehensive understanding about the world view.'

This was precisely the reason why the West rejected Heraclitus and Socrates and accepted Aristotle, and even Plato. It is easy to understand the language of logic than intuitive language. I believe in both, reasoning and intuition. But it is my firm belief that when it comes to grander understanding, logic or reasoning will not take you deeper.

❧ Wrap Up ❧

For the past 2000 years, 'western thinking' has been dominated by a 'dualistic approach'—either/or. Either something is good, or it is bad, desirable or undesirable, someone is an ally or an enemy.

Before he launched the war against Afghanistan, President George W. Bush made that infamous statement: 'Those who are not the allies of America are our enemies'. This is just a reflection of how much damage such a dualistic approach has done to our wisdom. The West accepted Aristotle and Plato and rejected both, Heraclitus and Socrates. The reason was simple. It was easy to understand logic than to comprehend intuitive wisdom. It was easy to see a thing either in black or white than to see a thing through millions, or rather, billions of nuances.

As mentioned in the beginning of this chapter, Heraclitus was the Lao Tzu of Greek philosophy. Plato was the Confucius of Greece. But in the West, the genuine message of Heraclitus was forgotten, and Plato's thoughts became the foundation.

Business has grown in the West—and it is no wonder that its foundation is embedded in logic. The western school of thought has accepted Aristotle and, thus, logic became an acceptable commodity in business management. The western world that has adopted a materialistic outlook cannot understand the subtlety of eastern philosophy.

It is possible to westernise the East but you cannot 'easternise' the West. There is no word like 'easternise' in English dictionary. That in itself speaks volumes.

15

Corporate Reality

Here is a test to find whether your mission on earth is finished.
If you're alive, it isn't.

—Richard Bach

We live in a well-knit web of uncertainties and interdependence: All existences great and small are linked through a web of inter-dependent relationships. Every relationship has a certain polarity and a certain order. The movement within and between beings in relationships is the source of generative and creative power.

One does not know what will happen in the next moment. As the second law of Murphy says, 'If something has to go wrong, it will!' One should not be content with one's success nor should he feel low and resentful when gripped by failure. Neither does the sunshine last nor does the darkness remain all the time! Both, success and failure are natural and constitute what we term as 'uncertainties'. Corporate management is no exception to this rule. If someone takes success for granted, the uncertainties of life will catch him unaware. As Dr. B.L. Maheshwari of the Centre for Organizational Development, Hyderabad fondly says, 'Sometimes companies with a track record of success fail because they have not understood the real factors that caused the success.'

Danger arises when a man feels secure in his position. Destruction threatens when a man seeks to preserve his worldly estate. Confusion develops when a man has put everything in order. Therefore the superior man does not forget danger in his security, nor ruin when he is well established, or confusion when his affairs are in order. In this way he gains personal safety and is able to protect the empire.

—**I Ching**
Great Commentary 2.5.9

If the new-age CEOs take the ancient mantras seriously, they can save several successful companies from dying out like withered trees. Ironically, the decadence sets in when the company thinks it is the most secure. When it finds itself on the top of the world, it becomes complacent. It is when we reach the heights that we are best poised for the fall. Old Master Lao Tzu says, 'Going up is coming down'. So the companies should never be oblivious to the danger of decline during their prosperity and should not forget to see the faint silver lining behind the dark clouds during the days of distress. The only certainty in life and business is 'uncertainty'. Confusion begins when our affairs are in order; danger swallows up someone when he thinks he is absolutely secure.

Ancient wisdom, though subtle, one can always sensitise by developing the intuitive instincts. Heedfulness is the path to deathlessness; heedlessness is the path to death. Those who heed ancient wisdom and cosmic principles will emerge as winners in new age.

☙ Hearing the Unheard ❧

Ancient monks, saints and sufis tried to create awareness to help attain enlightenment. The very approach was different. In the corporate world, it is important to be able to hear that which is unspoken or unheard. Here is an ancient parable that might enlighten the new-age managers. The parable has been published in many Chinese ancient books, including the *Harvard Business Review*.

Kink Ts'a sent his son, Prince Ta'i to a temple to study under the great master Pan Ku. Since Ta'i was to succeed his father, Pan Ku was to teach the boy the basics of being a good ruler.

The master sent the prince to the Ming-li forest alone. After one year, the prince was to return to the temple to describe the 'sound of the forest' When Ta'i returned, Pan Ku asked the boy to describe all that he could hear.

'Master', replied the prince, 'I could hear the cuckoos sing, the leaves rustle, the humming birds hum, the crickets chirp, the bees buzz and the winds whisper and holler.'

The master told the prince to go back to the forest and listen to what more he could hear. The prince was puzzled—Had he not discerned every sound already?

For days and nights on end, the young prince sat alone in the forest listening, but he could hear no sounds other than those that he had already heard.

Then one morning, as the prince sat silently beneath the trees, he started discerning faint sounds unlike those he had ever heard before. The more carefully he listened, the clearer the sounds became. A feeling of enlightenment enveloped the boy.

(Contd.)

(*Contd.*)

> When he returned to Pan Ku, he said, 'Master, when I listened more closely, I could hear the unheard—the sound of flowers opening, the sound of the grass drinking the morning dew.' The master nodded approvingly.
>
> 'Hearing the unheard', remarked the master, 'is a necessary discipline to be a good ruler. For only when a ruler has learned to listen closely to people's hearts, hearing their feelings uncommunicated, pains unexpressed, and complaints not spoken of, can he hope to inspire confidence in people, understand when something is wrong, and meet the true needs of his citizens. The demise of the state comes when leaders listen only to superficial words and do not penetrate deeply into the souls of the people to hear their true opinions, feelings and desires.

In order to manage through 'Intuilogy', it is essential to 'hear the unheard'. An enlightened manager listens to the 'unspoken' only when he finds himself close to the heart of his people. He realises and fully understands the pain that his people suffer even if they do not communicate it to him. Managers and CEOs sow the seeds of decline when they listen only to the words and are not

> *Love is the only way to grasp another human being in the immense core of personality.*
> —**Viktor Frankl**

sensitised enough to understand the feelings of their people. 'Feelings' is the language of soul. To understand people one must have a sensitive heart and a strong intellect that can scan feelings and comprehend the unspoken figure of language.

✺ Seeing the Unseen ✺

It is as important to see the invisible as to hear the unheard. I quote another ancient parable:

> *In the Royal Palace, amidst festivities one of the three disciples of Chen Cen enquired from his master, 'At the central table sits Xiao He. His knowledge of logic cannot be refuted. Next to him is Han Xin. His military tactics are perfect. The last is Chang Yang. He sees the dynamics of political and diplomatic rations in his palm. All this we understand and can see well. But what about the Emperor? Liu Band cannot claim noble birth, and his knowledge of logistics, fighting, and diplomacy does not equal that of his heads of staff. How is it, then that he is the Emperor?'*
>
> *The master smiled and asked his disciples to imagine the wheel of a chariot. 'What determines the strength of a wheel in carrying a chariot forward?'*
>
> *'Is it not the strength of the spokes, master?'*
>
> *'But then, why is it,' the master asked, 'that two wheels made of identical spokes differ in strength?'*
>
> *After a moment the master continued, 'See beyond what is seen. Never forget that a wheel is made not only of spokes but also of the space between the spokes. Sturdy spokes poorly placed make a weak wheel. Whether their full potential is realized or not, depends on the harmony between them. The essence of wheel making lies in the craftsman's ability to conceive and create the space that holds and balances the spokes within the wheel. Think now who is the craftsman here?'*
>
> *The answer was obvious! Wisdom dawned upon the disciples.*

The real strength lies not only in the individual excellence of people, but also in their ability to play as a well-knit team under able guidance. The space between people, which is invisible, is the most important aspect that determines team spirit and harmony. 'Seeing beyond what the eyes see', or 'seeing the invisible' is vital in day-to-day management practices. Unfortunately, most of us are not lucky enough to have the teachers who possess the third eye. On the contrary, we have teachers who help us distinguish between black and white and make us blind to the nuances that underlie a statement. Sturdy spokes that are poorly placed make a weak wheel. Likewise competent people wrongly placed will not add value to the organisation.

◖ Holistic Perspective ◗

Perspective makes all the difference. How should one develop the right perspective? I quote another parable that will explain, or rather depict, 'How difficult it is to develop different perspectives?' It is possible only through insight and perfect understanding?

In ancient China, on the top of Mound Ping stood a temple, where the enlightened master, Hwan dwelled. Lao-li was one of his disciples who was struggling to attain 'enlightenment'. Once, while he was meditating, a falling cherry blossom said to his heart, 'I can no longer fight my destiny.' Lao-li gave up all hope of enlightenment and informed his master of his decision to go back home. His great master agreed. 'Tomorrow, I will join you on your journey down the mountain,' he told Lao-li.

The next morning before their descent, the great monk looked out into the vastness surrounding the mountain peak and asked, 'Tell me, Lao-li, what do you see?'

'Master, I see the sun beginning to rise just below the horizon, meandering hills and mountains that go on for miles, and couched in the valley below, a lake and an old town,' said Lao-li

The master listened to Lao-li's response. He smiled and then they took the first step of their descent. On reaching the foot of the mountain, Hwan again asked Lao-li to tell him what he saw.

'Great wise one, in the distance I see the roosters as they run around barns, cows asleep in sprouting meadows, old men and women basking in the later afternoon sun, and children romping by a brook' The master remained silent. They continued to walk until they reached the gate of the town.

They sat under an old tree. 'What did you learn today Lao-li?' asked the master. 'Perhaps, this is the last bit of wisdom I will impart to you.' Lao-li was silent.

At last, after a long silence, the master continued, 'The road to enlightenment is like the journey down the mountain. It comes only to those who realise that what one sees at the top of the mountain is not what one sees at the bottom. Without this wisdom, we close our capacity to grow and improve. But with wisdom, Lao-li, there comes an awakening. We recognise that above one sees only so much—which, in turn, is not much at all. This is the wisdom that opens our minds to improvement, knocks down prejudices, and teaches us to respect what at first we cannot view. Never forget this last lesson, Lao-li—what you cannot see can be seen from a different part of the mountain.'

A holistic perspective can be developed only when you perceive truth from different levels, from different angles, from different focal points, from different perceptions. Remember, the sum total of segments does not give you a holistic picture. The big picture should be seen in its totality, not in segments.

☙ Introspection ☙

The model of universal harmony is the model of business management in the new millennium. The person who is virtuous without discrimination and takes care of those who practise virtue and selflessness as well as those who do not practise virtue and selflessness, shall be the role model for tomorrow's leadership—the virtuous leader. The virtuous leaders follow 'non-judgmental justice' and will lead both the virtuous and the non-virtuous while holding steadfast to their virtues. What is needed is the correct awareness of one's true nature.

Tomorrow's business organisation will be the enlightened organisation.

We have now learnt the simple truth and realised that the ancient wisdom is not something alien; it is relevant to the world of business. The true business guidance ought to be intangible; the universal integral way is beyond the limits of our minds. Success and failure in business depends on the 'universal law of energy response'.

I believe that our present way of understanding business management only in terms of tangibles is skewed. The longer we remain insensitive to our soft assets while stepping up the pace on the universal integral pathway, the farther we move away from those intangibles that really matter in managing tomorrow.

The various tag words that we have—business management doctrines, business principles, concepts, buzzwords, and watchwords—have their usefulness to the extent that they condition business acumen. If one has to understand the perfect cosmic management ethos, one has to remove the 'conditioning' and perceive the ''whole'—the big mental map! Snapshots do not reveal the big picture.

To survive in uncertainties today, always try to discover a new horizon. Keep looking for an alternative strategy even when you are doubly sure of success—there are no sure-fire solutions in management matters.

Imagine the cosmos as beautiful, just, perfect, balanced and expanding! The various principles will merge one into another and emerge as the 'integrated cosmic principles'. They would explain the panorama of life.

'We are, in the most profound sense, children of the Cosmos,' writes Carl Sagan in his *Cosmos*. 'Hidden within every astronomical investigation, sometimes so deeply buried that the researcher himself is unaware of its presence, lies a kernel of awe.'

✇ Concept of a Higher Power ᾬ

The subtle Cosmic One cannot be seen in any beautiful form, because to the Universal One there is nothing which can be considered as 'form'. The Universal One is truly imageless, yet in the attempt to make it conform to an image, people distort reality and separate themselves from It.

Business management is no different. In an attempt to comprehend the invisible, we conform to an image giving it some name. And while doing so, we distort reality and separate it from the truth.

Business management is within the realm of Universal Life. The intangibles are invisible! They go beyond the concept of measurement. When we start measuring the intangibles, they cease to be intangibles. 'Reality defined is reality defied': that is one of the angelic thoughts of Lao Tzu.

What lies within—and which researchers are unaware of—Is. The ancient wisdom Is. The cosmic principles Are. Both ancient wisdom and cosmic principles are relevant to the new age corporate world.

✎ The New Reality ✐

It is not just a question of whether you believe in values, virtues and wisdom in business management. The question is: If you believe, will you change? Would the managers change if they knew what awaits them in the New Age?

Here is what Richard Bach says:

> *A cloud does not know*
> *why it moves in just such a direction*
> *and at such a speed.*
> *But the sky knows the reason and the pattern,*
> *and you will know too,*
> *when you lift yourself high enough*
> *to see beyond horizons.*

It is time to discover new horizons. Trawl ancient wisdom to find the modern solutions in the new age. Take a holistic look with an intuitive eye to turn dreams into reality.

We must learn sometimes from fiction and our dreams. Sometimes our undying quest must go beyond the dreams. We must learn to dream, yet struggle not to lose touch with reality.